Teaching Talented Art Students

Principles and Practices

DISCARD

Jessica & Stanley Prescott

Making Art
Collection

Teaching Talented Art Students

Principles and Practices

Gilbert Clark • Enid Zimmerman

Teachers College
Columbia University
New York, NY 10027
www.tcpress.com

National Art Education Association
1916 Association Drive
Reston, VA 20191-1590

Dedicated to our fathers:
Gilbert Clark
Benjamin Deutchman

Published simultaneously by Teachers College Press, 1234 Amsterdam Avenue, New York, NY 10027, and the National Art Education Association, 1916 Association Drive, Reston, VA 20191-1590

Library of Congress Cataloging-in-Publication Data

Clark, Gilbert.
    Teaching talented art students : principles and practices / Gilbert Clark, Enid Zimmerman.
        p. cm.
    Includes bibliographical references and index.
    ISBN 0-8077-4445-X (pbk.)
        1. Art—Study and teaching—United States.   2. Gifted children—Education—United States.
    3. Children with social disabilities—Education—United States.   4. Community and school—United States.   I. Zimmerman, Enid.   II. Title.

    LC3993.265.C545 2004
    372.5'044—dc22   2003068738

    ISBN 0-8077-4445-X(paper)

Printed on acid-free paper

Manufactured in the United States of America

11   10   09   08   07   06   05   04   8   7   6   5   4   3   2   1

Contents

Copyright Acknowledgments

This is a list of permissions for materials used in our book. We believe these may have 500 words or more repeated from the original sources with minor word changes from the original texts. Since we are responsible for copyright issues for our book, we prefer to include the following sources to be listed as citations. We compacted the releases so they now are listed alphabetically and not by chapter so there is no repetition and the list is much reduced.

Clark, G. (1984). Establishing reliability of a newly designed visual concept generalization test in the visual arts. *Visual Arts Research*, *10*(2), 73–78.

Clark, G. (1992). Child art, art teachers and gifts: Implications of the concept of artistic giftedness. *Images*, *3*(3), 2.

Clark, G. (1993). Judging children's drawings as measures of art abilities. *Studies in Art Education*, *34*(2), 72–81.

Clark, G., & Zimmerman, E. (1978), A walk in the right direction: A model for visual arts education. *Studies in Art Education*, *19*(2), 34–39.

Clark, G., & Zimmerman, E. (1986). A framework for educating artistically talented students based on Feldman's and Clark and Zimmerman's models. *Studies in Art Education*, *27*(3), 115–122.

Clark, G., & Zimmerman, E. (1988). Views of self, family background, and school: Interviews with artistically talented students. *Gifted Child Quarterly*, *32*(4), 340–346.

Clark, G., & Zimmerman, E. (1992). *Issues and practices related to identification of gifted and talented students in the visual arts*. Storrs, CT: National Research Center on the Gifted and Talented. Research for this report was supported under the Javits Act Program (Grant No. R206R0001) as administered by the Office of Educational Research and Improvement, U.S. Department of Education. Grantees undertaking such projects are encouraged to express freely their professional judgement. This report, therefore, does not necessarily represent positions or policies of the Government, and no official endorsement should be inferred. This document has been derived with the permission of the National Research Center on the Gifted and Talented.

Clark, G., & Zimmerman, E. (1994). *Programming opportunities for students talented in the visual arts*. Storrs, CT: National Research Center on the Gifted and Talented. Research for this report was supported under the Javits Act Program (Grant No. R206R0001) as administered by the Office of Educational Research and Improvement, U.S. Department of Education. Grantees undertaking such projects are encouraged to express freely their professional judgement. This report, therefore, does not necessarily represent positions or policies of the Government, and no official endorsement should be inferred. This document has been derived with the permission of the National Research Center on the Gifted and Talented.

Clark, G., & Zimmerman, E. (1997). *Project ARTS: Programs for ethnically diverse, economically disadvantaged, high ability, visual arts students in rural communities*. Washington, DC: U.S. Department of Education. Research for this report was supported under the Javits Act Program (Grant No. R206A30220). The final project report and identification, curriculum, and assessment manual can be accessed through the ERIC database (ED 419 762 and ED 419 765).

Clark, G., & Zimmerman, E. (1998). Nurturing the arts in programs for gifted and talented students. *Phi Delta Kappan*, *79*(10), 747–756.

Clark G., & Zimmerman, E. (2001). Art talent development, creativity, and enrichment programs for artistically talented students in grades K–8. In M. D. Lynch & C. R. Harris (Eds.), *Fostering creativity in children, K–8: Theory and practice* (pp. 211–226). Boston: Allyn & Bacon.

Guskin, S., Zimmerman, E., Okola, C., & Peng, J. (1986). Being labeled gifted or talented: Meanings and effects perceived by students in special programs. *Gifted Child Quarterly*, 30(2), 61–65.

Thurber, F., & Zimmerman, E. (1997). Voice to voice: Developing in-service teachers' personal, collaborative, and public voices. *Educational Horizons*, 75(4), 20–26.

Wilson, T., & Clark, G. (2000). Looking and talking about art: Strategies of an experienced art teacher. *Visual Arts Research*, 52(2), 33–39.

Zimmerman, E. (1991). Rembrandt to Rembrandt: A case study of a memorable painting teacher of artistically talented 13- to 16-year-old students. *Roeper Review*, 13(2), 174–185.

Zimmerman, E. (1992). Assessing students' progress and achievements in art. *Art Education*, 45(6), 34–38.

Zimmerman, E. (1992). A comparative study of two painting teachers of talented adolescents. *Studies in Art Education*, 33(2), 174–185.

Zimmerman, E. (1994–1995). Factors influencing the art education of artistically talented girls. *Journal of Secondary Gifted Education*, 6(2), 103–112.

Zimmerman, E. (1995). It was an incredible experience: The impact of educational opportunities on a talented student's art development. In C. Golomb (Ed.), *The development of artistically gifted children: Selected case studies* (pp. 135–170). Hillside, NJ: Lawrence Erlbaum.

Zimmerman, E. (1997). Authentic assessment of a painting class: Sitting down and talking with students. In G. D. Phye (Ed.), *Handbook of classroom assessment: Learning, achievement, and adjustment* (pp. 448–458). New York: Academic Press.

Zimmerman, E. (1997). Excellence and equity issues in art education: Can we be excellent and equal too? *Arts Education Policy Review*, 98(4), 281–284.

Zimmerman, E. (1997). I don't want to sit in the corner cutting out valentines: Leadership roles for teachers of talented art students. *Gifted Child Quarterly*, 41(1), 37–41.

Introduction

Plate I.1 A student at the IU Summer Arts Institute generating a painting of another student playing the cello

Picture an artist in a well-equipped studio, engrossed in thought, seriously committed to creating new works of art, but "blocked," unable to work, because the artist's gallery director has established several rigid conditions for a new set of commissioned works. The artist is troubled and unsure the work can be done. The conditions the gallery director has imposed on the artist are the following:

1. Work without any reference to observed real-world objects (i.e., create all images from memory)
2. Focus upon expression of whatever mood or feelings the artist experiences
3. Move to new and untried media and invent techniques to be used
4. Create unique and different imagery in each new media

1

5. Create a completed work of art in each studio session
6. Avoid criticism or critiques by anyone
7. Observe only the works of others working under these same conditions
8. Avoid contact with art imagery that may bear some relationship to this commission. (Clark, 1992)

It is easy to sympathize with this artist's "block" and understand the inability to move ahead and create under the imposed conditions. A similar situation, however, occurs daily in school art classes, particularly in elementary schools: The art teacher is the gallery director, and the classroom is the artist's studio. This portrayal may be exaggerated, but it describes conditions that teachers often set for students working in their classrooms. The outcomes are predictable and self-fulfilling. In the name of achieving "child art" or creative self-expression outcomes, most teachers have been taught to set these conditions and even to criticize learning experiences in art that differ from them.

Being asked to create under such conditions is detrimental to the expressive abilities of most students and particularly those of artistically talented students. Like most high-ability students, artistically talented students are inherently precocious in that they learn more and faster than other students. They deal with abstractions more quickly, consciously understand generalizations with fewer examples, and have advanced abilities that facilitate their achievement in the visual or performing arts. Precocious students with highly developed abilities in the visual arts often demonstrate unusual perceptivity; they are more visually sensitive and observant than are other students. They have advanced sensitivity to issues that can be translated into meaningful visual images requiring an advanced sense of design, balance, colors, and composition for creating meaningful works of art. They create more meaningful artwork than other students because they value working with art media, they consider their creations important, and they have a sense of their emotive and communicative power. These abilities, skills, and understandings are not, however, simply the result of maturation. Like most human behaviors, they are

learned and are clearly the result of deliberate instruction.

Artistically talented visual arts students often face unfair challenges in schools due to beliefs and practices that do not support attention to their abilities and interests. Some beliefs prevalent among art teachers, and frequently reinforced by administrative practices at local, state, and national levels, predicate against best practices for development of art talent and education of artistically talented students. These beliefs are reinforced by lack of special programs or educational opportunities that meet the needs of artistically talented students.

One misguided belief is that, if left to their own devices, artistically talented visual arts students will develop effective skills and express themselves creatively on their own. We know, however, that these students' abilities and talents may never be actualized without the means to identify such students, to educate teachers to use appropriate strategies and resources to develop these students' talents, and to create educational programs and curricula and to plan educational settings that best serve their needs.

Another misinformed belief about art talent development is that students who come from privileged and/or specific racial, ethnic, cultural, or socioeconomic backgrounds automatically possess more talent than those in other groups. In fact, talented art students come from widely diverse backgrounds, with differences in gender, racial, cultural, and socioeconomic attributes that are found in all communities.

Still another erroneous belief is that all students are equally talented and that education can be a great equalizer in developing the art talent of all students. Rampant egalitarianism should not be equated with democratic practice. In a democratic tradition, excellence should be recognized and supported through educational programs; individual differences should be encouraged and every student should have the right to achieve to the best of his or her abilities. In schools of a democratic society, therefore, provisions should be made for educating all artistically talented students to their highest possible achievement levels in order for their abilities to be recognized, safeguarded, and rewarded.

ABOUT THE BOOK

This volume addresses contemporary concerns relevant to educating artistically talented students. Its content is based on more than 25 years of studying, conducting programs, reflecting, and writing about the education of artistically talented visual arts students. This book is intended to be used by elementary classroom teachers and art specialists, middle school and senior high school art teachers, teachers who wish to integrate the visual arts into gifted and talented programs, university art students and art educators, and administrators of programs for artistically talented students. It also may be of interest to parents, state directors of art and gifted and talented programs, and others concerned with developing students who are artistically talented in the visual arts.

Teaching Talented Art Students contains six chapters. Chapter 1 discusses current issues about art talent development, including the dynamic tension between excellence and equity, the integration of the arts and academics, current conceptions about art talent identification, and popular misconceptions about artistically talented students. Chapter 2 explores how to identify artistically talented students and offers practical suggestions for identification. In Chapter 3, the identification of talented art students and their characteristics are considered in several ways: from the viewpoint of students participating in special programs, in the perceptions of artistically talented girls, and through a case study of an artistically talented student. Characteristics of teachers of artistically talented students are considered in Chapter 4. Characteristics and strategies of two teachers of artistically talented students who promote art talent development are presented, followed by approaches for involving students in looking at and talking about art and ways of building leadership roles for teachers of artistically talented students.

Chapter 5 discusses several curriculum frameworks that foster art talent development, along with their practical applications. A program structure for creating a holistic art curriculum, models for differentiating curricula for artistically talented students, a framework for art talent development that is influenced by cultural consideration, and art curricula for talented students in rural communities all are included in Chapter 5. Programming opportunities and strategies for conducting authentic assessments of artistically talented students are offered in Chapter 6. These include locally developed assessments in a summer institute for artistically talented middle school and high school students and in communities that have diverse student populations.

We do not purport to cover in this book all issues or concerns related to education of artistically talented students. Rather, we identify areas we consider important in the field of art talent development and describe the relevant research and development contributed to the literature about educating artistically talented students.

RESEARCH AND DEVELOPMENT PROGRAMS FEATURED IN THIS BOOK

Three research and development programs we developed and coordinated will be referred to throughout this book. As an aid to the reader, full descriptions of the programs are offered here as background information. Components of these programs will be addressed in later chapters, but will not be described again in detail.

Indiana University Summer Arts Institute

For over a decade, we codirected the 2-week Summer Arts Institute that took place on the Indiana University campus. It was organized and implemented to serve artistically talented students entering Grades 7 through 10 who were seriously interested in studying the visual arts, along with music, dance, or drama. Students were identified as talented according to specific criteria. Our policy was to admit students who evidenced talent or had potential to develop special abilities and interests in the visual arts. The students lived for 2 weeks in a campus dormitory and about half of them were funded through scholarships. Most were from rural Indiana, but others attended from nearby states and other countries.

Principle goals were to extend knowledge, skills, and understandings about the visual arts and to provide opportunities for students to interact and work with others with similar interests and abilities, as well as with professionals in the arts. The arts were studied with the intent of enabling students to understand and appreciate feelings, ideas, and values communicated through art traditions of many cultures and to develop individual skills of expression.

Institute participants were assigned to major classes in drawing and painting and selected two elective arts classes from a variety each year. All classes were taught by fine arts faculty members from Indiana University. Major classes offered opportunities to explore media and techniques not usually available in the students' local schools. Elective classes offered opportunities for study in a variety of other arts activities, such as figure drawing, computer graphics, photography, ceramics, narrative drawing, choral singing, jazz, and modern dance or musical theater.

Counselors organized activities for afternoons and weekends that included swimming, playing games, working in open art studios, and visiting art galleries and museums. Special evening programs included lectures by guest artists, musical events, and a talent show.

The curriculum differed substantially from the students' regular art classes in their local schools. Teaching emphases were on problem finding and problem solving; students' individual solutions to problems were strongly encouraged. They were also taught to experience independent inquiry. Study was demanding and accelerated, designed to develop skills and introduce students to the worlds of past and contemporary art.

Artistically Talented Program

Educating teachers to become empowered and to assume educational leadership roles in their own classrooms and in community contexts where communal relationships are valued were the purposes of the Artistically Talented Program (ATP). It is important to help teachers gain confidence in speaking out, become challengers, take initiatives, and determine what and how to teach. Through collaboration and shared leadership, teachers can become empowered to social and political activism and become influential and valuable professionals. For 5 years we coordinated the Artistically Talented

Program with the support of grants from the Indiana Department of Education, and this program has continued to the present without that support. All teachers who attended were certified K–12 art teachers teaching in, or about to start, a program for artistically talented students. Accepted on a competitive basis, they received free room and board, tuition, supplies, and books, as well as a stipend for purchasing art resources. The ATP lasted 2½ weeks and two ATP classes were offered daily; the teachers also had responsibilities throughout the following school year. If they took five classes during 2 summers, they could earn a state endorsement in gifted and talented education.

Program objectives included helping teachers in the following ways:

1. Be challenged, question their assumptions, and examine their teaching strategies
2. Introduce content that was intellectually challenging
3. Become better able to determine what they needed to teach
4. Become a community and inspire one another to become leaders
5. Form cooperative teams in which they explored teaching thematically using traditional and new technologies
6. Be flexible and have broad ideas about what they would teach
7. Assume leadership roles and present their projects publicly at state conventions and local workshops

The teachers chose and developed their own themes and approaches to creating curricula for artistically talented students and formed groups of four or five based on similarities of ideas. The teams continued to meet throughout the next academic year and for several years after their involvement. Every year, alumni from previous years meet during the school year to share ideas and continue their previous networking and collaboration.

The ATP was designed specifically to educate inservice teachers to become proficient in serving populations of artistically talented students. Emphasis was on developing an understanding of the problems, issues, and research related to identification, teaching methods, program policies, program evaluation, and educational resources. Participants were encouraged to reflect on their attitudes and values and form personal positions about programs for artistically talented students. Instruction also focused on helping them become aware of, and critically evaluate, curriculum resources and materials related to educating artistically talented students. We attempted to create a family-like environment by eating meals with the ATP participants where conversations ranged from problems and issues related to art talent development to personal concerns and accomplishments. A substantial amount of time was spent participating in group activities that were both social and professional. All class members were encouraged to strive for high goals and afforded opportunities to achieve them.

Project ARTS

There is a popular focus on programs for students at risk in urban environments, where crime, homelessness, declining test scores, teen pregnancy, and other issues make front-page news. Needs and problems of students in rural communities are less visible and certainly less reported. Though sponsored by a federal agency that previously had funded mostly projects in urban schools for academically gifted students, Project ARTS was a research and development program designed to serve students with high abilities in the arts who attended seven rural elementary schools in Indiana, New Mexico, and South Carolina (Clark & Zimmerman, 1997). All of the schools served 55 to 99 percent of their students free or subsidized lunches, indicating that their local communities are economically disadvantaged.

Briefly stated, the main purposes of Project ARTS were to identify underserved, high-ability, visual and performing arts students; implement 2 years of curricula with the same students; and evaluate the successes of these efforts. The special focus of Project ARTS was to meet the needs of artistically talented students who were culturally diverse. Communities were chosen to participate because the vast majority of people in the communities represented well-established, rural subcultures.

The two Indiana communities were located in southern agricultural parts of the state where, over several generations, families had migrated from Appalachian regions of Kentucky and Tennessee.

They represented a distinctive culture with its roots in England and Scotland.

Two schools in New Mexico, each with a distinctive culture, participated. One served students of Hispanic descent whose families have lived in northern New Mexico since the mid-1500s. Their Spanish Catholic backgrounds were intermixed with that of Native Americans from nearby Pueblo cultures. Students in the other school were entirely Native American, living on a conservative, traditional pueblo on the Santo Domingo Indian Reservation, and speaking Spanish and English along with their native Keres language.

Located near the southern coastal tip of South Carolina, Beaufort is home to the Sea Islands and the African American people who developed the Gullah language and culture. They have lived there since the earliest days of their African ancestors' importation as slaves. Three rural schools in this area participated in Project ARTS.

The four cultural groups represented in the project are locally quite homogeneous in their respective locations. Each has a long and well-established history and culture. None of these schools, however, had included community arts or local culture in their curricula. In Indiana, schools that participated had both arts and gifted and talented programs. In New Mexico, there were no arts teachers, but there was a long-standing gifted and talented program. In South Carolina, there were arts teachers in the schools, but no gifted and talented program. The staff of Project ARTS emphasized a multiethnic approach by helping students understand and appreciate their local crafts, folk arts, popular arts, and cultural traditions of their families and communities. We encouraged teachers at each school to form parent and community advisory groups to help with identifying students, bringing local cultural resources into the curricula, and assessing the results.

Each school staff decided to emphasize history and cultural backgrounds and arts of their local communities. The arts of other cultures also were studied, and differentiated curricula were extended to include music and dance; these were then exchanged among all of the sites. Each group of students, therefore, was able to study and share ideas, values, and traditions associated with all of the students' cultures in the seven schools participating in Project ARTS.

1 Current Issues in Art Talent Development

Plate 1.1 A photo collage by a seventh-grade student at the IU Summer Arts Institute, which expresses her concerns with the negative effects of gossip at her junior high school

There are several current issues that bear directly on contemporary concerns about art talent development. One is the dynamic tension between elitism and egalitarianism in respect to nurturing art talents of highly able students, while at the same time providing quality art education programs for all students. Another issue is related to integrating the arts and academics for gifted and talented students, and a third concerns definitions and conceptions about relationships among giftedness, talent development, and creativity.

EXCELLENCE AND EQUITY ISSUES FOR ARTISTICALLY TALENTED STUDENTS

Conflicts between elitism and egalitarianism arise in all societies. To avoid creating elitist educational systems, the educational policies of many countries contain commitments to offer equal opportunities for all students. Americans have never been comfortable with confronting ideas about excellence and equity, and this discomfort often can be traced to deep-seated anti-intellectualism (Zimmerman, 1997e).

In liberal democratic traditions, the promise of democracy is attainable only when advantages available to one person are available to all. Smith and Traver (1983) defined *equity* as a desire for justice, fairness, or even mercy. They defined *excellence* as the desire to achieve the highest degree of human perfection. Within this tradition, the only way to produce good citizens or a good society is to have high expectations and demand excellence through independent, individual efforts. Others have defined *equity* in terms of educational interventions that match the needs of all students, from the learning disabled to the gifted, and believe that the outcome of a democratic education should provide maximal learning for every student. (Evans & King, 1994; Stevens, 1992).

It is obvious that a dilemma arises in balancing educational demands of equity and excellence, especially in an age of major demographic shifts. Stevens (1992) believed excellence and equity had been interpreted as mutually exclusive, but thought that equity and excellence could be merged. He defined *equity* as equality of opportunities offered to each individual. *Excellence* would occur when each individual's specific educational needs were met and a student could progress as far as his or her abilities allowed. This explanation of a quality-oriented paradigm of excellence and equity brings to the fore important questions about whether such a synthesis is possible or desirable, or whether excellence and equity should be viewed as dichotomous.

Questions of equity and excellence in education have always been asked when values of equal op-

portunities for all appear to be in opposition to the perceived tradition of high achievement. Gardner (1961) noted that there are three competing principles—hereditary privilege, "equaltarianism," and competitive performance—and that tension is created between an "emphasis on individual performance and restraints on individual performance" (p. 28). He believed this tension should never be resolved. He used the term *equaltarianism* to define education that benefits each individual and seeks to establish excellence in a context of concern for all. According to Gardner, a democracy must foster excellence in education in order to survive, but excellence must be sought in a context of concern for all. Society must provide opportunities and rewards for all individuals so that they can realize their potentials, perform at their best, and not resent those at other levels. A democratic education should include a balance of these discrete, competing arguments; and care must be taken not to move toward aristocracy or totalitarianism.

The excellence versus equity argument raises the question, What is meant by equity in a nation that purports to offer equal opportunities for all citizens? If standards are important, the same standards must apply to all. If equal opportunities are important, different resources must be offered to different students. School interventions must ensure that no student is held back by others' rates of progress. Excellence without equity is elitism, and equity without excellence produces mediocrity. Balanced policies, therefore, are needed to uphold a dynamic tension between excellence and equity.

Historical Background

It is important to review, briefly, the history of excellence and equity in the context of American education from the polar beliefs evidenced in Jacksonian and Jeffersonian conceptions to present-day concerns about educational opportunities and practices. Opposing stances about education are not new and their roots are grounded in a legacy of education that has as much relevance today as it did during the period from 1789 to 1877. At that time, differences between Jacksonian and Jeffersonian conceptions of excellence and equity took form and citizens took sides. Jefferson believed a liberal arts education should be available to people from all social classes and he supported the establishment of colleges where superior students would be educated and prepared for leadership roles in society. Jefferson thought superior students from any class could rise to leadership positions, based on ability, not just students from the privileged class.

Jackson viewed public education as a great leveler, providing common bases for building a cohesive society, free of aristocratic patterns of European societies. He believed that all people could take leadership roles and that the attainments of a well-educated farmer and a scholar were equal. He sought to establish free school systems in which every high school graduate, regardless of ability, could attend a state university and study vocations needed by society.

In 1893 the Committee of Ten, consisting of prominent educators appointed by the National Education Association to study high school curriculum, advocated a uniform, traditional high school curriculum in the United States. Anyone who completed high school was to be accepted into college, and all students were to receive the same education. In terms of equity, there would be no distinction between non-college-bound and college-bound students. By the 1920s immigration laws changed and notions about the need for a stratification of society surfaced. Deeper issues of inequity in respect to race, class, and gender, however, were not addressed. The early 1920s and 1930s also witnessed popularity of the testing movement that emphasized psychometric advances in measurement of intelligence as related to school achievement. Reactions to this movement became influential in the late 1930s and 1940s: Stress was placed on interrelatedness of individuals, schools, and society, and educators questioned the value of standardized tests and instruction that relied heavily on test results. Time was ripe for the emergence of Lowenfeld's (1954) notions of self-expression and creativity that quickly became popular and dominated art education theory and practice for the next 5 decades. The creative self-expression approach places great emphasis on student-centered art activities. The focus is on the use of a variety of art materials and teachers' roles

are to nurture and motivate students directly in techniques and skills, rather than to instruct. Students are expected to develop naturally with a minimum of adult intervention.

During the post-Sputnik era of the 1950s, there was an intense interest in developing mathematical and scientific capabilities of high-ability students. Grouping and tracking became popular, with placement based on individual differences determined by standardized ability tests. In the early to mid-1960s the emphasis on educational excellence was replaced by a focus on practices that contributed to achieving educational equity. Attention shifted from academically talented students to those who were underprivileged. Long-neglected societal issues that addressed the nation's minorities and underrepresented groups were championed through federal legislation. In the 1970s there was a renewed interest in disadvantaged students and issues related to social justice, flexible curricula, and individual learners.

The equity focus in the 1960s and 1970s did not yield satisfactory educational results. The late 1970s, therefore, witnessed a waning of interest in social equity and a shift toward educational excellence manifest in the back-to-basics movement. In this new global environment, academic achievements of U.S. students did not equal those of other developed nations. In the 1980s numerous public and private studies and reports were published about the status of public education. Within the first few years of the 1980s, over 200 reforms at national and state levels were introduced, and the conclusion was reached that public education had failed to provide high standards for academic excellence, particularly for gifted and talented students. The idea surfaced that there should not be a standardized curriculum for all students although there should be a basic set of requirements for all academic subjects. Most people were in agreement about the importance of academic subjects in school curricula, but they varied in their support and value for arts education.

The early 1980s also witnessed establishment of the Getty Center for Education in the Arts, which emphasized fostering excellence in art education through intellectual attainment of skills and understandings in art criticism, art history, aesthetics, and art production. This notion was preceded by a number of research and development seminars, institutes, and publications that supported discipline-centered art education. This discipline-centered movement quickly became popular because its philosophy was right for the times. Resources and support provided by the Getty Center enabled art education reform practices to take place rapidly.

In the final period of this historical survey—the early 1990s—the emphasis on excellence in education continued, along with a growing interest in parent and community involvement in schools and attention to issues of pluralism and diversity. Issues in this school reform movement included multiculturalism, inclusion, collaboration, teamwork, and empowerment.

Gifted and Talented Programs

As mentioned earlier in this chapter, concepts of excellence and equity need not be incompatible, according to many educators involved in the education of high-ability students. If egalitarianism means giving equal opportunities for gifted and talented students suited to their needs, as has been done for those who are mentally or physically challenged, every student should receive a qualitative education appropriate to his or her needs. This means different children will receive different kinds of education; but as Gallagher (1993) asserted, "the equal treatment of unequals is not equal" (p. 19).

Programs of enrichment and acceleration usually have a great potential for positive effects on student learning. In his research about ability grouping, Kulik (1992) found that highly talented students profit greatly from working in accelerated and enrichment classes. Benefits were slightest for students in programs that group students by ability but prescribe common learning experiences for all students. It has been shown in many research studies that grouping of high-ability students produces significant academic benefits for all students. Students in lower ability groupings are not harmed academically and in many cases are helped. High-ability students' achievements decline in heterogeneous settings and rise when they are grouped according to their abilities (Kulik & Kulik, 1992). Those with special talents should have opportunities to cultivate those talents, and such opportunities therefore should not be viewed negatively.

Special programming for gifted and talented students does not necessarily mean that such students are always segregated from their age peers. In-class enrichment, ability grouping within a heterogeneous population, pull-out programs, after-school programs, summer programs, mentorships, and internships are examples of educational settings and practices that do not segregate high-ability students from other students. Not all educators agree that homogenized grouping is egalitarian, and some have charged that ability grouping is discriminatory, unfair, and ineffective. Others have argued that regular classroom teachers cannot meet the educational needs of talented students in regular classrooms and suggest that grouping options need to remove high-ability students from their classrooms. They recognize that high-ability students need time with similar peers so they can master more complex ideas than those presented in regular classrooms.

Improving the quality of education for all learners requires sensitivity to their needs and carefully planned educational experiences. There should be a balance between quality of opportunity and equality of treatment in education. High-quality education should be available to all students, but the nature of those services should vary according to diagnosed needs. Educational provisions should vary when applied in different contexts with students from diverse backgrounds and abilities.

A concomitant issue concerns integrating arts and academic subjects in programs for gifted and talented students so that they receive appropriate educational opportunities. It also is important for an equitable and excellent education, if art talent development is to take a prominent place in school programs, that arts abilities are recognized as cognitive abilities that require intelligence and are linked to academic abilities.

INTEGRATION OF THE ARTS AND ACADEMICS FOR GIFTED AND TALENTED STUDENTS

It was a warm day on our university campus, and teenage students were pouring out of cars to attend a 2-week institute for academically gifted students. Since we were directors of a similar institute for artistically talented students, the director of the academic program asked us, "Why have so many of these students brought guitars or other instruments? After all, this is an academic program." We replied that we thought it was natural because students often have potential abilities in any number of talent areas. Why is it assumed that someone with high science or mathematics scores does not have advanced interests or talents in the visual or performing arts? Why is it assumed that someone with high arts abilities doesn't also have high abilities in other school subjects? Why haven't school programs for academically able and artistically able students integrated their efforts? Such questions have been dealt with casually in education literature (Clark & Zimmerman, 1998). We will respond to these questions here and set forth a case for including art talent development as part of all programs for high-ability students.

There are many programs for high-ability visual arts students, but these often do not address academic areas or press students toward levels of high academic achievement. There is a need for the education of both high-ability academic students and artistically talented students to incorporate visual and performing arts as integral parts of their education because these needs often are ignored. A decade of administering a summer enrichment program and more than 25 years of research have shown us that students identified as gifted in academic programs often are also visually talented and students identified as talented in the visual arts often are highly able in academic subjects.

The Javits Gifted and Talented Students Education Act created a number of programs and research projects. *High-ability students* were defined as those identified by educators as having outstanding abilities and being capable of high performance in intellectual activities, academic aptitudes, creative or productive thinking, leadership abilities, or visual and performing arts abilities. These students require services not ordinarily provided by schools in order to fully develop their capabilities.

Definitions of the terms *gifted* and *talented* have been appropriated by researchers and educators and have been given specific meanings. In the past, *gifted* meant having generally superior intellectual abilities in academic subjects and *talented* meant having outstanding abilities in the visual and per-

forming arts. Recently, however, *gifted* has retained its meaning and *talented* has been defined as possessing superior abilities in language arts, science, mathematics, and other subjects. Abilities associated with the arts, however, often are considered subject specific, not requiring cognitive abilities.

The Relationship Between Academic Ability and Art Talent

There are several points of view about interrelationships between abilities of highly able students in academics and arts areas. One is to ignore art talent development as a component of programming for academically talented students. Another is to view students' academic achievements as separate from abilities in the visual arts. Often researchers claim little evidence that students with talent in the arts also are talented in academic areas.

Gardner (1983) claimed a positive relationship between arts and intellectual and academic abilities, whereas Sternberg (1985) argued that art abilities are not related to intellectual capabilities. Winner (1996) suggested that artistically talented students have abilities that cannot be measured on an IQ test. Dichotomizing arts and academic abilities often results in programs where arts are not valued in the education of high-ability students. The arts, however, offer much to support achievements of high-ability academic and art students.

Our own research has indicated direct relationships between academic achievement and arts abilities. During a study of teenage students attending our Summer Arts Institute, *all* reported positive reactions to schooling and were outstanding in academic subjects. In a case study, Zimmerman (1995) found a multitalented student able to express himself both discursively and nondiscursively in the visual arts, music, language arts, and science. Accelerated learning resulted in his being able to complete assignments in classes in many ways, including through both visual and verbal problem solving. The benefits of programs that allow high-ability students to develop both academic and arts abilities are demonstrated by this case study and other research.

Eisner (1994) claimed that affect and cognition are *not* independent processes that can be separated. Cognition is expanded through different kinds of intelligence as people confront and solve problems. Decisions to use language arts, science, social studies, mathematical, or visual and performing arts skills and understandings to confront meanings are rewarded differently in different cultures. There are traits, characteristics, and behaviors universal to talent development and these all have consequences in a variety of cultural contexts. If a culture places less value on arts than academic education, high-ability students will have little exposure to the arts and few opportunities to express their abilities in expressive areas. It is important to educate students to use their imaginations and spatial abilities as they attempt to solve problem without relying solely on their mathematical or verbal skills. On the other hand, an artist working as a graphic designer needs to use mathematics, language arts, and personal skills effectively, as well as visual thinking.

As a discipline, arts education should help all students understand and appreciate ideas and values that art traditions communicate in diverse cultures and forms. Chapman (1978) described purposes and goals of art education this way: "School art programs . . . facilitate the child's quest for personal fulfillment . . . studies of artistic heritage provide children with a knowledge of art as a significant form of human achievement" (p. 118). These goals have great relevance for a holistic and comprehensive education that incorporates the arts for all students. Arts are both basic and essential in curricula that focus on talent development and building social, personal, expressive, and cognitive skills necessary for responsible participation in a democratic society

Achter, Benbow, and Lubinski (1997) advocated more comprehensive assessments with appropriate ability and preference tools aimed at "revealing the richness, multidimensionality, and diversity within intellectually talented populations" (p. 13). Unfortunately, American education has promoted intellectual talent and abilities only in predominantly academic areas and has made the arts peripheral to this enterprise. A multidimensional view of highly able students should incorporate all areas of talent development, including those in the visual and performing arts.

Sensitivity to the fact that students may have multiple gifts and talents in several domains (such as mathematics and music) or in several arts areas (such as visual arts and dance), or may have specializations within one area (such as painting or sculpting) has prompted the use of multiple criteria systems of identification of high-ability students. One justification for this is the desirability of selecting students with talents in a number of different areas.

Understandings about characteristics and abilities of artistically talented students often are based on uninformed judgments and can affect how students are identified, what curricula are planned for them, and how their accomplishments are assessed. Although visual arts identification programs often emphasize a superior final product or performance, attention also should be paid to arts processes that may ultimately lead to products and performances. More emphasis on processes of arriving at solutions should be part of identification programs for students with high abilities in academic and arts domains. Although all high-ability students may not produce superior products or performances, evidence of their progress and achievement, for example, can be found in process portfolios at elementary and secondary levels. Students' methods of discovery and delving deeper into productive questions sometimes can be more indicative of arts understandings than their actual solutions to problems.

GIFTEDNESS, CREATIVITY, AND ART TALENT DEVELOPMENT

Definitions and conceptions about relationships among giftedness, talent development, and creativity have been considered for the past 5 decades (Clark & Zimmerman, 2001a). Yet intellectual ability and academic aptitude still dominate identification procedures and design of programs for students with high abilities in a variety of areas. There is a lack of consensus about what constitutes creativity in educational programs, and developing operational definitions of the term *creativity* is difficult. Sternberg and Lubart's (1999) definition of *creativity* as "the ability to produce work that is both novel . . . and appropriate" (p. 3) is one that has been widely accepted. Many psychologists and educators agree that creativity is a complex process that can be viewed as a system of relationships among persons, processes, products, and social and cultural contexts (Csikszentmihalyi, 1996; D. H. Feldman, 1999; Gardner, 1996; Sternberg, 1999). According to Sternberg, all creative work occurs in one or more domains, and a person, act, or product cannot be considered creative unless judged by a community of experts within that domain, such as the visual arts.

Although a number of scholars agree that creative achievement is reflected in the production of useful, new ideas or products that call for finding and solving a problem in a novel way, others distinguish between adult creative acts and those of students. Csikszentmihalyi (1990, 1996), D. H. Feldman (1982), and Winner and Martino (1993) all refer to creativity as inventiveness within a domain of knowledge, where a creative individual revolutionizes that domain. No talented children, they claim, have caused the reorganization of a domain of knowledge. If these concepts were applied to student acts, it would be rare that a student would create a work of art that is original, appropriate, and qualitatively different from products made by mature artists, although students can create products that are novel to themselves or those of their peers.

Some traits associated with creativity that are related to artists' processes of conceiving ideas and producing artworks may have significance for educating artistically talented students. Problem finding, problem solving, divergent and convergent thinking, self-expression, and flexibility to adapt to new situations are traits commonly associated with creativity (Mumford, Connely, & Baughman, & Marks, 1994; Runco & Nemiro, 1993). We do not advocate that artistically talented students should be involved in activities identical to those of adult artists. Rather, certain processes used by arts professionals can suggest educational interventions that enrich differentiated programs for artistically talented students.

Csikszentmihalyi (1996) claimed that talent differs from creativity because talent focuses on innate abilities and people can achieve success without evidencing talent. He explained that talented individuals fit under domains of knowledge that exist in their cultures. Members of a field relevant to their interests and abilities recognize talented people as highly competent. Creative people, however, often do not fit in a domain and only after

sustained effort and time are their accomplishments recognized and valued. Sternberg (2001) differentiated between intelligence, as advancing societal norms, and creativity, as opposing old and creating new norms.

Hunsaker and Callahan (1995) described three ways a relationship between creativity and talent development can be formulated:

1. Giftedness and talent can be viewed as separate abilities.
2. Creativity can be seen as a fundamental concept of giftedness.
3. Creativity can be considered as a separate category or style of giftedness.

Another view is that gifted is a fixed concept, not amenable to influence of education. Talent and talent development, however, are active concepts and students can be nurtured to develop special abilities where education plays an important role (Feldhusen, 1994). Feldhusen's conception of talent development is viewed in direct relation to academic school subjects students will pursue in their careers as adults.

Within the past 15 years, there has been a major shift in theory and practice in the field of visual arts education from child-centered to subject-centered curricula. This shift, referred to as *discipline-based art education* (DBAE) or *comprehensive art education*, emphasizes art in the general education of all students. Discipline-based art education differs significantly from *creative self-expression*, an approach to art education that had been dominant for over 45 years. The goal of creative self-expression was to develop each student's inherent creative and expressive abilities. Creativity was represented as being innate and developing naturally without imposing adult conceptions on a learner's creative development. The teacher's role in a creative self-expression program was to provide motivation, support, resources, and supplies. In DBAE, students are taught directly through articulated and required curricula in which disciplines are emphasized and works of adults, from diverse cultural contexts, serve as motivators.

Khatena (1982) and others claimed that visual and performing arts abilities are closely associated with creativity as a measurable construct. Recently, Clark tested over 1,200 third graders in four ethnically diverse communities and found strong correlation among drawing ability as measured by Clark's Drawing Abilities Test (CDAT), creativity as determined by a modified version of Torrance Tests of Creative Thinking (TTCT), and statewide achievement tests (Clark & Zimmerman, 2001b). Clark concluded that the correlation indicates performance on drawing, creativity, and achievement tests may be affected by other factors such as intelligence or general problem-solving abilities. Burton, Horowitz, and Abeles (2000) also found high-ability art students received high scores on Torrance Tests.

Characteristics of Artistically Talented Students

Characteristics associated with artistically talented students are well-developed drawing skills, high cognitive abilities, interest, and motivation. Other characteristics include intensity of application and early mastery of cultural forms typical of art exceptionality, production of a large volume of work over a sustained period of time, nurturance from family and teachers, and thematically specialized work (Pariser, 1997). These students also create imaginative worlds, are intensely involved in a specific domain, and experiment with spatial and naturalistic renderings (Winner, 1996). Milbrath (1998) found that artistically talented children began drawing representationally 1 to 2 years earlier, evidenced a high degree of creativity and originality, demonstrated deep commitment, and drew in qualitatively different ways than their peers. In research about world-class artists, Pariser (1991, 1995) found that, as young children, these artists did not evidence outstanding capacities. However, they did exhibit inventiveness and were able to render subjects accurately and enthusiastically.

We believe the ability to depict the world realistically should be considered only one among many indicators of talent in the visual arts. Some artistically talented young people concentrate on realistic depiction of objects and are influenced by Western spatial conventions. Others may concentrate on using art to depict visual narratives creatively, through use of themes and variations, humor, paradoxes, puns, metaphors, and deep emotional involvement. Popular culture and new conceptions of art talent development need to be addressed in programs for artistically talented students. Although skill with specific media may indicate precocious talent, it may not be a salient indicator for other students.

Educational Interventions, Creativity, and Art Talent Development

Recent research demonstrates that problem-finding and problem-solving skills can be taught and students' productive thinking and creative problem solving can be nurtured (Treffinger, Sortore, & Cross, 1993). Talent development can be enhanced in a supportive, flexible, and intellectually demanding environment by encouraging students to work consistently and responsibly when confronted by frustration. According to Feldhusen (1992), students can be taught to find and clarify problems and use appropriate skills when attempting to solve them. They also can be taught to monitor their own learning and seek and test alternative solutions.

Student creativity also can be developed by adapting teaching strategies that balance generation of new ideas, critical thinking abilities, and abilities to translate theory into practice (Sternberg & Williams, 1996). D. H. Feldman (1980) studied children who were prodigies in many different areas including the arts, and was convinced that all progress in learning is the result of intensive and prolonged instruction. Successful teachers of highly able students are knowledgeable about their subject matter, able to communicate instruction effectively, and select important learning experiences that lead their students to attain challenging and advanced levels of achievements. To develop art talent and creativity, therefore, it is important that art teachers be sensitive to the needs of artistically talented students and go beyond teaching skills to encouraging independent thought, spontaneity, and originality. These are traits not typically encouraged in classrooms, although they often are evidenced in the behaviors of artistically talented students.

Educators have suggested a number of strategies that support creativity and talent development in students who use them. These include the following:

1. Practice problem finding as well as problem solving.
2. Use unfamiliar materials that elicit more original thinking and lead to new ideas.
3. Experience convergent (structured) and divergent (unstructured) tasks.
4. Rely on both visual and verbal materials.
5. Be exposed to curricula with open-ended outcomes that allow for unpredictable results.
6. Follow individual interests and work in groups, as well as independently.
7. Choose environments that support individual talents and creativity.
8. Encounter a wide range of tasks intended to reinforce and enhance emerging talents. (Csikszentmihalyi, 1996; Feldhusen, 1995; Mumford et al., 1994; Runco, 1993; Runco & Nemiro, 1993; Starko, 2001; Sternberg & Williams, 1996).

In addition, Csikszentmihalyi (1996) suggested that talented students should be exposed to, and become involved with, a domain that interests them early in life, even if it is not what they may pursue as adults. Such students may be interested in many domains; however, this breadth of interest is not often encouraged in schools.

From a Western perspective, creativity is defined as culminating in a product that is both novel and appropriate within a particular cultural context. Problem-finding and problem-solving initiatives are strategies that are in harmony with a product-oriented cultural context. Creativity, therefore, is more likely to occur in a society where new ideas take less time to be disseminated and accepted (Lubart, 1999; Sternberg & Lubart, 1999). In many Eastern cultures, for example, collaboration, cooperation, conformity, and tradition are valued more than novel solutions to problems and circumstances within a culture.

In this postmodern age, the notion of recycled objects that can be used to create artworks has been accepted (Efland, Freedman, & Stuhr, 1996). An implication is that contemporary concepts about creativity and art talent development may need to be reconsidered if creativity is defined only as producing something novel or original within a particular culture. Peat (2000) suggested that renewing and revitalizing something already accepted tradi-tionally can be viewed as a creative act, and innovation and rapid change may disrupt traditional societies.

CONCEPTIONS AND MISCONCEPTIONS ABOUT ART TALENT DEVELOPMENT

Even when the terms *giftedness*, *creativity*, and *art talent development* are clarified and defined for purposes of identification, curriculum development, and assessment, some conceptions and misconceptions, myths about art talent development and stereotypes about artistically talented students, still continue to exist. It is important to make these misconceptions and misunderstandings public so that characteristics and abilities of artistically talented students that are related to identifying, teaching, and providing programs, services, and settings appropriate to their educational needs are taken into consideration.

Many people believe that artistically talented students' artwork is easy to recognize in classrooms. Many students, however, demonstrate their talents in activities that only occur outside of schools, and teachers are often unaware of the rich visual expressions that students create in such situations (Clark, 1984; Wilson & Wilson, 1976). Many students, especially adolescents, mask their art abilities because such abilities are misunderstood or considered strange by teachers and other students. Students who conform to classroom expectations and perform well in art often are judged as talented, although the obvious difficulties of such labeling have been noted (Guskin, Zimmerman, Okola, & Peng, 1986). Gallagher (1985) claimed that many gifted and talented children remain unrecognized because their school performance is inconsistent with teachers' expectations. Many children demonstrate superior abilities only in extracurricular activities because such events are more rewarding and less threatening than those that occur in their regular school classrooms (Fine, 1970).

Another common misunderstanding is that above average intelligence is not a requirement for superior artistic abilities. Prominent educators have claimed that intelligence tests do not indicate artistic giftedness (Sternberg, 1986; Winner, 1996).

Such beliefs are reinforced when schools place students with low intellectual abilities in art classes because it is thought that such children can succeed there even though they may not be successful in other school subjects. An even more detrimental practice is counseling students with superior academic abilities away from art classes in the mistaken belief that such classes make no contribution to their future needs.

Arbitrary separation of intellectual and artistic performance has been questioned for many years. In 1936 Tiebout and Meier summarized their years of research with the conclusion that both artistic potential and general achievement are dependent largely on intellectual capacity. Other researchers have asserted that positive relationships exist between intelligence and abilities in art (Eisner, 1994; Ziegfeld, 1961) and that high-ability academic students also may be talented in the arts (Schubert, 1973; Vernon, Adamson, & Vernon, 1977). Although not all high-ability academic students possess art talent, they often possess abilities necessary for acquiring advanced techniques and skills for producing superior artworks (Luca & Allen, 1974; Schubert, 1973).

Adult artists are often caricatured in the United States as social outcasts, misfits, nonconformists, or loners, and children with superior art abilities often suffer from such caricatures by adults, although these caricatures often are false. So, too, are stereotypes of gifted children as socially inept, physically immature, or emotionally unstable. Numerous studies have shown gifted and talented students to be social and intellectual leaders, physically superior to their peers, and emotionally well adjusted (B. Clark, 1979; Guskin et al., 1986; Terman & Oden, 1947; Tuttle & Becker, 1980). The common stereotype of artistically talented children as social isolates is refuted by evidence that gifted and talented children frequently are chosen as preferred companions and have above average social contacts and relationships (Gallagher & Gallagher, 1994).

A major misunderstanding is that talented students need no instruction or that teaching in the arts will harm creative self-expression. Statements such as "One cannot teach art. . . . Artists are born" (Viola, 1942, p. 35), "Let children do what they please, their creativity should be entirely unconstrained" (Fritz, 1930, p. 22), and "Where rigid plans are made . . . the experience may be disap-

pointing and frustrating" (Brittain, 1961, p. 283) have led teachers to believe talented children should not be taught, that talents develop simply as a result of maturation, or that talented children can make it on their own. As a consequence, they believe that programs for talented students need not be planned and that commonly available art materials are sufficient to meet their needs.

Studies of intellectually and artistically talented students have shown that directive instruction is essential to the development of superior abilities (D. H. Feldman, 1979; Robinson, Roedell, & Jackson, 1979; Zimmerman, 1995). Talent in the arts must be encouraged, exercised, and practiced in order to flourish, and students with superior abilities need differentiated assignments, time schedules, and instructional guidance. Beliefs that all children are equally talented or that only a few are endowed with art talent predicate against sound education in the visual arts and lead to programs detrimental to the needs of superior students (Zimmerman, 1997e). Teachers with these misconceptions believe that all children are creative or that everyone can draw. They also lead children to say, "I can't draw a straight line" or "I can't make anything look right."

A New Look at the Concept of Art Talent

Intelligence is a fairly universal concept, identified by scores on tests or teacher assignments. It also is believed to be normally distributed, with some students receiving low scores, most students receiving midrange scores, and some students receiving high scores. Intelligence, therefore, includes many deviations above or below a mean. Giftedness or talent often is described as obtaining scores significantly above the mean. Research establishes that art talent is normally distributed, dependent upon societal norms, and subject to cultural interpretation. Reliable and valid instruments, such as Clark's Drawing Abilities Test, have demonstrated that students have little, average, or superior art talent; with a normal distribution as a consequence (Clark, 1984). Everyone can be viewed, therefore, as possessing some art talent; some will have small amounts, some average amounts, and some high levels of art abilities.

Art educators, classroom teachers, researchers, and theorists all have discussed artistically talented children, and their conclusions often are contradictory. All children develop their own style of drawing, while some will develop a qualitatively richer style than others. Some researchers reported that differences between students with varying levels of talent were in degree, not in kind (Lark-Horovitz, Lewis, & Luca, 1967; Lark-Horovitz & Norton, 1960; Meier, 1939). Another contribution to understanding art talent as normally distributed was reported in the National Assessment of Educational Progress (1977, 1981) and the National Center for Educational Statistics (1998). These measured the skills and abilities of students and yielded scales of naive to sophisticated solutions. Neither children nor adults are cognitively able or not able, nor are they talented or not talented. Ability often is measured on scales that range from minimum to average to superior. All children possess art talent in similar ways; the amount of talent each child possesses will effectively limit his or her capabilities to learn and perform tasks related to the arts.

We have outlined a generalized curriculum content for teaching all of these stages of art talent, related to understanding the works of artists, art historians, art critics, and aestheticians (Clark & Zimmerman, 1978b). This model can be used to create an organizing framework for reporting needed research, reporting completed research, and defining art talent as normally distributed. If the naive to sophisticated stages in this model are superimposed over a normal distribution, the standard deviations might be seen as describing parallel levels of development of talent in the visual arts (see Chapter 5 for a detailed description of this model). This distribution is important because it implies that art education researchers could categorically group products or other measures as evidence of naive to sophisticated abilities. We could then think of art talent as normally distributed with predictable deviations above or below a mean. This creates a new model for identification of artistically talented students.

CONCLUSIONS AND RECOMMENDATIONS

In a democratic society, policies are needed that uphold the dynamic tension and competing de-

mands of excellence and equity. In art education, creating a balance between excellence and equity demands that students, parents, teachers, administrators, and community members need to take responsibility for action. They need to stress excellence and demand equity and the exploration of a diversity of perspectives. Curricula and assessments should be designed to develop standards that serve the needs of all students and are high enough to challenge artistically talented students. Gifted program standards have been supported by the National Association of Gifted Children (Landrum, Callahan, & Shaklee, 2001) to provide benchmarks for measuring program effectiveness, criteria for program evaluation, guidelines for program development, and recommendations for minimal requirements for high-quality gifted and talented programs. Opportunities in the visual arts for economically disadvantaged students and students from diverse backgrounds also should be provided so that barriers to success are removed and opportunities for achievement in art are open to all. Rather than having all students complete tasks at grade level, according to minimal standards, schools should provide the most excellent and equitable education for all students so that no students are kept behind.

All citizens need to strive toward establishing meaningful goals and values for art education. It is one thing to assert that art should be taught in all schools and another to set forth clear goals and objectives about what and why this should be taught. Students, teachers, parents, administrators, and community members should all have input about how art is taught in their schools and realize there are commonalities and differences between what is taught in their communities and what is taught in other communities. They must decide what goals and values are important for achieving an equitable and excellent art education program in which all students, including those with superior artistic talent, are best served.

Research should be conducted to evaluate the effectiveness of program options, such as mixed-ability grouping, ability grouping, and acceleration for artistically talented students. Universities and colleges as well as private, federal, and state agencies should be encouraged to support large-scale research studies that address issues in art education about art content and program opportunities including size, purpose, design, selection, curriculum, funding, and arts-related experiences that are offered. There is a need for program designers to establish a clearly defined theoretical basis for including all highly able students in programs that emphasize both academic and arts abilities and understandings that are qualitatively different from those generally offered in schools. The importance of developing enriched programs for artistically talented students cannot be underestimated. It is apparent that students need to be prepared for a new information age. Students who will later become practicing artists should be prepared to think creatively and develop skills and abilities appropriate in a rapidly changing world. There also is a need to prepare appreciators and consumers of art who, as future leaders, will make decisions about the arts in their local communities and beyond.

Following are our recommendations for nurturing art talent in comprehensive education programs for high-ability students.

Recommendation 1: Students should be offered differentiated programs that integrate arts and academic areas. High-achieving science students need access to well-equipped, up-to-date laboratories in which they can explore problems related to those that resemble the work of contemporary scientists. In the same way, artistically talented students need access to spaces and facilities that resemble studios and other workplaces of artists solving current visual art problems.

Recommendation 2: The arts should be included as part of all comprehensive gifted and talented programs. Every student is entitled to the education he or she needs; different students need different educational programming. Schools should provide the most excellent and equitable opportunities to study the arts to all students as part of comprehensive programs. Learning the role of the arts in societies and cultures is vitally important to full understanding of all peoples in all parts of the world.

Recommendation 3: Parents, teachers, and administrators need to be educated about the content

of gifted and talented education programs. Schools often encourage students who have high abilities in academic and arts areas to take classes in the former and view the latter as an area of study to be mastered outside the school environment. Administrators should provide financial support for high-ability students' education in all talent areas.

Recommendation 4: Academic and arts educators who teach academically and artistically gifted and talented students should communicate and collaborate in planning programs. Relationships between the arts and academic areas need to be integrated without the arts becoming subservient to the goals of academic programs.

Recommendation 5: Resources and teaching strategies need to be developed that incorporate the arts in comprehensive programs. If the arts are to become integral parts of all high-ability programs, teaching strategies need to be developed that incorporate the arts into programs that are appropriate to the learning styles and cultural backgrounds of individual students. Teachers of highly able students should address how best to educate students so the arts are successfully represented with both equity and excellence in gifted and talented programs across the country.

Recommendation 6. There is a lack of consensus about definitions of creativity, giftedness, and talent and their interrelationships. Our position is that it is most appropriate if talent development and aspects of creativity are defined in terms of educational practice and how they are responsive to educational interventions. In visual art education, there has been a shift in emphasis from creative self-expression to comprehensive art education, where creativity and talent development are related to the world of art and the work of artists. There also is emerging evidence that art talent development, creativity, and academic achievement may all be correlated.

Recommendation 7. Persons who have studied artistically talented students have countered popular misconceptions about art talent with evidence and counter claims. We presented a new conception with parallels between representation of achievement on a normal distribution and of

Plate 1.2 A pastel drawing of another student by a sixth-grade IU Summer Arts Institute student that depicts personal feelings about growth and renewal

talent in art on a naive to sophisticated continuum. In this new construction, every person has talent, but in varying degrees. Implications of this new concept of talent should create teaching practices and program designs that lead to new opportunities for students at all talent levels, including those with superior abilities in the visual arts.

2 Student Identification

Photo 2.1 IU Summers Arts Institute students deeply involved in drawing activities

Near the beginning of Chaim Potok's book, *My Name is Asher Lev* (1992), the principle character explains his lifelong obsession with creating images. Later he describes his uncontrollable need to create images and how he drew in his family's Bible and defaced it. Although this story is fiction, there are a great number of young people across the country who share this interest and overwhelming desire to create expressive imagery. Unfortunately, most of them are provided neither the support nor instruction they need to realize their abilities. Many are not even acknowledged to be artistically talented. In this chapter we explore how to identify artistically talented students and offer practical applications. First, we will introduce a series of contemporary issues that bear upon the subject. Next, we will describe the ramifications of these issues and then relate some of these to current practices. Finally, we will generate a series of research recommendations about identifying artistically talented students.

ISSUES RELATED TO THE IDENTIFICATION OF ARTISTICALLY TALENTED STUDENTS

Our concerns about identifying artistically talented students are based upon our histories as teachers and our dedication to improving their education. Since we coauthored *Educating Artisti-*

cally Talented Students (1984) and *Resources for Educating Artistically Talented Students* (1987), there has been a heightened interest in the education of such students. Concurrently, several authors have written about problems of defining, describing, screening, and identifying artistically talented students as well as developing programs for them. Here we will discuss two groups of issues: (1) defining visual arts talent and (2) identifying artistically talented students.

Definition of Talent in the Visual Arts

There are no commonly accepted definitions of the terms *gifted* or *talented*. As discussed in Chapter 1, the term *gifted* refers to students with superior intellectual abilities, while *talented* has come to mean possessing superior abilities in a single subject, including mathematics, language arts, science, or the fine arts. The term *gifted and talented*, in some contexts, has been replaced by *talent development*, driven by an emphasis on processes of developing talents rather than working with predetermined gifts (Feldhusen, 1994, 1995).

In a preview of research about identification procedures and instruments for artistically talented programs, one writer concluded that talent in the visual arts is desirable, but criteria to identify students as intelligent or talented have yet to be agreed upon. This is especially true for students from economically disadvantaged families or minority groups (Richert, 1987). The term *talent*, as used by art teachers, generally refers to high-ability students in a specific arts area. Few agree, however, on how to define high abilities in the visual or performing arts because identification recommendations for specific programs are idiosyncratic. Current writers have moved away from a single definition and have endorsed multiple criteria identification practices. Many schools have avoided this problem by specifying program contents and goals first, and then selecting only students appropriate to their programs.

Is a true definition of *talent* possible, with accompanying research examples, for identifying high-ability art students? We are aware that such a definition would guarantee meaningful discussions and arguments about students' abilities. We are also aware that visual arts talents are mani- fested in many ways. They can be manifested in visual arts media, processes or potential, performances or products, creative expression, problem-solving skills, abilities to produce adultlike products, or personality characteristics and values. In fact, Weitz (1961) argued for an open-ended definition of *visual arts* and concluded that a closed definition is impossible because there cannot be a true statement of all necessary and sufficient properties for all works of art. Teachers, Weitz believed, should go to theories for suggestions about how to teach, rather than for true definitions. We agree that a conclusive definition of talent in the visual arts, to be used to identify students for school programs, is not possible or even desirable.

Culture

Feldman and Goldsmith (1986a, 1986b), writing about case studies of child prodigies in several subjects, stressed that "cultures vary in the importance they attach to mastery of different domains at different times" (1986a, pp. 13–14). What is considered talent in one culture may not be valued in another. Artistically talented students are dependent on instruction that can be communicated effectively within their cultures. Feldman and Goldsmith claimed that potential talent cannot be developed without access to an effective symbol system and a domain that values the symbol system. Only those areas of expression valued by a culture are developed sufficiently to have organized symbol systems and domains that can be communicated to artistically talented students and others. A student, therefore, can only be identified as talented in areas a culture values.

Student Characteristics

Claims about characteristics of artistically talented students are varied and contradictory. Researchers working in different contexts and times have used different sets of characteristics, and artistically talented students have been categorized in many ways. Although examining art products for evidence of talent is common, it also is possible to observe behaviors that indicate a predisposition to create art products. We analyzed over 75 years of claims from research about characteristics of artistically talented students and grouped them as observable characteristics of both art products and students. Hurwitz and Day (2001) referred to task commitment and cognitive, artistic, and creative characteristics of art students as ways of defining artistic intelligence. Pariser (1997) cited other characteristics, including a burning desire to create artwork, precocious ability to depict imagery that reflects cultural values, creation of a body of work, support from teachers and family members, and artworks that are theme-oriented. It is clear that there are many ways to describe and categorize characteristics of artistically talented students and no single set of characteristics will ever adequately describe all manifestations of such talents.

Creativity

As we pointed out in Chapter 1, the concept of creativity is poorly defined. There are numerous definitions of creativity related to education of high-ability students; many are idiosyncratic to persons writing the definitions and are not based on research. Indeed, there is no adequate definition of creativity that can be measured by a single test. The term *creative*, as used in common language, generally describes students able to rearrange and integrate objects and ideas into new patterns, although these often are manifestations of normal development. In the visual arts, young students who produce "x-ray views" (showing exterior views and interior contents simultaneously) or multiple perspectives often are judged to be creative when, in fact, they simply are evidencing normal passage through symbolic stages of development. Researchers and educators have cast definitions of creativity as either conceptual (setting forth definitions) or operational (setting forth procedures) to assign values. There have been conceptual definitions that describe creative processes as distinct from creative products. Torrance (1963) argued that creativity is "the process of sensing gaps or needed elements; of forming ideas or hypotheses concerning them; of testing these hypotheses; and of communicating the results" (p. 90). Gallagher (1985) wrote, "Creativity is a mental process in which an individual creates new ideas or products, or recombines existing ideas of products, in a fashion that is novel

to him or her" (p. 303). These and other definitions require that a creative process or product be qualitatively better than those that preceded it and appropriate to a given solution.

Some researchers have questioned using creativity measures to identify students as gifted or talented. Renzulli (1982) claimed that creative performance on a test might have little or no relation to a person's life work. High scores on creativity tests, according to several authors, have questionable value, lack validity, and do not correlate with other measures of school performance, including performance in the arts.

Skills, Cognitive Abilities, and Affective Abilities

Some writers contend there might be two separate indicators of visual arts talent and either might be used for identification processes: (1) when a student has an advanced level of drawing abilities and (2) when a student generates original ideas, inventions, and innovations in art works. Another indicator occurs when students combine well-developed drawing skills with high-level cognitive abilities. Stalker (1981) included cognitive complexity (manifesting many solutions to problems), executive drawing abilities (superior skills in drawing), and affective intensity (strength of emotional responses and judgments) as parts of her definition of visual arts talent. Jellen and Verduin (1986) did not address problems of identification, but suggested concepts that define gifted and talented students in terms of cognitive (intelligence and imagination), affective (empathy and sensitivity), and connotative (interest and motivation) intensities. These seem parallel to Renzulli, Reis, and Smith's (1981) more familiar factors of intelligence, creativity, and task commitment.

If any of these constructs is accepted as a definition of visual arts talent, many problems still remain. Gardner (1989) pointed out that "there are separate developmental sagas which govern skills of perception, reflection, and critical judgment . . . the orchestration of perceptual, productive, and critical skills turns out to be a complex undertaking" (p. 160). According to Gardner, development in any skill area proceeds separately; they may never be present at the same levels at the same time.

Potential and Process Versus Performance and Product

Controversy about identification solely on the basis of clearly demonstrated superior abilities in any field of endeavor, in the past, was popular with research and practice in gifted education. Criticism of those practices arose and charges of elitism and lack of fairness were expressed by many writers. Today, however, many programs for artistically talented students are still based on defining art talent as an ability to create superior products or perform in a distinguished manner. Such programs have studio portfolios or performances in conjunction with other identification methods as a requirement for acceptance. Superiority of performance clearly is weighted heavily. Conversely, some arts educators are eliminating such requirements and expressing concern for students' interests, desire to participate, and potential. Some programs even offer "first-come, first-served" policies for students with potential talent in the arts.

Although definitions of art talent often emphasize a superior final product, many writers have emphasized attention to forming processes that lead to outstanding products. They claim processes students select and pursue are more important to the definition of high abilities in the arts than final products. An ability to depict the world believably is certainly only one indicator of talent in the visual arts; uses of paradoxes, puns, metaphors, and deep emotional involvement may be others. Others have stressed the importance of using process portfolios to assess learning. Getzels and Csikszentmihalyi (1976) studied college art students and concluded that their methods of discovery, envisaging, and delving into productive questions often were more indicative of high abilities than their solutions to problems.

Intelligence was generally viewed as a single, measurable trait until the 1980s when researchers challenged the popular notion of intelligence as a single construct. Gardner (1983) posited the existence of seven intelligences: linguistic, logico-mathematical, musical, spatial, bodily kinesthetic, interpersonal, and intrapersonal. Sternberg (1985) described aspects of high intelligence that include abilities to think at high levels, process information effectively, achieve insights and solve problems, and use efficient metacognitive processes. Sternberg's abilities were related to general intelligence and Gardner's intelligences were related to separate abilities.

Within various arts areas, vastly different behaviors and abilities are required for success. Students with superior drawing or painting abilities will have different sets of sensibilities than those whose talents are three-dimensional. Even within two-dimensional visual arts, clearly different sensitivities and abilities are needed to be a photographer, printmaker, painter, or political cartoonist. Intelligence needed for success in the arts clearly cannot be defined as a single characteristic, but as a phenomenon that contains multiple ways of dealing with knowledge (Hurwitz & Day, 2001).

Distribution

No discussion of issues about defining talent in the visual arts would be complete without acknowledging how talent is distributed in the world's population. Many have argued that talent in art should be conceived as normally distributed among all students and adults. In 1977 and 1981, the National Assessment of Educational Progress, and in 1998, the National Center for Educational Statistics, reported normally distributed results of arts examinations of national samples of 9-, 13-, and 17-year-old students. Professional acceptance of the concept of visual arts talent as normally distributed has the potential to lead to new, and substantially different, identification criteria and procedures and a more open-ended definition of talent.

Talent in the Visual Arts

The foundations for identifying gifted and talented students were laid by researchers such as Binet and Terman who were pioneers in the development of IQ tests. Over time, as the concept of intelligence was extended to include other kinds of abilities and skills, dependence on standardized tests as the only identification measures has been seriously challenged. It obviously would be difficult to devise a single test to identify leadership or visual and performing arts abilities, even though these have been identified as forms of giftedness or talents in state and federal legislation. Other measures that can be used to predict art talent are information about students' backgrounds, ages, personalities, life histories, and values.

Testing

At the state level, in 1990, about 23 locally designed visual arts achievement tests were in use (Sabol, 1994). Most attempts to develop standardized tests for use within a state have resulted in emphases on basic abilities that have been used as measures in other content areas. Hausman (1994) warned that these state tests have an "undue emphasis . . . on formalist and factual approaches . . . that lend themselves only to short term answers and multiple choice, machine scored items" (p. 38).

There are a number of common misunderstandings about the relationship of intelligence tests, creativity tests, and achievement tests with the identification of visual arts talent. One is that above average intelligence is not a requirement for superior performance in the arts, even though the separation of intelligence and performance in the arts has been questioned for many years. Relationships between intelligence and art talent have not been pursued in recent research partly because IQ tests have been challenged by many educators and researchers (Feldhusen & Hoover, 1986; Gardner, 1983; Sternberg, 1985; Treffinger & Renzulli, 1986). Despite such challenges, other educators and researchers continue to advocate for the use of IQ or achievement tests for the identification of gifted and talented students, although always in conjunction with other measures (Borland, 1986; Kaufman & Harrison, 1986; Shore, 1987). During the 1970s a number of researchers demonstrated that highly intelligent students also are highly able in the arts (although not all highly intelligent students possess art talent) and that most highly able arts students are also highly intelligent (Luca & Allen, 1974; Schubert, 1973; Vernon, Adamson, & Vernon, 1977). A high degree of intelligence has been claimed as necessary for acquiring the kinds of advanced techniques and skills required for superior arts performance (Luca & Allen, 1974: Schubert, 1973).

Several researchers have developed creativity tests, and creativity has become a byword in the education of high-ability students. Originally, creativity tests were used to measure general problem-solving abilities applicable to various situations. Then some authors developed instruments to help identify creativity of artistically talented students. It should be noted, however, that Torrance (1972) reported creative achievements in science, writing, and medicine were more easily predicted than in business, music, or the visual arts.

Standardized instruments have been developed and used to measure educational gains in reading, mathematics, social studies, language arts, and science. They have not been recently developed for visual arts education because arts are not considered basic subjects in most schools. An exception is Clark's Drawing Abilities Test, shown to be reliable and valid in a variety of educational contexts (Clark, 1984, 1993). Even when standardized arts tests exist, however, their usefulness as sole identification measures of art talent can be questioned. Studies have confirmed the importance of such factors as motivation, task commitment, drive, persistence, and self-confidence for the identification of artistically talented students, and all of these have more important roles in adult achievement than test scores.

Backgrounds, Personalities, and Values

The issue of identifying artistically talented students in diverse populations is currently a concern of many researchers and educators. Students from diverse backgrounds, particularly from minorities and low socioeconomic groups, usually are underrepresented in identification programs for educational opportunities. All students differ in their interests, learning styles, rates of learning, motivation, personalities, and work habits, as well as in their ethnicity, sex, economic backgrounds, and social class. Yet these characteristics often are ignored in identification programs for academic or arts programs in schools.

Other researchers have used life history information to predict art talent, academic achievement, or leadership abilities. Such biographical instruments are not culturally or racially biased, compared to traditional identification instruments.

Other researchers are attempting to develop identification instruments for art talent for specific racial and cultural groups, but this research needs to be more developed before such measures can be used effectively and fairly for general populations.

Age

There has long been disagreement among advocates of gifted and talented education about age and appropriate uses of formal identification procedures. This subject has not been discussed in depth or developed theoretically by art educators. Winter (1987) claimed that art talent will emerge in young children and can be recognized early. Others, such as Walters and Gardner (1984), claimed that musical and mathematical talent will emerge at earlier ages than talent in the visual arts. Still others claim that different students will manifest talent in the arts at different ages or grade levels (Bloom, 1985; Khatena, 1989). At this point, few definitive answers exist to guide decision making about appropriate ages to identify artistically talented students. Age remains an important and unresolved issue in the development of art talent.

Multiple Criteria

If all artistically talented students were obvious in demonstration of special abilities, interests, and dedication to art, it would be easy and expedient to identify them for special arts programs. Since that is not the case, most current educators support the use of multiple criteria systems in identification programs for all high-ability students. A justification for multiple criteria identification is awareness of the need and desirability to select students appropriately matched to a program's purpose and content. Multiple criteria systems should include diverse measures of various aspects of students' abilities, backgrounds, behaviors, interests, skills, achievements, and values, because different students, at different ages and from different backgrounds, respond optimally to different kinds of tasks. People now advocate using identification measures expressed through authentic real-life situations, with integrated, complex, and challenging tasks that encourage the expression of higher level thinking skills and achievements.

CHILDREN'S DRAWINGS AND CLARK'S DRAWING ABILITIES TEST AS MEASURES OF TALENT

One of the greatest difficulties facing program designers and administrators in identifying artistically talented students is the continuing existence of myths about talent, or being talented, and not enough knowledge grounded in research or practice. Talent is not simply an untutored or unlearned gift or natural endowment. According to D. H. Feldman (1980), abilities of superior young people "are not achieved without intensive, prolonged, educational assistance" (p. 125). He asserted that crucial factors in development of art-related talents are interventions of teaching and learning.

Nevertheless, an enthusiasm for the study of children's drawings as a measure of art abilities and talent has been expressed among art educators and others since the 1800s (Clark, 1987). In London, Ebenezer Cooke (1885) published an analysis of children's drawings that influenced both teachers and subsequent researchers. Another early writer, the Italian Carrado Ricci (1887), began his research into children's drawing the day he ducked into a train station to avoid being soaked by a drenching rain. There he became fascinated with children's graffiti on the walls of the station, noting the differing character of lower, midlevel, and highest drawings on the walls. From this experience, he published *L'Art dei Bambini* (The Art of Children) in which he discussed the development of children's drawings, based on his analysis of over 1,350 drawings and 20 clay figures made by children. Thus began the study of children's drawings and along with that attempts to produce tests to measure drawing ability in terms of aptitude and achievement.

The Study of Children's Drawings

Dale Harris (1963) grouped the study of children's drawings into three historical periods:

1. 1885–1920, descriptive investigations that intensified during 1890–1910
2. 1926–1940, experimental and correlational studies that compared drawing abilities with intelligence and other capabilities

3. 1940–1963, psychological, projective studies that concentrated on content and "afford[ed] a basis for organizing much of the observed phenomena of children's drawings." (p. 11)

In early writings, Ayer (1916) and Manuel (1919) described several methods used in the study of children's drawings. They pointed out that collection and study of children's drawings have proceeded from objective to subjective methods. Objective methods included:

1. The Gross Products Method, which begins with indiscriminate collection of large numbers of drawings
2. The Special Products Method, which requires pupils to create drawings related to a specific theme
3. The Comparative Products Method, based on collection and comparison of a group of subjects that may or may not require gross products or special products and assignment

Subjective methods included:

1. A Single or Biographical Method based on the analysis of drawings by a single subject, or a limited group of subjects, over a period of time
2. The Experimental Method in which one or more drawing tasks are carried out in a relatively controlled experiment

From 1900 to 1920 more than 50 studies of children's drawings were reported in western European countries. In Germany, Kerschensteiner (1905) collected more than 52,000 children's drawings that had been created to design a book and a plate pattern. In the United States, Thorndike (1916), Whipple (1919), and Manuel (1919) all conducted extensive studies about children's art development and were major figures in psychometrics and testing.

Clark's Drawing Abilities Test

Early test development in art failed to produce a body of standardized tests as were created in academic subjects. Some standardized art tests (Meier Art Tests, Horn Art Aptitude Inventory, and the Graves Design Judgment Test) created from the 1920s through the 1960s, and a number reissued in the 1950s and 1970s, were critiqued in several editions of Buros's *Mental Measurements Yearbooks*, as being dated, failing to prove their assumptions, and not being successful as diagnostic achievement tests (Clark, 1987). It should be noted that none of these tests are diagnostic of drawing ability and several are still in use. From 1966 to 1985 there were about a dozen art tests in use, of which half were drawing ability tests. Of these tests only one, the Silver Drawing Test (1983), is standardized; however, it is used to identify students who are experiencing disabilities and not those who are artistically talented. We do not know of any other standardized art drawing tests currently available for use in identification of talented visual art students, except for Clark's Drawing Abilities Test.

In 1983 Gilbert Clark received a grant to develop an instrument to test the assumption of normal distribution of visual arts–related abilities among school-age children. Following an extensive survey of uses of the terms *talent* and *talented* in art education as well as gifted and talented education literature, and conceptual analyses of many instruments and scales that had been used in the past to identify high-ability art students, he decided to limit the instrument to a few specific drawing tasks based on extensive precedents in previous research (Clark, 1989).

One reason drawings have been used often in research is that they are the easiest mode of visual arts expression to assign, administer, and evaluate. More important, drawing has been recognized as basic to expression in all art forms by a number of research professionals. In addition, drawing may be a particularly apt task for identification of high ability in the visual arts because persistence in drawing is relatively unique. DiLeo (1977) pointed out, that "with the approach of adolescence . . . drawing will be replaced by other more satisfying forms of self-expression [although] the gifted will persevere" (p. 167). Finally, an assumption that underlies this research is that drawing abilities are evidence of skills and knowledge. "The ability to draw well . . . depends not only upon developing skills and increasing awareness of the world, but also upon knowledge of the problems of art and artists" (Wilson, Hurwitz, & Wilson, 1987, p. 43).

Clark's Drawing Abilities Test (CDAT) consists of four drawing tasks and a scoring guide that have been used in a series of ongoing studies. It has been used and tested with over 5,000 upper elementary, middle school, and high school students throughout the United States and in eight other countries. On the basis of this history and research, the CDAT has been shown to be valid, reliable, and highly effective as a standardized screening and identification instrument for artistically talented students. However, this instrument should not be used as the sole basis for accepting or rejecting applicants into a program for high-ability students; it is not intended for, and never should be used for, labeling or classifying students except on a very short-term basis. It is clear that scores on the CDAT are very amenable to change through instruction, and the test can be used to identify not only students who exhibit evidence of drawing ability at a high level, but also to identify students whose drawing abilities fall below the norm and may need remediation to further develop their drawing skills.

Drawing Tasks in the CDAT

Major problems confronted during the development of Clark's Drawing Abilities Test were selecting appropriate drawing items and constructing a scoring procedure that could be used easily by others (Clark, 1989). A number of drawing tasks were developed and tested, then reduced to four that had been used in previous research. The four tasks are:

1. Draw an interesting house as if you were looking at it from across the street (see Figure 2.1).
2. Draw a person who is running very fast (see Figure 2.2).
3. Make a drawing of you and your friends playing in a playground (see Figure 2.3).
4. Make a fantasy drawing from your imagination (see Figure 2.4).

In Figure 2.1, below-average drawings of houses are stereotypical; they are drawn with little detail and display no evidence of perspective or size relationships. In average drawings, there are attempts to introduce more realistic size relationships, details, perspective, and a variety of lines, shapes, textures, and patterns. Perspective and details are depicted more accurately in above-average drawings and indications of specific environments and other details are included. There are also unusual placements of houses in the compositions, and sensitive uses of lines, textures, patterns, and positive and negative spaces.

In Figure 2.2, below-average drawings of simplified running figures are drawn immaturely with respect to body parts. Average drawings resemble people running and indicate movement with a variety of lines or textures. Above-average drawings demonstrate awareness of accuracy of body parts and figures in motion, appropriate use of contexts, and more unique depictions of running figures.

In Figure 2.3, below-average drawings of children in a playground are conceptually immature and demonstrate a lack of relationships of figures to their contexts. Average, simplified figures are shown in appropriate contexts and there is awareness of a whole composition and varying line qualities. In above-average drawings, figures are contextualized into imaginative settings and are recognizably engaged in play activities, with sensitive uses of lines, dark and light contrasts, and textures.

Item 4 is deliberately more open-ended and lacks the specified content of the previous three items. In Figure 2.4, below-average drawings are immature and lack meaningful narrative content. Average drawings are more representational, conceptually stronger, and show awareness of how to depict people and objects in space. Characteristics of above-average drawings are imaginative uses of popular culture imagery, ability to tell a story with interest, self-expression, and creativity, and use of drawing techniques at skillful levels.

These tasks call for the demonstration of very different abilities, skills, and expressive responses, and this may explain their past popularity. Drawing a house requires depicting perspective, textures, meaningful shapes and sizes, and recognizable details. Drawing a person running requires portrayal of actions, as well as body proportions and recognizable details. Drawing a group of persons on a playground requires portraying figures accurately, composing in receding space, and grouping figures in that space. The final fantasy drawing task provides opportunities for subjects to use their imaginations to portray whatever they wish, including

Figure 2.1. Sixth-Grade Students' Responses to Item 1 on the CDAT, Draw an Interesting House as if You Were Looking at It From Across the Street

BELOW AVERAGE

BELOW AVERAGE

AVERAGE

AVERAGE

ABOVE AVERAGE

ABOVE AVERAGE

Figure 2.2. Sixth-Grade Students' Responses to Item 2 on the CDAT, Draw a Person Who Is Running Very Fast

BELOW AVERAGE

BELOW AVERAGE

AVERAGE

AVERAGE

ABOVE AVERAGE

ABOVE AVERAGE

Figure 2.3. Sixth-Grade Students' Responses to Item 3 on the CDAT, Make a Drawing of You and Your Friends Playing in a Playground

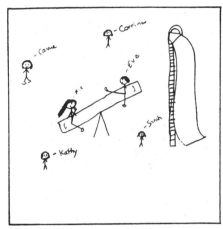

BELOW AVERAGE

BELOW AVERAGE

AVERAGE

AVERAGE

ABOVE AVERAGE

ABOVE AVERAGE

Figure 2.4. Sixth-Grade Students' Responses to Item 4 on the CDAT,
Make a Fantasy Drawing From Your Imagination

BELOW AVERAGE

BELOW AVERAGE

AVERAGE

AVERAGE

ABOVE AVERAGE

ABOVE AVERAGE

things they know and draw well. These four tasks are scored on originality, expressiveness, and creative solutions as well as drawing skills.

Validity of the CDAT as a Test of Artistic Talent

In a series of field tests, the CDAT was used with groups of students in college classes, public school classes, and summer classes for artistically talented students. Resulting data yielded normal distributions, and this finding supported the original research hypothesis that talent is a normally distributed characteristic.

In order to explore validity questions, teachers' rankings of students' performance in three Summer Arts Institutes also were collected, inasmuch as it had been speculated that a major criterion for measurement of success in a program would be teacher ratings of children on performance (Feldhusen, Asher, & Hoover, 1984). All teachers at the institute were asked to rank all of their students in categories of superior, above average, average, and below average, based on their own criteria of success in their classes. The most important finding regarding correlation is that scores on each item of the CDAT correlated significantly with teachers' rankings of student success in all of their classes.

Every possible correlation of the four drawing tasks with one another on the CDAT also was significant. This internal consistency was verification of the power of each of the tasks and partially explains the instrument's effectiveness as a research or identification device. Many who were asked to score the instrument expressed concern that the fantasy drawing (Item 4) would be inconsistent with results on the other items because it is open-ended. In scoring, however, there was a significant correlation between performance on this item with all other items.

Another concern with the CDAT was that the scoring criteria reward representational or realistic drawings, which might place students with other skills at a disadvantage. This is not true, however, because students who take this test are at developmental levels where they are consciously and deliberately developing emerging abilities to depict things realistically. It should be noted that only 3 percent of the fantasy drawings (from well over 5000 examples) are nonobjective or lack realistic references.

In addition, very high levels of agreement in scoring were found among several sets of judges with varying degrees of experience with children's art works. As a result, many people have asked Clark to specify a cutoff score on the CDAT that would segregate high ability students from others; however, that is not possible because performance on the instrument varies significantly from school to school, community to community, or situation to situation.

IDENTIFYING TALENTED VISUAL ARTS STUDENTS IN RURAL COMMUNITIES

In recent years, there has been a focus on special programs for students in urban environments; the needs of students from rural communities often go unnoticed and unacknowledged. Books and journals about educating gifted and talented students are filled with references to programs and advantages offered to urban and suburban students because most opportunities for students with high abilities have been offered in cities and the areas surrounding them. There are few year-round programs or projects for artistically talented students from distinctly rural communities, with ethnically diverse backgrounds, offered in local schools.

Definitions used in rural programs should be broad-based because it is important to be expansive when identifying arts performance levels in populations of rural students who do not have previous learning experiences in the visual arts. Restrictive identification measures, such as specific creativity or achievement test scores, often are used in urban or suburban school districts. Certainly, such cutoff scores would not be appropriate to use in most rural schools, particularly those serving economically disadvantaged and/or ethnically diverse students. Few of these students would be accepted into art talent development programs on the basis of these types of test scores.

Due to their distance from large population centers, students in rural schools often do not have easy access to traditional cultural resources, such

as large art galleries, major museums, large librar-
ies, concert halls, and similar facilities found in
major urban areas (Nachitgal, 1992). Thus students
from rural schools do not have the same exposure
or opportunities to explore the kinds of arts resources and experiences available to students in
more heavily populated urban and suburban parts
of this country. What they often have, however,
are rich cultural heritages and strong community
support networks. Schools seeking to identify high-
ability visual arts students in smaller, rural communities usually have not identified enough students
to warrant specialized teachers, appropriate instructional resources, or access to mentors. At this time,
there is a great need for the development of identification measures and program opportunities for
students with art talent potential and abilities who
live in smaller, rural communities across the United
States.

Description of Project ARTS

In an effort to serve the many needs of artistically talented students in rural schools, Project ARTS
was designed as a 3-year research and development
project. Its purpose was to identify underserved,
high-ability, visual and performing arts students in
third grade in seven selected rural schools in the first
year and to implement differentiated curricula appropriate to those students during the following two
years, and also conduct assessments during the third
year. The staff began with testing over 1,000 third-
grade students in seven schools, with input from
teachers, parents, administrators, artists, and other
concerned community members. These advisory
groups were established to offer advice about local
populations and appropriate expectations for students in each community. Third-grade students at
participating schools were administered an entire
range of local measures adopted at each site. In addition, Project ARTS staff also required each school
to administer two standardized instruments that
were to be used for research purposes. These standardized instruments were an adapted Torrance
Tests of Creative Thinking (TTCT) and Clark's Drawing Abilities Test. In addition, standardized state
achievement test scores were used as part of the
research we conducted with all participating schools
in Project ARTS.

Standardized Tests and Project ARTS

As we stated earlier in this chapter, there are
few nationally standardized art tests available to
measure drawing abilities, and tests that do exist
have been questioned. Most state art achievement
tests do not require students to produce artwork or
respond to questions about the arts (Sabol, 1994).
These situations raise questions about identifying
high-ability students in rural schools, which may
not emphasize standard language, arts skill development, or provide frequent standardized testing
experiences.

The Torrance Tests of Creative Thinking and
Clark's Drawing Abilities Test were chosen for
Project ARTS as two reliable and valid tests to be
used for research purposes only. Due to cooperating school districts' rules about confidentiality,
scores obtained on TTTC, CDAT, and standardized
achievement tests were given anonymous codes;
therefore, these scores could not be compared with
scores students received on local identification
measures (Clark, 1997).

Torrance Tests of Creative Thinking. An adapted
Torrance Tests of Creative Thinking was administered to all third-grade students in participating
schools specifically to assess its use for identifying
high-ability students in schools with rural, culturally diverse populations. TTCT scores often have
been used as an identification measure for visual
arts programs in urban and suburban settings in the
United States (Torrance, 1972). The abbreviated
TTCT version we used consists of three tasks:

1. List as many unusual uses of junked automobiles
   as you can
2. Make some pictures with titles (in four, preprinted rectangles)
3. See how many objects you can make from 12
   preprinted triangles on a page

This TTCT was used as evidence of fluency, flexibility, and elaboration, and subjects received a nu-
meric, quantitative score.

Clark's Drawing Abilities Test. Many researchers
believe that art talent is relatively stable and normally distributed and that the amount of talent a

person develops will effectively control and limit that person's capabilities in the visual arts. In other words, all students possess talent, but some will develop it to a small degree, most to an average level, and some to considerable heights. To test these beliefs, an instrument was required that would demonstrate common differentiation of art abilities among students, based on the work-sample technique. Work samples require completion of the same task, using the same amount of time, with the same materials and instructions by all students in order to compare student performance. Completion of the same task by all students provides a more legitimate basis for analyzing and comparing children's art development than examination of different products rendered in a variety of media. Past uses of the CDAT have been analyzed and reported based on age, gender, grade, and SES demographic data about subjects and in relation with achievement scores (Clark, 1989, 1993; Clark & Wilson, 1991). The CDAT was administered to all third-grade students in all schools cooperating with Project ARTS.

Standardized State Achievement Tests. Project ARTS students also were administered standardized achievement tests as part of each district's testing program. These tests were idiosyncratic for each state and scores across sites could not be compared. Results of these tests can be compared in each state, however, with results from the TTCT and CDAT. Analysis of variance (ANOVA) was used to assess the results on achievement test scores, although these findings are reported specifically only for each state. TTCT and CDAT scores were compared by the gender of subjects and these findings also are reported by state.

Local Identification Procedures

Although standardized tests were used for research purposes, each school was encouraged to develop local identification measures for the identification of students for Project ARTS. Currently, there are no agreed-upon criteria about the validity of using local identification measures, or about the interrelationships between them. These measures, nevertheless, often are recommended for use in school identification programs. Students from

rural areas often possess unique characteristics that should be taken into consideration when identification procedures are being developed or selected (Zimmerman, 1992b, 1992d). For populations being served by Project ARTS, it was decided that attention also should be paid to processes that might lead to advanced products from students who might not receive high scores on standardized tests. Each cooperating school was encouraged to require identification tasks or measures related specifically to their local populations.

At each Project ARTS school, local committee members' advice about what constituted art talent in each of their communities was taken into consideration when identification measures were formulated. Several tasks at each site were designed specifically as local identification measures for their populations. Although each site developed local instruments, some measures used did not vary to any extent. (See Figure 2.5 for a summary of identification procedures administered in Project ARTS.)

Indiana Identification Procedures. Methods used in Indiana schools incorporated nine locally designed measures, including nominations by students, parents (see Figure 2.6), teachers, and peers; standardized class assignments; assessments of student portfolios and out-of-school projects; previous art grades; and observations of students.

These were designed to be as inclusive as possible and grading criteria were developed locally at each school. One Indiana school used a museum field trip as a unique identification procedure. Volunteers, parents, and teachers recorded students' behaviors and responses at the museum on a form designed by the local art teacher. At this school, all peer nomination forms required both boys and girls to be listed in response to a number of descriptive statements about art talent (see Figure 2.7). It was felt that stereotypic role definitions were learned early in this rural community and many peer selections might result in single sex groupings.

New Mexico Identification Procedures. Methods used in New Mexico schools included seven locally designed measures: nominations by students, parents, teachers (see Figures 2.8 and 2.9), community members (see Figure 2.10), and peers; and assessments of summer sketchbooks, works shown

Figure 2.5. Identification Procedures Used in Project ARTS Programs in Indiana (IN), South Carolina (SC), and New Mexico (NM)

	IN	NM	SC
Self-nomination forms	√	√	√
Parent nomination forms	√	√	√
Teacher nomination forms	√	√	√
Peer nomination forms	√	√	√
Collage design work-sample task			√
Storyboard for teacher-read story			√
3-D clay animal task			√
Student attitude questionnaire			√
Sketchbook (for summer use)		√	
Other standardized class assignments	√		
Community art exhibition		√	
Student portfolios	√	√	√
Out-of-school projects	√		
Observations of students (in class and on field trips)	√		
Previous art grades	√		

at a community art exhibition, and student portfolios. Procedures of special interest were sketchbooks distributed at the end of the school year to all second graders, who were asked to return with them at the beginning of the next school year.

Although only a small percentage of the sketchbooks were returned, these indicated high interest and commitment by the students who completed them. All students in one New Mexico school were invited to submit artwork for a community exhibition held at a local gallery and judged by adult artists on a set of commonly agreed-upon criteria, including originality, technique, and composition. In the pueblo school, a local artist who had worked with many of the students for several years and knew their artwork well nominated a number of them to participate.

South Carolina Identification Procedures. Methods used in South Carolina schools included nominations by students, parents, teachers, and peers; scores on three work samples; and student attitude questionnaires. Three unique measures and criteria that resulted in work samples were developed to be sensitive to cultural influences of students from Gullah backgrounds and were judged with local criteria by art teachers in the cooperating schools. Because pattern and design are important to artists from this area, one identification procedure was a torn-paper collage design (see Figure 2.11). Storytelling is an art form embedded in the Gullah culture, so a second procedure had students illustrate a story in a sequence of four prepared panels (see Figure 2.12). A third procedure involved having all students

Figure 2.6. Project ARTS (IN): Parent Information Form

Student Name _____ Date _____

Parent Name _____

Directions: If your child has special talents or interests in any of the areas on this form, please fill
                them out. Fill out only the categories that fit your child. Return this form to your child's
                teacher by _____. Thank you for your help.

My Child

1.   **Fixes things**: _____yes   _____no

        If yes, what kinds of things?

        How long has he or she done this?

        Can you remember (and tell us) any stories about this? Or send a sample to school?

2.   **Makes things**: _____yes   _____no

        If yes, what kinds of things?

        How long has he or she done this?

        Can you remember (and tell us) any stories about this? Or send a sample to school?

3.   **Writes things**: _____yes   _____no

        If yes, what kinds of things?

        How long has he or she done this?

        Do you have some samples of work that you can send to school?

4.   **Reads a lot:** _____yes   _____no

        If yes, what kinds of things?

5.   **Something that hasn't been mentioned that I would like to tell you about my child**:

Plate 2.2 A drawing by a third-grade Project ARTS student at Orleans Elementary School that displays observation of daily life on the farm where he lives

make clay animal figures because this procedure was thought to be sensitive to skills used by rural students who often find materials with which to experiment and create three-dimensional objects (see Figure 2.13).

Results of Standardized Tests in Project ARTS

As we mentioned earlier, an abbreviated version of the Torrance Tests of Creative Thinking test was administered to students in third grade at all seven schools participating in Project ARTS. Scores on the TTCT indicated a wide range of creative behaviors as defined by this measure. In a normal distribution, the midpoint of scores would occur in the center of a diagram. Skewed distributions, with midpoints to the left or right of the center, are the result of atypical conditions. The Torrance Tests and CDAT diagrams shown in Figures 2.14 and 2.15 are skewed to the left because students in Project ARTS had little or no previous experience with these types of measures. Clark's Drawing Abilities Test also was administered to third graders at all seven schools. Distribution of scores on the CDAT identified a broad range of differentiated art abilities, including some students with low ability levels, most with midrange ability levels, and some with obviously high ability levels although they were skewed to the left, as were the TTCT scores (see Figure 2.15).

Tasks on the TTCT and CDAT measure different expectations, execution, product outcomes, completion, and scoring criteria. Nevertheless, correlation between these two tests was highly significant. The TTCT measures fluency, flexibility, and elaboration and is based on both verbal and visual responses. It also measures inherent abilities relatively unaffected by past experiences and skills. The CDAT measures problem-solving skills and differential drawing abilities, but scores are sensitive to past experiences and previously learned skills and techniques. CDAT scores usually accelerate with age and instruction, whereas scores on the TTCT remain relatively constant over time.

One important finding was that, for third graders at each school, there was a positive correlation among scores on the TTCT, CDAT, and achievement tests. Although the correlation may not be as high as in more affluent, suburban communities, we often have speculated about a positive correlation of high scores on achievement tests and high abilities in the visual and performing arts. An interesting confirmation of that was obtained in this study. Each of the three states used a different standardized achievement test, yet students with high scores on the CDAT and TTCT also had high scores on each of the different standardized achievement tests. In other words, students with higher levels of creativity and drawing abilities also obtained substantially higher scores on language, mathematics, and reading tests in the three states. This con-

Figure 2.7. Project Arts (IN) Classroom Assessment Form

Room _____   Date _____

1. Which student or students in your room sing well?
    Girls:
    Boys:

2. Do you know of any students in your room who play the piano or an instrument?
    Yes or No?
    Who?

3. Which students in your room draw well?
    Girls:
    Boys:

4. Which students in your room are good at making things such as 3-dimensional projects or using clay?
    Girls:
    Boys:

5. Which students in your room are good at using color or painting?
    Girls:
    Boys:

6. Which students in your room enjoy and like science?
    Girls:
    Boys:

7. Which students enjoy learning about history?
    Girls:
    Boys:

8. Which students enjoy learning about other countries?
    Girls:
    Boys:

9. Which students in your room know a lot about how things work or are put together?
    Girls:
    Boys:

10. Which students in your room know a lot about nature, plants and animals?

11. Which students in your room like to read?

12. Which students in your room like to write stories or poems?

Figure 2.8. Project ARTS (NM): Teacher Nomination Form

Student _____   School _____

Classroom Teacher _____   Grade _____

Art Instructor _____   Date _____

This student has shown exceptional art skills in

_____

_____

_____

_____

_____

I feel this student should be recommended for Projects ARTS participation because

_____

_____

_____

_____

The checklist below is a rating of the student's abilities and behaviors as a gifted student from a tribal/cultural perspective.

1 = No evidence

2 = Little evidence

3 = Possesses traits to some degree

4 = Possesses traits more than an average degree

5 = Possesses high degree of abilities, qualities, and behaviors

Tribal Cultural Awareness	(1)	(2)	(3)	(4)	(5)
1. Respectful of tribal elders					
2. Respectful of others					
3. Understands tribal history					
4. Understands tribal culture					
5. Ability to produce tribal arts					
6. Storytelling ability					
7. Tribal language competence					

Total Score_____

Figure 2.9. Project ARTS (NM): Native American Student Creative Behaviors Form

---

Student's Name: _____ Age: _____

School: _____ Grade: _____

Note: Behaviors listed may or may not be observed in a classroom environment. Panelists stated that the Native American student would be more likely to display some of the behaviors among other Native Americans, at social gatherings, or at home and that some students may not necessarily express creative behaviors verbally.

Direction: Circle the number that best describes this student as you know him/her.

    1 = never   2 = rarely   3 = sometimes   4 = frequently   5 = always

1. Displays intellectual playfulness: fantasizes; imagines; manipulates ideas by elaboration or modification   1 2 3 4 5

2. Is a high risk taker; is adventurous and speculative   1 2 3 4 5

3. Has a different criteria for success   1 2 3 4 5

4. Displays a keen sense of humor reflective of own cultural background   1 2 3 4 5

5. Is individualistic; does not fear being different   1 2 3 4 5

6. Predicts from present information   1 2 3 4 5

7. Displays curiosity about many things; has many interests   1 2 3 4 5

8. Generates large number of ideas of solutions to problems/questions   1 2 3 4 5

9. Demonstrates exceptional ability in written expression; creates stories, poems, etc.   1 2 3 4 5

10. Is sensitive to color, design, arrangement and other qualities of artistic appreciation and understanding   1 2 3 4 5

11. Is sensitive to melody, rhythm, form, tone, mood, and other qualities of music appreciation   1 2 3 4 5

12. Demonstrates exceptional ability/potential in one of the fine arts (depending on experience and nurturance)   1 2 3 4 5

13. Demonstrates unusual ability in one of the practical arts (wood, handicrafts, metal, mechanics, etc.)   1 2 3 4 5

14. Demonstrates exceptional skill and ability in physical coordination activities   1 2 3 4 5

15. Shows interest in unconventional careers   1 2 3 4 5

16. Improvises commonplace materials   1 2 3 4 5

17. Is emotionally responsive (may not overtly respond in classroom environment)   1 2 3 4 5

18. Demonstrates ability in oral expression (may not be orally expressive in classroom environment)   1 2 3 4 5

19. Is aware of own impulses and open to the irrational in self   1 2 3 4 5

Figure 2.10. Project ARTS (NM): Community Survey Form

Our school is participating in Projects ARTS—a project to identify artistically talented students in 3rd grade. If you know of any child in the community who may be talented in any of the following areas, please write his or her name, the name of his or her parents or guardians, and school. Please nominate only 3rd graders.

ART: drawing, painting, sketching, wood carving, sculpture, jewelry making, pottery making, cartoon art, sewing, weaving, etc.

Name	Parent	School

DRAMA: acting in plays, community productions, activities, church productions, school plays, writing or making up plays or dramas, etc.

Name	Parent	School

DANCING: dancing in traditional community dances; recreational dancing; dancing in school, church, or community programs; dancing classes such as ballet, tap dancing, square dancing, Ballet Folklorico, etc.

Name	Parent	School

MUSIC: plays an instrument in school, at home, within the community or church; sings at home, school community or church; participates in concerts, talent contests, etc.

Name	Parent	School

Name: _____

Organization: _____

Plate 2.3 A drawing by fourth-grade Project ARTS student at Santo Domingo
Pueblo Elementary School of a group of horses that he often views near his home

sistency across all three states confirms that populations of high-achieving students, in general, will include high-achieving, visual arts students.

Two other findings should be noted. First, gender performance for these rural students is relatively coequal on the TTCT, CDAT, and standardized achievement test in language, mathematics, and reading. In elementary schools, generally, girls are expected to exceed boys in achievement scores and general school performance. No evidence was found to confirm this. Second, performance for all third graders on the CDAT and TTCT were also not sensitive to the age of subjects. Neither the TTCT nor CDAT scores were significantly correlated with age of subjects, although this may indicate only that these tests are not sensitive to age differences in small incremental measures.

Results of Local Procedures in Project ARTS

Results of local measures used in each school or community were discussed with the Project ARTS staff, although the data were not correlated with the standardized tests because of the small number of students who were assessed in each school. In order to correlate the scores from the local measures with the standardized tests many more students would have to be involved in each school to make any accurate interrelationships among the standardized tests and local procedures. In addition, even if we desired to see relationships among standardized and local assessments, students were anonymous to us as researchers in respect to their standardized scores and thus there was no means to correlate local and standardized scores. Groupings of students who performed well on local measures and were identified for Project ARTS, however, were visited and observed on several occasions during the subsequent 2 years. When students' progress and achievements were assessed after the project was concluded, there was evidence that most students chosen for the program developed skills and understandings about art and increased their awareness and appreciation of the arts in their local communities. In interviews, a few teachers expressed concern about using some tasks (even though these were locally designed and

Plate 2.4 A drawing of a classmate by a third-grade Project ARTS student at J.J. Davis Elementary School indicates careful attention to details of the figure and her dress

Project ARTS continue to use some of the instruments their teachers developed to identify students with high abilities in the visual arts.

Lessons Learned from Project ARTS

Basically, the importance of developing identification procedures in Project ARTS indicates that artistically talented students can be found in almost any school in any part of the country. Identifying artistically talented students in rural communities may require bending the rules in atypical situations and having local community groups, in cooperation with local teachers, develop instruments to identify high-ability students in their schools. A few students entered these programs who may not have been correctly identified, but being open about procedures offered many students with high potential or high abilities opportunities they may never have experienced. Many local procedures proved to be appropriate when they were used in conjunction with other locally designed procedures. The most difficult step was to convince some teachers to respect the potential and abilities of their students and have faith in their own abilities to identify them as artistically talented.

We recommend that a number of different measures—several local measures, the CDAT, and achievement test scores—be used in programs that have similar populations to those in Project ARTS. Although many elementary teachers claim that the arts offer students who are not academically able the opportunity to achieve that is not available to them in other school subjects, our findings indicate that high achievement in the visual arts is most likely to be attained by students who are generally high achievers in other school subjects.

CURRENT PRACTICES USED FOR IDENTIFYING ARTISTICALLY TALENTED STUDENTS

There are some general recommended practices for administrators who wish to use various identification procedures to identify students for an artistically talented visual arts program. Before identification decisions are made, however, administrators considering implementing a program for

administrated) and expressed faith in their own perceptions of students' abilities. The majority of teachers, however, felt the local measures were appropriate for the identification of artistically talented students. The most successful identification measures, according to staff observations and teacher endorsements, were work samples, community exhibits, teacher observations, and self-nominations. Today, many schools served by

Figure 2.11. Project ARTS (SC): Collage/Design Project

DIRECTIONS: Ask these questions: "What is a design?" (a group of patterns, lines, and shapes). "Where do you see design?" (everywhere). "How is design different from a picture?" (a design doesn't have to look like a real thing). Give these directions: "Today you will make a design using line, shapes, and colors. You may tear paper into shapes or cut them with scissors. Next, you will arrange your shapes on your background paper and glue them with small dots of glue. Do not use too much glue because puddles of glue may ruin your work. You will use only red, blue, and yellow paper, and a black marker. Do not ask for other colors."

"Put your name, grade, and teacher's name on the back, please. You will have 30 minutes to complete your design. I will tell you when half the time is gone and at five minutes before cleanup." Pass out to each child, a 12 x 18 manila tag, one 9 x 12 red, blue, and yellow construction paper, a black marker, scissors, and glue.

Collage Design Criteria	(rated on a 1–5 scale)					
balance	0	1	2	3	4	5
repetition and variation	0	1	2	3	4	5
movement	0	1	2	3	4	5
unified composition	0	1	2	3	4	5

artistically talented students need to make decisions about program size, character and purpose, student population, and available funding. Procedures currently used typically admit from 5 to 15 percent of local school populations. Decisions about program size obviously dictate identification procedures designed to achieve the desired population. Identification procedures also can be used to screen students as appropriate to classes offered. Desirable critical skills, abilities, and experiences would differ for different kinds of programs in different parts of the country. The age group, types of instruction, and goals of a program should guide decisions about the number and kinds of students to be admitted.

If school personnel are initiating a new program for artistically talented students, they may decide to have less-rigorous entrance criteria than if they had a long-established, popular, and well-funded program. Screening procedures for identifying artistically talented students also can be modified in light of a decreasing applicant pool. Administrators can choose from a range of screening procedures: A "first-come, first-served" procedure would be least selective, followed by nonstructured nomina-

tions by self and others; structured nominations by self, peers, parents, teachers, and others; grades in art courses, academic records, and achievement test scores; informal art tests or work samples; and reviews of slides or videos. Portfolio reviews, auditions, interviews, and observations would be most selective and most costly to administer (see Figure 2.16).

We recommend that multiple identification procedures, at appropriate ages, always be used in identification programs in schools. Interviews, academic records, and self-nominations, however, may not be appropriate at primary grades. They can be used with confidence at intermediate and secondary levels. (See Figure 2.17 for the application of identification procedures at various grade levels.)

Nominations: Nonstructured and Structured

Nonstructured nominations simply ask nominators to recommend prospective students. Students, peers, teachers, parents, counselors, and others can provide valuable insights about candidates that

Figure 2.12. Project ARTS (SC): Story Illustration Project

DIRECTIONS: "This project will show your ability to tell a story without words. You will do this on one piece of paper that will be folded into four sections." Pass out paper and demonstrate folding, then number the boxes 1–4 and have students do the same. "Turn your paper over and write your name, grade, and homeroom teacher's name. You are not to draw on this side; do not turn the paper over until I say to. Listen carefully, I can read this story only once." Read the following story:

"Once upon a time, there was a baby fish who ran away from home. His Mama had told him to stay close to her: 'Do not speak to strangers,' she said. 'Stay away from underwater caves, huge rocks, forests of sea weed, and giant fish.' But this baby fish didn't listen to his mama. He swam, and swam, and swam. He swam past some strangers, he swam past huge rocks, and he swam past forests of seaweed. Suddenly, an enormous, gigantic, monstrous fish appeared. Gulp!"

"Now tell this story with pictures. Draw it in sequence, from beginning to end. The first part will be in box 1, what happens next will be in box 2, and what happens next will be in box 3. Draw the end of the story in box 4. You will use pencil and draw the story with as much detail as you like. You will have only 20 minutes to draw the whole story. I will tell you when to go on to the next picture so you can finish drawing the whole story."

Story Illustration Project Criteria	(rated on a 1–5 point scale)					
illustrations appropriate to story	0	1	2	3	4	5
details and elaboration	0	1	2	3	4	5
completion of sequence	0	1	2	3	4	5
size relationships and perspective	0	1	2	3	4	5
compositional arrangement	0	1	2	3	4	5
expressive qualities	0	1	2	3	4	5

they nominate. The value of such nominations depends upon the nature of information and quality of insights provided by nominators. Their bias, as well as lack of previously specified criteria, often results in too little valuable or too much inappropriate information. Nonstructured nominations can provide important insights about candidates and can be used to place them in appropriate classes, but they are weakened by a lack of standardized criteria.

Structured nominations that ask all respondents to answer the same questions are important to receive along with open-ended responses. They control information reported and facilitate comparison of responses found on different applications. Struc-

tured nominations provide useful information because they require similar information from all applicants and can be tailored to stated purposes of a program. They also can be solicited from prospective students, parents, peers, teachers, and others familiar with the criteria used. Nomination efficiency requires forms that are appropriate to program goals, clear and easy to use, and easily assessed by program staff. Commonly available structured nomination forms consist of prepared lists of behaviors in specific categories, and users are asked to check or rate observations of specific behaviors. When rating is added, each behavior is judged for its frequency or strength as well as its presence. Forms used to record degrees of

Figure 2.13. Project ARTS (SC): Clay Animals Project

DIRECTIONS: Ask these questions: "How are animals different from people? How many of you have pets? How many of you have been to a zoo? How many of you can think of animals that are no longer around (unicorns, dinosaurs, dragons . . .)? Do you have a favorite animal?"

Give these directions: "Today, you will make an animal with clay. You can make any animal you want. It can be real or imaginary and you will all receive the same amount of clay. Remember, the clay all stays on the table in this room."

Pass out 3 x 5 cards and pencils. "Put your name, grade, and teacher's name on these cards. Keep them clean. When you finish your clay piece you will turn it in on top of this card. You will have 30 minutes to finish your animal. When the clay and tools are passed out, you may begin." Pass out clay and tools. Mention remaining time at 15 minutes and 5 minutes before cleanup. When students are finished, say, "Please bring your animals to me now. Be sure to bring them on top of the card with your name."

Clay Animal Criteria	(rated on a 1–5 scale)					
elaboration and details	0	1	2	3	4	5
texture	0	1	2	3	4	5
skillful construction	0	1	2	3	4	5
recognizability	0	1	2	3	4	5
effective use of clay	0	1	2	3	4	5
shows expression	0	1	2	3	4	5
shows movement and balance	0	1	2	3	4	5

differentiation provide better results than simple checklists.

Self-Nominations

Student desire and interest are probably the most salient indicators for identifying artistically talented students, because intense interest and persistence of expression are critical characteristics for later progress and achievements. Applicants to arts programs for high-ability students might be nominated by a teacher or principal and meet a number of entrance criteria, but they also should be asked to write a short essay about why they want to attend. Their statements may indicate successful art experiences in the past, talent in one or more areas, humor and problem-solving abilities, and high motivation.

Artistically talented students often are very self-critical, but also are able to assess their own interests, skills, and abilities more perceptively than others. A self-interest inventory can identify pertinent abilities, hobbies, and interests that relate to the goals of a program, and can yield data about students' beliefs, goals, and values related to achievement in the visual arts.

Peer Nominations

Although many highly talented students may conceal their abilities from teachers and other adults, they generally are well known to their peers from school, extracurricular, and out-of-school activities. Asking students to list other students they believe are talented, however, simply elicits a list of names. More useful information is gathered by

Figure 2.14. Distribution Obtained With Modified Tests of Creative Thinking
(Note: $SD = 2.67$; $M = 9.32$; $N = 1,021$)

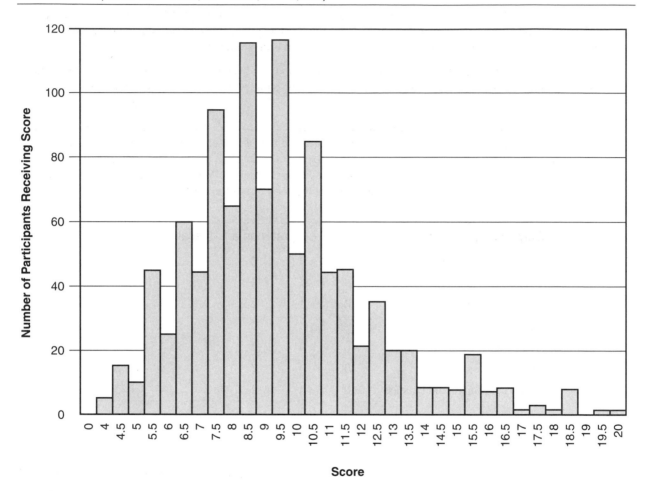

asking students to nominate specific individuals for specific tasks and to rate the frequency of their art-related behaviors. By asking for comments, useful information can be obtained that may help guide selection procedures.

Parent Nominations

Parents often know their children better than teachers or administrators because they see their children in multiple, social situations beyond schools and at home. Parents, however, often are biased. They may overemphasize or underemphasize their child's accomplishments for various reasons. This potential for bias precludes using parent nominations exclusively, although parents often supply types of information with which school personnel or peers may not be familiar. Parent nominations may be either an open invitation to write a letter or a request to fill out a structured form where they rate frequency of art-related behaviors and generally describe interests and activities that help indicate potential success in a selective school program.

Teacher Nominations

Evidence presented by researchers often has demonstrated that open invitations to teachers to

Figure 2.15. Distribution Obtained With Clark's Drawing Abilities Test
(Note: *SD* = 29.96; *M* = 73.2; *N* = 946)

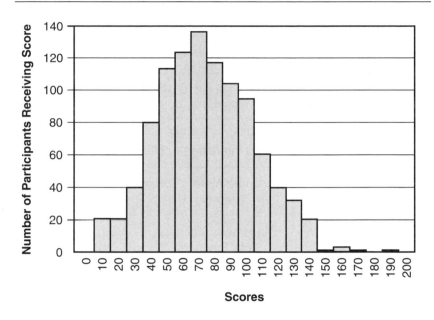

nominate gifted and talented students have yielded very poor results. It is possible, however, to greatly improve the effectiveness of teacher nominations by providing nomination forms that state specific criteria and by providing in-service education about the use of criteria and methods prior to the nomination process. We suggest that various combinations of checklists and subjective questions are superior to either used in isolation. Both nonstructured and structured nominations are important because they yield very different kinds of information and responses.

Standardized Tests

The use of standardized achievement test scores have been recommended by some people, and the usual criteria are scores 2 or more years above grade level. This is based on research that has shown that students who are artistically talented usually are achieving above grade level in other school subjects. (Such achievement often is demonstrated, although not always, by superior grades in academic subjects and the arts.) We recommend that

if achievement test scores are mandated for screening purposes, they should not be used exclusively.

We cannot, at this time, recommend use of any currently available standardized visual arts test (e.g., Graves, 1978; Horn, 1953; Meier, 1942) except Clark's Drawing Abilities Test (Clark, 1993; Clark & Wilson, 1991), which has been proven to be reliable and valid (see discussion of CDAT earlier in this chapter). Many questions also have been raised about using creativity tests for the identification of artistically talented students (see Chapter 1). Despite a possible correlation between the CDAT and the TTCT, and creativity tests always should be used in combination with other measures for the identification of artistically talented students.

Informal Art Instruments

Many administrators of visual or performing arts programs, especially at junior or senior high school levels, administer group drawing tests, ask students to submit slides of their art work, or require students to send a portfolio as screening pro-

Figure 2.16. Screening Procedures Used for Identifying Artistically Talented Students in Order of Selectivity and Cost

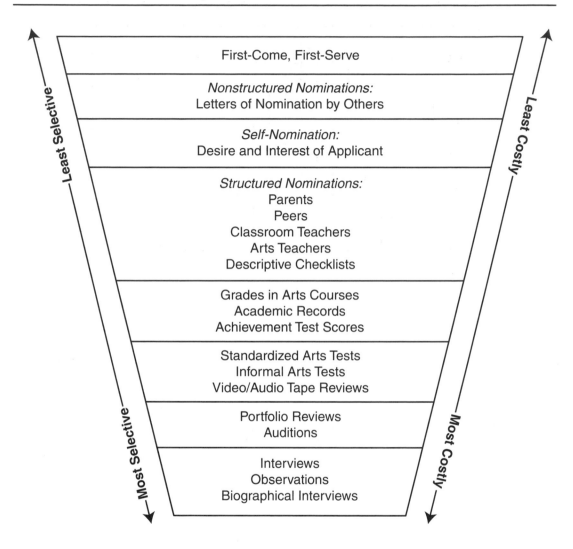

cedures. Students often are not given information about specific criteria that will be used to judge their works. Locally created criteria frequently are used to make selection decisions and these are stated, if at all, in very open-ended or ill-defined terms. Such decisions often fail because they are based on subjective reactions of teachers. The work-sample technique offers an alternative and does not incur most of the criticisms we have just listed. In a work-sample procedure, a common assignment, or group of assignments, is given to all applicants, and evaluation criteria are established to grade results, thus making comparisons of results possible. Many informal instruments, however, are not trustworthy enough to be used as sole criteria for selection of applicants for an artistically talented program because they lack sufficient reliability or validity.

Portfolio and Performance Review

The advantages of being able to view and critique each student's work and/or performance are obvious. Viewing a student's artwork in a variety of media can give judges insights about the student's

Figure 2.17. Applications of Identification Procedures at Various Age/Grade Levels in School

	Primary Ages 6–9	Intermediate Ages 10–12	Secondary Age 13+
Nonstructured nominations:			
Others	√	√	√
Self		√	√
Structured Nominations:			
Self		√	√
Peer		√	√
Parent	√	√	√
Teacher	√		√
Grades in art courses		√	√
Academic records			√
Reviews of slides or video presentations		√	√
Informal instruments	√	√	√
Portfolio review			√
Interview		√	√
In-class observations	√	√	√

abilities to use skills and techniques and demonstrate use of media. Demonstrated abilities, however, should not be the only factor assessed in portfolio reviews; attention also should be paid to potential ability and processes that might lead to superior products or performances. Process portfolios can be used as part of an identification process and may take the form of files or folders that provide summaries of an individual's achievements (Gitomer, Grosh, & Price, 1992; Zimmerman, 1997a, 1997b).

Exclusive use of portfolio reviews usually eliminates the identification of students with unproven potential talent, because students who have taken prior arts classes obviously are advantaged in this process. Candidates who submit portfolios also may be asked to create a related product under controlled conditions while being observed by judges to assess their processes. Candidates should be told specific portfolio requirements and criteria that will be used

to assess them. Judges should be educated to use portfolio reviews equitably and fairly and attend to potential as well as demonstrated abilities.

Interview Procedures

Interviews are conducted as identification procedures in a number of programs after preliminary screening or immediately after a portfolio review. Interviews give both participants opportunities to interact and share information in an open exchange. Interviews also should be used to give applicants information about a program and collect information about applicants. Interviewers, when possible, should have opportunities to examine each candidate's application materials prior to the interview. They can familiarize themselves with strengths, interests, and goals expressed by candidates and can then tailor questions to students' interests and strengths. Interviews are costly and time consuming, however, and should be used only at the end of a screening process. Upon completion of an interview, a biographical inventory can be compiled to summarize the applicant's responses from application materials, observations, judgments, and interviews.

Observation Procedures

Trained observers can be very accurate when identifying artistically talented students by observing them working in classrooms and other settings. Information about students should emerge as an observer spends time with a subject. Many people have recommended observation as an important aspect of identification procedures, but it has two major limitations: It is costly and requires trained, perceptive observers who are not regular participants in a student's environment.

CONCLUSIONS AND RECOMMENDATIONS

In 1992, we reported a limited number of then current identification practices, standardized art tests, and screening procedures used at state and local levels. Since that time, numerous programs for artistically talented students have appeared, and many states have prepared guidelines for the identification of gifted students, including artistically talented students. Most of these guidelines advocate use of multiple criteria systems and include descriptions and examples of a variety of nomination forms, checklists, and other resources. There still are some limitations to effective and efficient identification of artistically talented students. Although there has been a progression from using single identification instruments to using multiple criteria systems, decisions about which measures to use often are based on simple speculations. Currently, there are no agreed-upon criteria derived from research findings about interrelationships of these measures; thus a diverse battery of identification procedures is highly recommended. Procedures currently used or recommended periodically need to be examined critically and evaluated in light of the most recent research findings and re-

ports of successful implementation in artistically talented programs throughout the country.

The following recommendations are derived from our reviews of issues and practices related to the identification of talented students in the visual arts (Clark & Zimmerman, 1992). A brief discussion and suggestions for further research follow each recommendation.

Recommendation 1. The term *artistically talented* is recommended for research and practice relative to the identification and education of highly able visual arts students. The implication is that art talent should be conceived of as multidimensional, with emphases on cognitive complexity, affective intensity, technical skills, and interest and motivation in the arts.

Recommendation 2. Art talent, like achievement, should be conceived of as normally distributed, with students with highly developed art abilities or poorly developed art abilities in relatively small numbers; the majority of students will be identified with average abilities. Acceptance of art talent as normally distributed should lead to new and substantially different identification criteria and procedures in which artistically talented students can be identified as separate from the general population.

Recommendation 3. Creativity tests are supported by some researchers and writers and questioned by others as useful for the identification of artisically talented students. There is a need to analyze past creativity research and conduct new research about their conceptual and operational definitions and relationship to the identification of art talent.

Recommendation 4. The identification of artistically talented students should be based on careful attention to student potential and works in progress as well as final performance and products. Researchers are challenged to develop new methods for identifying artistically talented students and to assess emerging skills, cognitive abilities, and affective abilities through observations and works in progress.

Recommendation 5. We recommend the use of Clark's Drawing Abilities Test to assess the drawing abilities of artistically talented students, but researchers also need to develop effective alternatives with general applications for identification at different grade levels with a variety of populations, such as process portfolios, work samples, and biographical inventories. Also, local application of procedures, such as those developed in Project ARTS, should be created to identify students with talent in other two-dimensional areas such as painting or collage making and three-dimensional aspects of the visual arts such as sculpture and ceramics.

Recommendation 6. Students' backgrounds, personalities, values, and age need to be considered as factors in the identification of artistically talented students. All students differ in their interests, learning styles, rates of learning, motivation, work habits, and personalities, as well as in their ethnicity, sex, economic backgrounds, social class, and age when art talent emerges. These characteristics should be studied as aspects of identification programs for all artistically talented students.

Recommendation 7. Use of multiple criteria systems is recommended in all identification programs for supporting art talent development. When multiple criteria systems are used, they should include a number of different kinds of identification instruments and procedures. It is important to avoid using just one or two similar methods. Although there has been a progression from using single identification instruments to using multiple criteria systems, decisions about which measures to use, what criteria are appropriate, and how these factors interrelate still need to be studied and researched.

3 Student Characteristics

Plate 3.1 A self-portrait drawing by a seventh-grade IU Summer Arts Institute student that is sensitively rendered

Characteristics of students who are identified as possessing art talent can be explored from a number of vantage points so that programs that meet their needs can be planned and developed. In this chapter, conceptions about giftedness and talent held by students participating in both academic and art summer programs are explored. The first concern addressed is students' reactions to being labeled gifted and talented. Next, talented art students' views of self, views of family and home environment, school and studying art, and reactions to enrollment in a summer arts programs are described and interpreted. In a separate section, artistically talented girls' perceptions and life situations are contrasted and compared with academically gifted girls as well as artistically talented boys. Then in an even finer focus, one student's experiences with educational opportunities and how these influenced his art talent development are discussed. Finally, we make some recommendations about educating artistically talented students, based on student characteristics.

PERCEPTIONS OF STUDENTS LABELED GIFTED AND TALENTED

While researchers have extensively explored the labeling of handicapped children, there have been few studies about labeling gifted and talented students. Questions such as those suggested by Becker (1964)—who applies a label to whom, what consequences the label has for persons labeled, and under what circumstances a label is successfully applied—need to be given attention in the field of gifted and talented education. Categories and labels have the power of making services, opportunities, and programs available for exceptional children that may otherwise not be open to them. Labeling can facilitate passage of legislation and provide structures for organizing programs that address their needs.

In the 1960s, some research was carried out concerning perceptions of gifted and talented students. Weiner and O'Shea (1963) developed questionnaires and attitude scales about gifted students that were administered to university faculty and students, administrators, supervisors, and teachers. Attitudes of supervisors were found most favorable, followed by administrators, university faculty,

teachers, and graduate students in that order. In a subsequent study, Weiner (1968) found that school psychologists and psychometrists were favorable to establishing programs for high-ability students.

B. Clark (1979) discussed the ambiguousness of the label *gifted*. Many times students labeled gifted are placed in all accelerated courses, whether or not they are advanced in all subjects. She stressed that labels create expectations, and if students are labeled to improve their educational opportunities, negative aspects of labeling should be taken into account and avoided.

Some writers have speculated that the label *gifted* may affect students negatively. Others have noted that children labeled as having high intellectual ability often are viewed as having been given this label rather than earning it. Thus gifted students often are viewed with suspicion or hostility. Sandborn (1979) believed many gifted children do not like being called gifted and that *gifted* and *talented* often are categorical terms that lack meaning to individuals so labeled. Zaffrann (1978) noted that the term *gifted* often is defined as removed from the norm and problems of isolation, boredom, and resentment often are attributed to students with such labels.

Being Labeled Gifted and Talented

Research about labeling specifically of students highly talented in the arts is limited, and research findings about academically gifted students do not necessarily apply to those who are talented in the arts. The label *talented in the arts* may affect students in an entirely different manner than the label *academically gifted*.

It was decided, therefore, to investigate conceptions of giftedness and talent held by students participating in art and academic summer programs that included their recollections and interpretations of earlier labeling experiences and their perceptions of others' reactions to their being labeled (Guskin et al., 1986). Although theory is not well developed in what might be called the social psychology of gifted and talented children, a parallel body of theoretical formulations has evolved in the social psychology of handicapped students (Guskin, 1978). One of the more widely used frameworks is labeling theory.

When applied to gifted and talented students, labeling theory suggests that others are likely to react differently to persons labeled gifted; labeling effects will result in patterns of behavior and experiences that can lead to irreversible life patterns that are very different from ones of those who are not labeled. Assumptions aside, labeling theory provides a useful framework for asking questions addressed in this study:

1. When are children first identified as gifted or talented and by whom?
2. What leads a child to see himself or herself as gifted or talented?
3. What implications are drawn from this by the child?
4. Does a child sense changes in his or her expectations as a result of being labeled gifted or talented?
5. What changes in his or her life occur consequent to such labeling?
6. Are labeled children treated differently by other parents or peers?
7. Do they view themselves as different from others?
8. Do they anticipate a different future from that of their peers?

Methodology

Participants were 47 students attending the Indiana University Summer Arts Institute and 248 students attending the College for Gifted and Talented Youth. All were entering Grades 6–10 in the fall and ranged in age from 9 to 15. Forty-four percent (129) were girls and 56 percent (166) were boys. Both groups lived in campus dormitories for 2 weeks. The College for Gifted and Talented Youth was designed for academically gifted students and the Summer Arts Institute was designed for artistically talented students in the arts. Following guidelines provided by these two programs, students were nominated by school personnel and required parent approval to enter either program.

Data Collection and Analysis

Fourteen students were interviewed prior to participating in one of the summer programs, and questionnaires were developed based on their responses. Questionnaires then were administered to all students ($N = 295$) during their participation in the summer programs. Twenty open-ended questions, followed by a checklist of labels for self-description (e.g., "brilliant," "talented," "creative," and so forth) and three 35-item adjective rating scales (one each for "typical academically gifted teenager," "typical artistically talented teenager," and "you") were used. Responses to the 20 open-ended questions were categorized using content analysis procedures and reliability of the content analyses was established independently by two coders. Frequency distributions of responses to the checklist of self-descriptions and the rating scales were derived separately for academically gifted and artistically talented groups. Chi-square tests were used to determine significance of group differences.

Results of the Study

Responses to the checklist of self-description words and phrases indicated that most academically gifted or artistically talented students characterized themselves "as good in school" (88.5%), "imaginative" (80.4%), "creative" (79.7%), "smart" (79.0%), "talented" (74.5%), "intelligent" (71.0%), "successful" (65.4%), and "gifted" (64.3%). Only a small proportion checked "average" (22.7%), "brilliant" (22.6%), or "outstanding" (28.7%). Approximately half characterized themselves as "good in the arts" (45.8%) or "special" (53.1%). The only significant differences between the two groups were more frequent checking by the academically gifted group of the adjective "successful" (69.0% vs. 45.5%) and by the artistically talented group of the adjectives "average" (40.9% vs. 19.4%) and "good in the arts" (81.8% vs. 39.3%).

On the three rating scales on which students indicated agreement or disagreement with 35 adjectives and phrases drawn from the literature and interviews describing a "typical academically gifted teenager," a "typical artistically talented teenager," and "you," terms agreed with, or disagreed with, by at least two-thirds of the subjects indicate many commonly held stereotypes. Findings suggested that stereotypes of both groups were highly positive, similar to one another, and to their positive self-descriptions. Items agreed with included "self-confident," "likes challenges," "enthusiastic," "competitive," "born with talent," "sensitive," "full of life," "popular," and "makes friends easily." Terms commonly disagreed with were "not interested in school," "immature," "dislikes lots of people," "brags a lot," "gets jealous easily," "tries to attract attention," "a smart aleck," "stuck up," and "bugs the teacher." Thus, accepted terms described consistently positive traits and rejected terms were consistently negative. Academically gifted students were more likely to be seen as learning on their own, getting good grades, and as student leaders. Artistically talented students were more often viewed as making friends easily, attractive, and less likely to be seen as studying all the time. Self-descriptions included being good in sports, being attractive, making friends easily, and getting good grades. Both groups' self-descriptions denied the concept of studying all the time.

Students responded to 20 open-ended questions in which their opinions of giftedness and talents and their personal experiences with labeling were probed. They were asked questions relating to the determinants of gifts or talents, and when asked, "Can anyone have special abilities and skills?" 65 percent answered yes. One-third responded that everyone has special abilities and talents. Half the students thought anyone could be specially able or skilled if they were motivated, worked or studied hard, or used their abilities. Those who disagreed thought one needed to be born with gifts and talents. When asked why some people have special abilities or skills, 44 percent referred to motivation, hard work, practice, or time spent learning; and 23 percent referred to innate capacities. Emphasis on hard work, motivation, and practice was greater when asked, "What must happen for a person with special abilities to become outstanding?" In general, these students did not view gifted or talented persons as very different from others, except in the effort initiated to develop their skills and abilities.

Subjects were also asked, "Do people treat you differently because of your abilities?" and over a third (35%) answered no. Differential treatments reported included higher expectations or demands (14%), generally good treatment (11%), encouragement or support (8%), and praise or pride (7%). These results are consistent with findings by other researchers who have suggested little negative reaction to students being labeled gifted or talented (Ford, 1978; Lutz & Lutz, 1980) and differ from speculations that gifted students often face rejection (e.g. Sandborn, 1979).

Discussion and Conclusions of the Study

Findings of this study suggest that these students have highly favorable views of themselves and of gifted and talented students generally. They believe that gifts or talents can be attained by hard work and that gifted and talented students are not very different from others. They perceive themselves as being treated no differently or no more favorably than others. Only a small minority reported negative reactions from their peers.

What do these findings suggest about the applicability of labeling theory to academically gifted or artistically talented students? The gifted or talented label is seen as a mixed blessing, associated with high status, especially in the eyes of parents and teachers. Like any differentiating label or category, it contains the risk of separating an individual from his or her peer group. Thus, while these students are quite willing to view themselves as competent and personable, they do not want to be seen as outstanding or too different from others. They want gifts and talents to be the result of effort, rather than immutable. Although they did not report negative consequences, they seem very aware of the potential for rejection if they were to be set apart as "elite." Thus this study demonstrates the utility of labeling theory for defining researchable questions about gifted or talented students and suggests that labeling students as gifted or talented does not have negative consequences in schools.

In this study the focus was on comparing and contrasting student views about being labeled academically or artistically gifted and/or talented. As a result of conducting this study we decided to research talented visual arts students at the Summer Arts Institute in greater depth. There was a dearth of literature about this topic and especially about students of middle and high school ages.

CHARACTERISTICS OF ARTISTICALLY TALENTED STUDENTS IN A SPECIAL PROGRAM

Although information is available about characteristics of students talented in the visual arts, findings often are confusing because they have been generated at various periods of time, use differing methodologies, and emphasize divergent research questions. Researchers in psychology and art education have conducted interviews with young art students or artists in the early years of their careers to gain access to their early reminiscences. Getzels and Csikszentmihalyi (1976) interviewed young artists when they were college art students and after they left school. They attempted to construct a pattern of socialization into art and answer questions about how a person becomes an artist and creative problem finder. Bloom and his associates (1985), through interviews with subjects, siblings, and parents, examined processes by which individuals reach high levels of accomplishment before the age of 35. They included two art groups, concert pianists and sculptors, as well as high achievers in other fields. Bloom felt information they needed could be secured through retrospective accounts of people who had already achieved high levels in selected fields.

A few researchers have interviewed young artistically talented students to gain information about their perceptions and life situations. Chetelat (1982) interviewed six artistically talented students to discern differences and similarities of specific characteristics and their living and learning environments. He also studied early childhood experiences of six eminent artists recorded in their autobiographical accounts. Using interviews and open-ended questionnaires, Guskin et al. (1986) studied artistically talented and academically gifted students in order to understand how they view themselves and interpret their abilities. Taylor (1986) interviewed artistically talented students to determine how they developed a commitment to one or more art forms and identified or empathized with art objects.

Interviews with Artistically Talented Students

Use of interviews by researchers in psychology and education to study life situations of artistically talented students has suggested questions that can be applied in a variety of settings. We decided to interview students at the Indiana University Summer Arts Institute (IUSAI) and questions were categorized into topics about early art talent, adult and peer encouragement, position in a family, future expectations, early interest in reading and looking

at art books, schooling, and perceptions of art abilities (Clark & Zimmerman, 1988b). These categories were addressed in an effort to gain more information about characteristics of artistically talented students. Although the study by Bloom (1985) involved accomplished professionals and Getzels and Csikszentmihalyi's (1976) subjects were college-age, we believe reminiscences of these populations would probably differ in degree and intensity, but not in kind, from reminiscences of junior high school art students.

Results of this study will be compared with findings of the researchers cited in order to expand available knowledge and create a foundation that may lead to understanding artistically talented students as a specific population. Teachers and others who work with them need to understand how this population differs from other students in order to identify them, provide appropriate services, and best meet their educational needs.

Methodology

The Summer Arts Institute was the setting for this study. Participants were 20 students attending the institute during the summers of 1986 and 1987 who were nominated by art teachers or other school personnel as artistically talented. Because we were interested in investigating similarities and differences between international and U.S. students, one-third of the students interviewed were born outside the United States, although they represented only 9 percent of the total institute population. Students from the United States were chosen randomly, and all students who were interviewed volunteered to participate.

All students interviewed were entering Grades 7 through 11 and ranged from 13 through 17 years of age. Of the 112 students who attended the 1986 and 1987 institutes, 20 students were interviewed. Twelve students were female (60%) and eight were male (40%), although each gender was represented by 50 percent of the total institute population. The majority of the students were from Indiana, although five were from other states, three were from other countries, and seven had lived in the United States for less than 3 years. Eight of the students interviewed were, or were originally, from Brazil, Korea, Malaysia, New Zealand, Singapore, Spain,

Taiwan, and Vietnam. One-third of the students attending the institute and one-third of those interviewed received financial aid. Of the twelve students from the United States, eight were from communities of less that 50,000 people, two were from communities with between 50,000 and 100,000 people, and two were from large cities with well over 100,000 people. All international students were from large cities in their home countries. The number of children in the families of students who were interviewed ranged from 1 to 14, with 6.92 the average. This figure is skewed, however, because three students came from very large families. The majority of students came from families with one to three children and only one student was an only child. Eighty percent of the students were the oldest or youngest in their families.

Data Collection and Analysis

We conducted our interviews with participants during out-of-class times. The interviews lasted from 1½–2 hours and were tape recorded and transcribed. Interviewers were curious about similarities and differences between international students and students from the United States. Our interview protocol contained nine categories, with three to six questions for each, and was used to guide interviews, although students' responses determined the dialogue used. All categories were covered with each student, but not necessarily in the same order.

Content analysis described by Mostyn (1985) has been used extensively to analyze unstructured, open-ended research material that results from "nondirective questions which, by their nature, impose as few constraints on respondents' answers as possible" (p. 115). Mostyn contended that in qualitative research, if the sample is small, interviews usually last more than one hour, respondents react to questions in a general framework, and the objective is to expand the knowledge base gained by previous data. Results were analyzed by content analysis, and the final report was based on understanding students' attitudes and behaviors.

Results of the Study

Large categories, resulting from analyses of interview data, were labeled

1. Views of self
2. Views of family and home environment
3. Views of school and studying art
4. Views of aspects of the Summer Arts Institute

Views of Self. Most students remembered becoming interested in art at a preschool or primary level and some remembered doing fantasy or realistic drawings when they were young: "When I was younger, I liked to sketch. Ever since I remember, I was drawing, but the earliest picture I remember was when I was 4. It's in sections and it's got a home, a hell place, and a heaven place." Most students remembered specific people and incidents as triggers to when they first became interested in art: "My father has a friend who is an artist and he made a book for me. It was really good, and I would just stare at this thing forever. I drew a lot from that."

Boys, more than girls, stated a concern for developing technical skills and did not report creating art for expressive reasons: "When I draw . . . I concentrate on it, look at the different outlines, the shape of it, think about what it's like, how it looks in different positions and then I draw." Girls, more than boys, reported beginning with an emotional need and then learning skills to help them express themselves: "When I am happy and when I am upset, I always draw mostly black. I mean, the color's usually dark and dreary and everything."

Both boys and girls reported their favorite subjects were observed objects, places they had been, landscapes, human figures, and fantasy places, in that order. The most commonly used medium was pencil because they had the most experience with it and it is inexpensive and readily available. Five students indicated they liked to draw realistically; they did not copy but used illustrations as sources. Five others mentioned they copied from comic books when they were young and still look at illustrations for ideas: "When I'm drawing my own characters and stuff, I go in my closet because I've got a lot of books and I get out a couple and I take bits and pieces."

A majority of students felt good about themselves and their abilities and could accept criticism to improve their work: "I don't mind being criticized. It's like you have to accept it, you can't go through life thinking that you're doing everything

Plate 3.2 A drawing of a superhero by an eighth-grade student in the Visual Narrative class at the IU Summer Arts Institute demonstrates how comic books often influence art talent development

right. I'm 15 years old and I've still got a lot to learn." Some students expressed an interest in having a career in the arts as cartoonists, painters, interior decorators, or in advertising. More girls than boys wanted to be artists, although three girls mentioned pressure from their families to marry and raise a family and to view their art as an avocation: "Ever since I was small, I always knew that I was

going to be an artist. You know, when other kids say, 'I want to be an astronaut,' well, I always wanted to be an artist and parents would look at me like I've been watching too many movies."

Views of Family and Home Environment. Most students (70%) reported they were encouraged in their artwork by their mother, father, or both. Fifteen percent noted that family members other than parents encouraged them, and three students (15%) reported that no family members encouraged or supported their art interests. No differences were noted between boys and girls in these findings. Only three parents and one sibling were reported as having studied art or doing artwork as a hobby. Ten students (50%) mentioned that none of their friends were interested in art, and five (25%) noted that they did have friends interested in art.

Thirteen students (65%) reported they had a place to do artwork in their homes; the remaining seven (35%) did not. Those who reported working in their homes did not have special facilities: "When I work at home in my bedroom, I like to be quiet and get away from everything. I just lie on my floor or bed or whatever to draw." Of eighteen who responded, twelve (60%) remembered having illustrated comics or wildlife books in their homes. Students from the United States tended to have stayed in a local area and not to have traveled far from home. Most international students mentioned having moved a number of times and had traveled to one or more countries. One U.S. student said: "I have traveled, but only to places like to our cousins in North Carolina. The places I really want to see are Chicago and Manhattan."

Views of School and Studying Art. Many students from rural areas said school offered them their only access to a social community: "The first semester of school is when I really like it. I enjoy seeing my friends; I live out in the country. In the summer, I don't really get to see my friends." Most, however, mentioned difficulty in finding friends at school who shared common interests in art: "I don't really have a group I can relate to at school."

Fifteen (75%) students took art classes in their regular schools, and five (25%) reported they didn't have time to take art classes due to pressure to complete an academic curriculum: "I don't take art right now in high school, but I used to. It's an elective class and I have to take a foreign language." Most students reported taking arts classes outside their schools; eight took visual arts classes and four were enrolled in performing arts classes; and an equal number of these were boys and girls. International students tended to take private lessons with teachers who emphasized skills and techniques, and most U.S. students took group lessons at a university or museum that emphasized creative self-expression.

Nearly half of the students mentioned the impact of winning awards as helping maintain their interests and contributing to support from their families: "After my paintings started winning in the art show, my mother started looking for teachers to teach me, because I wanted to paint." Negative aspects of awards also were mentioned, including the effects of perpetuating adherence to a rewarded style, creation of tension between winners and nonwinners, and lack of awareness of how competitions were judged. "I did get ribbons and I'd think about the past things I've done and that's what I'd usually draw."

All the students reported receiving good grades and subjects they liked most were science, English, history, or mathematics. A few international students mentioned they disliked studying English (to them a foreign language). Typical reports of grades were high, including mostly As or Bs by both girls and boys. "I am interested in art and biology. I was thinking it would be nice to combine them. The cells of animals and things like that are really interesting to me." "I have a 4.0 average in school. I like history and algebra because I like working with figures and stuff. I like them all."

Three images of regular art teachers emerged. One was supportive, but not challenging. Another was challenging, but failing to reinforce or support accomplishments. The third was supportive, but not offering instruction about how to succeed. "I get sick of being told everything I do is good. I know it is not perfect, but she's like 'It's great!' and I never get satisfied with my work." "I work hard and think I'm doing my best, but she always tells me I could do better but won't tell me how." Students who had lived in other countries reported their art classes tended to be more crowded, were taught more formally with an emphasis on techniques, were based on specific assignments from workbooks, and were stricter and more rigorous. They also reported they had to pass examinations in both art and art history.

Views of Aspects of the Summer Arts Institute. Most students found that teachers at the institute

1. Challenged them more than those in their regular schools

2. Taught them to use new media
3. Made them think about what they were doing
4. Made them look more carefully and accurately
5. Taught them to consider how to express themselves through careful use of techniques

"I couldn't draw. . . . He said I was looking at what it was, and my brain was drawing what I know it looks like. Once I learned that, my drawings got one hundred percent better."

The majority of students expressed pleasure at being grouped with others with similar interests and abilities: "It is fun because there's a lot of people who think like us 'cause in school they're not really interested in art." Most students enjoyed working at a high level of difficulty, felt they were doing better work than in their regular classrooms, and realized how much they had learned.

Most expressed pleasure at the openness of conversations outside of classes, when they shared ideas and critiqued each other's artwork: "One thing, we enjoy ourselves so much that we want to work. I feel if I enjoy myself, I can do more and my work will come out better and better." A number of students expressed awareness of having learned a lot about themselves socially and through learning new techniques and means of expression: "Sometimes, when we've been standing up and drawing for 2 hours straight, that's kind of tiring and everybody gets all edgy. Later on, you think about it and it's all clear."

Most students reported that they were surrounded by other students of comparable or superior abilities and they had to work hard to do well and meet teachers' expectations. A few were reluctant to abandon their own styles or change their approaches to creating art because they had been rewarded for these things in the past: "The institute is not as good as I had hoped. I'm not used to painting this way. I like my own style, and I don't want a different one forced on me."

Most students mentioned that their smaller classes encouraged better communications and instruction: "In my IUSAI class, there are only thirteen. We can really be more of a group and if it's too big, you can't get to know everybody." New

Plate 3.3 An ink drawing by an IU Summer ARTS Institute sixth grader combines multiple and complex points of view while at the same time maintaining a focus on the posed figure

experiences for most students, such as going to an art museum, hearing an art historian lecture, or visiting an art store were mentioned as memorable events: "I enjoyed just everything. Going to the art store. That's the first time I've ever been into a real art shop. Then going to the artist's studio, that was a real experience."

Discussion and Conclusions of the Study

In this study most students were found to be aware of their talents, interested in improving their abilities, and introspective about the role of the arts in their lives. Many were aware that they possessed unusual interest and abilities in the arts and had favorable views of themselves and talented students in general, as did subjects in the Guskin et al. study (1986). Bloom (1985) and Chetelat (1982) also found that young people with talent in the arts find art-making experiences rewarding. Although Getzels and Csikszentmihalyi (1976) reported that emotional crises were stimulants to creating art, students at the institute spoke about being stimulated to make art by pleasurable experiences and did not indicate they were using art for emotional release. More girls than boys, however, described their art making as a means of self-expression, rather than building techniques or skills.

Findings by Getzels and Csikszentmihalyi (1976) were similar to findings in this study:

1. Young people talented in art drew many of the same images (cartoons and comic book heroes) as others of similar age.
2. Their drawings were praised more than those of other students in their classes.
3. They devoted a great deal of time to drawing.
4. They remember drawing from ages 6 to 8.

These findings were not consistent with those of Chetelat (1982) who found a high degree of solitary art making among his subjects. Students at the institute were almost equally divided between favoring solitary work and working in or with groups of other students.

In this study most students' families encouraged them to maintain their interest in art, even though they did not have art backgrounds and did not travel extensively. Few of the students had friends interested in art, yet they continued to maintain their participation in art activities. Bloom (1985) and Chetelat (1982) reported strong support and encouragement from both parents, and subjects in this study reported similar support. This contradicts findings by others that young art students frequently receive support only from their mothers and had harsh memories of their fathers.

Bloom (1985) reported that parents of talented students varied greatly in the level of education they had completed, their type of work, their economic level, and their avocational interests and activities. In this study students' responses verified similar findings. Bloom reported homes that emphasized music and the arts; but few subjects in this study were offered such opportunities. Chetelat reported that all of his subjects showed a great interest in viewing books and were stimulated by book illustrations. Few subjects in this study recalled having illustrated books at home, although a few reported recollections of comic book illustrations and their own drawings.

Most students reported that their school offered a social community, although they did not have many friends with similar interests. Many took art classes outside of school and perceived winning awards both positively and negatively. Almost all earned high grades and enjoyed school, and their art teachers were recalled as encouraging them, although they often expressed a need for more rigorous and supportive instruction. Students' recollections of their art teachers varied widely; although many recalled specific teachers who rewarded and encouraged them, not all recalled their art teachers positively. In this study, being selected to exhibit their artworks, participating in an art club, or being praised for specific achievements motivated and encouraged them to continue to make art.

All subjects in this study reported positive reactions to schooling and were excellent students in most subjects. Recollections of art teachers agreed with Bloom's (1985) descriptions of early teachers as being child-centered, using approval and praise, and making early learning pleasant and rewarding. Institute students perceived their need both to be challenged and taught at higher ability levels that would improve their art works. In this, they anticipated their need for advanced teachers who were experienced with artistically talented students and who demanded high achievement and commitment to their talent areas that Bloom described as important to development of talent in the arts.

Our IUSAI students recognized major differences between classes at the institute and their regular classes. They were pleased to be grouped with others like themselves, and they enjoyed and were stimulated by others with similar abilities. They became more conscious and critical of their own abilities and took advantage of the many university facilities available at the institute. Highly talented students have been described as having illuminating experiences that changed their lives through encounters with original works of art. In this study students who had never previously visited an art museum, attended a concert, or visited an artist's studio reported similar experiences. Analysis of findings from this study verified or called into question results of previous research about artistically talented students.

THE ART EDUCATION OF ARTISTICALLY TALENTED GIRLS

In 1986, when we interviewed artistically talented students about their perceptions of themselves, their families, and schooling in respect to their art talents, our focus was not on gender differences. We noted, however, that there were some differences in the ways boys and girls talked about these topics. For example, girls talked about their artwork as fulfilling emotional needs and then learning skills for self-expression. Boys focused on developing skills as a primary concern. We decided, therefore, to conduct another study that focused on perceptions of artistically talented girls at the Summer Arts Institute (Clark & Zimmerman, 1988b).

Influencing Factors

Identification and analysis of sexism in art education have been the concern of feminist art educators who have suggested that art educators study art-related sex differences in student learning and document gender bias in art content, classroom practices, and status of art teachers and public school art programs. The purpose of this study was to contrast and compare findings cited in reviews of research (Kerr, 1987; Reis, 1987; Silverman, 1986) about perceptions and life situations of academically gifted girls with findings about similar issues in the lives of artistically talented girls. In addition, comparison of gender differences was made with those we originally found in previous studies at the IUSAI (Zimmerman, 1994/95).

Methodology

The Summer Arts Institute was the setting for this study by Zimmerman. Participants were nominated by their art teachers or other school personnel based on criteria developed by staff. Seven boys and 12 girls who were in one painting class participated; they were entering Grades 7 to 11 the following semester. The mean grade level was 9.3 for boys and 8.8 for girls. All students interviewed were from Indiana; 14 were from small towns in rural areas and 5 were from larger communities.

Data Collection and Analysis

During the first week of the institute, along with the head counselor, we conducted interviews in out-of-class time. These interviews lasted from 1½–2 hours, were tape-recorded, and later transcribed. An interview guideline (not designed to differentiate gender differences) was used in previous summers and also was used in this study. The interview protocol contained nine major categories relative to art talent development, adult and peer encouragement, occupations of parents, future expectations, interest in doing art work, position in a family, familiarity with artists, schooling and art abilities, teachers, and attending the institute. This protocol was used to guide the interviews, although students' responses determined each dialogue. Each relevant idea found in subjects' responses was recorded in their own words and sorted by themes and the sex of the students. Large categories were labeled (1) views of self, (2) views of family and home environment, and (3) views of schooling and studying art.

Results of the Study

Results included information about the subjects' siblings and their parents' occupations. The number of children in their families ranged from 1 to 7, with 3.2 the average for girls' families and 3.7 the average for boys' families. More than half of the respondents were the youngest child (58% girls and 57% boys) in their families. Parents' occupations were widely distributed and included executive, administrative, managerial, crafts, repairs, laborers, and service positions.

Views of Self. Most students remembered becoming interested in art at preschool ages or in primary school. Art activities recalled were drawing, finger painting, making holiday cards, creating collages, and using modeling clay. One girl reported, "I did coloring books. We had a Barbie house you could take apart and do architecture with, and I used books that you put water on and paint appeared."

Boys remembered youthful experiences creating art; 57 percent recalled using wooden blocks, Lego blocks, Tinker Toys, or Lincoln Logs to build forms. The same percentage also recalled creating monsters: "I made Godzilla burning other Godzillas. . . . I drew monsters with fire coming out of their mouths and the cities they destroyed." Most boys and only half the girls remembered being aware of possessing art talent when they were young: "I don't recall knowing I had special talent, but I loved to draw." One boy remembered, "in the third or fourth grade, I knew I was good in art and other kids would have me draw stuff for them, and I still do."

Six of the girls (50%) and five of the boys (71%) recognized their emerging art talent and recalled the importance of approval by teachers and students and that receiving awards contributed to their feelings. Eight girls (67%) and three boys (43%) remembered specific people who triggered their interest in art. Some girls remembered grandfathers who encouraged their early experiences; other support came from fathers, uncles, cousins, and an aunt. One girl recalled, "I put my hand on [my grandfather's] when he was painting and drawing. He showed me how to do strokes." Boys were gen-

erally less specific about people who influenced their art talent, although they mentioned fathers, sisters, cousins, and uncles.

An equal proportion of girls and boys (58%) explained that engaging in artwork alleviated emotional needs, such as frustration and depression. Three boys (43%) stated they had a compulsion to draw. One explained, "I guess I was addicted to drawing; I would stay up late and neglect my homework to draw." No girls expressed this, although three (25%) explained they had a great need for their art work to be perfect. One stated, "My art teacher says I'm really accurate and take too long to do my art work. I'm too much a perfectionist and want everything just right."

Girls expressed interest in using color to make things look realistic. Acrylics, watercolors, oil paints, pastels, and tempera paints were mentioned as media they enjoyed. One girl remarked, "I have watercolors, oil paints, and tempera paints and always avoid black or white." All of the boys favored superheroes and fantastic imagery, and pencil was their favorite medium. One boy said, "I draw anything that goes against the mainstream . . . superheroes, fantastic, outrageous."

Sixty percent of the girls felt they were inadequate in relation to other students and were concerned about what others thought of them, but one girl said, "I think more about what I'm doing and not so much about whether others like it." Another girl explained she didn't speak up at a slide lecture because, "I thought I'd say something and be vulnerable and everybody would look at me." Seventy-one percent of the boys were positive about their art abilities, and none expressed feelings of inadequacy.

Two-thirds of the girls and half of the boys stated they preferred to work alone, and several girls (25%) felt that in a group "someone is always watching me and I have to do everything perfect." Four girls claimed they didn't have time to do artwork because of their homework and other commitments. When asked what an artist needs to be successful, one replied, "An artist needs to be confident and creative about his or her work, have a good imagination, find something to like, and have everyone else like it." Most boys (85%) mentioned practical necessities and vocational interests. One

Plate 3.4 A self-portrait by a sixth grade IU Summer ARTS Institute student reflects her interest in creating an image of herself as an attractive young woman

remarked, "You have to be able to make decisions, make contacts, and have 4 years of college and a company to work with."

Half of the girls interviewed expressed a desire to become a fine artist. Others anticipated related careers, such as art teacher, art therapist, photographer, or commercial artist. One girl explained, "I want to be an artist. You don't have a boss. I wouldn't like a boss telling me what to do." Six boys (86%) spoke about art careers that would lead to job security, such as being a computer artist, commercial artist, art teacher, architectural engineer, or medical illustrator. The boys were concerned with financial difficulties; one explained, "I'd like to become an architectural engineer. You won't make any money if you're going to be a private artist."

Views of Family and Home Environment. Most girls (75%) and boys (71%) reported they were encouraged in their artwork by their mothers, although fathers also encouraged 25 percent of the girls and 57 percent of the boys. Grandparents, siblings, and neighbors also were cited as encouraging their artwork. On the other hand, about a fourth of the girls and boys reported their parents were not interested in art and did not support their art interests. Ten girls (83%) and five boys (71%) claimed they had friends interested in art; half of the girls reported their friends did not do artwork, but "they think I'm really neat 'cause I can do art well."

Views of School and Studying Art. Most of the girls (66%) and boys (57%) who lived in rural areas enjoyed going to school and found a community of friends there with whom they shared interests. One girl explained she liked the family atmosphere in her school because "it's so small and you know everybody." Another girl said, "I like going to school; there's no other place you could get a social life, meet all those people, and learn a lot, except in school." One boy complained that his friends were not from his school, because "I go to a hick school and they're all a bunch of farmers."

Almost all girls and boys reported being good students and receiving mostly A or B grades. Girls stressed being good students and getting along well with others; boys admitted they received good grades, but were not always committed to being good students. One said, "I just draw in class a lot and wander off in my schoolwork." Half of the girls preferred mathematics; other classes they favored were art, English, sports, music, science, and social studies. Fifty percent of the boys preferred science, industrial arts, gym, and English classes.

Half of the girls (50%) and some boys (29%) were involved in special art classes for talented students. A few were not taking art classes in high school because of tight scheduling of academic classes. Most girls (75%) and boys (86%) took art-related classes outside of school. Three girls could not attend after-school classes because they were needed at home to work on their families' farms.

Most girls (75%) and boys (71%) indicated their local art teachers were supportive, encouraging, and interested in their artwork. Two girls and a boy reported their art teachers did not show preferences for one student over another: "She never acted any differently to me than anyone else. She didn't like to discriminate, so she didn't ever say she didn't like something." Two girls and two boys complained that their teachers wanted them to conform to specific standards and were not open to accepting certain subject matters they depicted in their artworks. One boy recalled his teacher saying, "I don't know why you draw stupid stuff; you could be a good artist if you drew nice stuff."

Three-fourths of the girls volunteered how much they enjoyed attending the institute. One girl admitted she had never been to an art museum or concert and "had never really got to experience those things, being from a small town." Another girl realized she did not have to feel intimidated by others' abilities: "At first I felt everybody is better than me, but you have to realize it could be for a lot of reasons. It could be they have more experience or are older." Almost all of the girls claimed they liked being away from home; 50 percent had never spent more than one night away from their homes before attending the institute.

Discussion and Conclusions of the Study

In this study cultural stereotyping was apparent in the choices of subject matter and media that girls and boys remembered using at an early age. Girls' activities were more passive than boys, who demanded active engagement with their environments. Although all the boys realized they possessed special talents, only half of the girls were aware of their capabilities in art; they were either not being given clues or not acknowledging them. Half of the girls remembered a grandfather who greatly encouraged their early art talents, and all of the girls remembered a male as an early influence and supporter.

Boys were more engaged in art-making activities and evidenced a compulsion to create, a finding not reported by any of the girls. Boys appeared to develop a stronger sense of identity with their artwork than girls. A fourth of the girls evidenced a perfection complex, and 43 percent of boys' descriptions of their compulsion to draw were self-motivated. Lack of self-esteem was evidenced by 66 percent of girls who felt they were not as good as other students. Reis (1987, 1991) described how such poor self-esteem contributes to females' lower levels of achievement. Some girls indicated they lacked time to do artwork because of school commitments, and several boys stayed up late to complete artwork. Boys were less concerned with grades in their classes than girls. Boys appeared to be more independent and less involved with achieving through conventional means.

Ninety percent of the boys and girls were able to name favorite artists. Except for Beatrix Potter, all artists named were male, and most were old masters. The need for girls to have knowledge of female artists as positive role models was apparent. Ninety-one percent of the girls had idealistic concepts about what artists must do to achieve success. They stressed personality characteristics as essential, whereas boys emphasized vocational skills and practical abilities. Half of the girls anticipated careers as artists; most boys preferred art careers that would lead to job security. Lack of realistic and practical planning for future careers was more apparent in girls' responses than in boys.

Although parents' occupations were widely distributed, 41 percent of the girls' mothers and 42 percent of the boys' fathers had professional careers. This may indicate the girls may look forward to professional achievements. Silverman (1986) found that successful women often had mothers as positive role models, and she described successful, gifted women as only children or first-born. In this study more than half the students were the youngest children in their families. Mothers, as well as friends, were viewed by the vast majority of all these students as being supportive and encouraging them in their artwork. Silverman (1986) stressed the importance of parents and others who encouraged their daughters and emphasized the importance of male support and assistance.

A majority of girls and boys, mostly from rural areas, found school a place where they could learn and enjoy a social community. Almost all the students had taken art classes in school and some had taken out-of-school classes. Because most lived in rural areas, locating and getting to extracurricular activities indicated parental support. Some girls reported they could not attend classes after school because they were needed at home. No boys reported missing extracurricular activities for this reason.

Most girls were model students, interested in getting good grades and admired by their teachers and peers. They evidenced what Loeb and Jay (1987) referred to as a need for achievement through conformity. Boys were less interested in being well behaved or conscientious about their schoolwork and were more independent and self-reliant. Both boys and girls based their likes or dislikes of school subjects on how interesting or challenging they found the classes. For girls, the most preferred class was mathematics, the subject most disliked by the majority of boys. Reis (1987, 1991) referred to male dominance in mathematics and science as an issue that deters women from success in these fields. Girls in this study, however, did not fit the stereotype of having math anxiety.

Art teachers were viewed as supportive and encouraging, although a few demanded more conformity and adherence to rules than was acceptable. Kerr (1987) indicated that females who achieved in their adult lives had a strong sense of identity and took responsibility for themselves and their lives. Art teachers who stress conformity may be encouraging traits in girl students that are not conducive to future success in life. A vast majority of the girls enjoyed being away from home and exposed to activities and places not available in their home communities. Some realized that although they might be the best artists in their schools, they could comfortably study with others who possessed talents and abilities beyond their own, and they were not intimidated by these experiences.

Counselors, parents, teachers, and community members should be educating artistically talented girls to be independent, have a mission in their lives, develop a strong sense of identity and self-esteem, and achieve in contexts free of sexual stereotypes or negative influences (Reis, 1987). This is a very challenging agenda for bright, talented girls

Plate 3.5 A photo-collage based on the theme, All about Me, by a seventh grade IU Summer Arts Institute student in which she parodies what most girls think their future will involve when they are married

in rural areas whose backgrounds are family-oriented and who often are encouraged to marry, have children, stay in their communities, and follow traditional ways of conducting their lives (Kleinsasser, 1986). In this study, however, there was no evidence of direct family pressure for girls to raise families or avoid careers. One girl said, "I think most girls my age say all they care about is boys and hair and how their face looks. I think they should try to do something they are talented in. A lot of girls don't realize their talents or they just don't care."

THE EFFECTS OF EDUCATIONAL OPPORTUNITIES ON A TALENTED STUDENT'S ART DEVELOPMENT

Although we gained much important information and many insights about the education of talented visual arts students at the Indiana University Summer Arts Institute from the studies already reported in this chapter, we lacked in-depth knowledge about individual students and educational opportunities that were offered to them. It appeared appropriate to focus on a case study of a highly talented art student and his educational opportunities to see how these might inform our understanding of student characteristics and art talent development.

There have been a number of case studies about the work of talented young artists who evidenced precocious abilities in the visual arts (Gardner, 1980; Goldsmith, 1992; Golomb, 1992a, 1992b, 1995; Milbrath, 1995; Wilson & Wilson, 1980). All of these studies emphasized spontaneous artwork done by precocious youngsters from early childhood through their adolescence or emphasized separate time periods during their development. Only a few case studies highlighted the effects of schooling and differential programming opportunities on the development of art talent (Nelson & Janzen, 1990). It is an underlying assumption of this case study that early educational opportunities in art classes can enhance and accelerate the art development of talented young artists.

Gardner (1980) presented a case study of spontaneous drawings by a 16-year-old artistically talented adolescent who grew up in an environment very supportive of the arts. Gardner claimed formal instruction did not have much impact on the artist's development. In case studies reported by Goldsmith (1992) and Golomb (1992b, 1995), formal art lessons or directed art experiences were viewed as inhibiting the visual art development of artistically gifted and talented students. Sloan & Sosniak (1985) studied accomplishments of 20 sculptors and concluded the absence of formal art education before college did not have a negative effect on their development or success. Conversely, Wilson and Wilson (1980) studied positive effects of enriched art learning on a student with high visual arts abilities. They credited his teacher with encouraging his talents by stressing the value of popular narrative models, rather then only emphasizing fine arts instruction. Milbrath (1995) did mention, in her case study of a talented art student, that he received differentiated art instruction that made a positive impact on his artwork at the high school and college levels.

Case Study: Eric, An Artistically Talented Student's Development

In this case study Zimmerman (1992c, 1995) describes the works of her son, Eric, whose early

art experiences began in preschool, developed in elementary and high school, affected his interests and abilities when he studied art in college, and eventually influenced his choice of an art-related career. Similar to the young people in Gardner's and Goldsmith's case studies, Eric's parents had interests and abilities in the visual arts and nurtured his talents; he also had encouragement from a number of his teachers, who likewise encouraged his developing art talents.

Methodology, Data Collection, and Analysis

Eric's spontaneous early artwork (from ages 3–17) will be discussed in respect to perceptual qualities, expression and skills with media, and conceptual qualities, including themes, puns, paradoxes, and metaphors. The impact of accelerated and enriched formal art experiences on Eric's development through these years also will be considered. Sources included 15 hours of audiotaped conversations, over 350 artworks (including paintings, drawings, ceramics, sculptures, games, and school projects), slides and photographs of artworks, school notebooks, and written class work.

Content analysis was used to discover themes, and comparative analysis was used to interrelate these themes throughout Eric's discussions and reactions to his artworks. A case study approach was emphasized, in which implications were drawn from themes that emerged from the data. It was believed that graphic development could best be understood by interviewing an artistically talented young adult who was old enough to be insightful when discussing his artworks but not yet removed from his childhood art creations.

Results of the Study

Family Background and the Culture of Schooling. From his earliest days, Eric watched his parents making art, talking about art, and discussing art education theory and practice. He was a frequent visitor to art museums, and in his early years there was much art making at home. Eric's artworks received much encouragement and criticism because his parents were aware of his burning desire to create art and were able to help him choose educational opportunities that would further develop his art abilities and interests.

Eric's first special art class was in the fourth grade, when he attended a class for students with high interest and abilities in the visual arts. His first extra-school opportunity was to study with a private art teacher when he was in the fifth grade. Next, he attended the Indiana University Summer Arts Institute as a rising seventh grader and continued for the next three summers. Eric took advanced drawing and painting classes at his high school during his junior year and attended a summer painting course for high school seniors at Indiana University. Eric also was academically advanced and attended accelerated classes in such subjects as calculus and advanced physics at his local high school. In addition, he was active in his school's music program, played clarinet and saxophone in an all-state orchestra, performed regularly as a member of a Baroque recorder ensemble, took art classes at Indiana University, and attended the Interlochen National Music Camp.

He graduated from the University of Pennsylvania with a Bachelor of Fine Arts degree. During his junior and senior years there, he was awarded a teaching assistantship and taught color theory to undergraduate and graduate students in the Fine Arts Department. Eric then earned a master's degree from Ohio State University in the Multi-Media Arts program at the Advanced Computer Center for Arts and Design. He currently works as a creative consultant and game designer for his own company, guest teaches graduate courses at several universities in communication theory and game design, and mentors graduate students at several universities. In addition, he is an educational curator of a new digital art museum in New York City and a practicing artist who exhibits work and conducts workshops in the United States and abroad. He has received a number of awards for games he has created in collaboration with others. In 1999 he was named by *Interview* magazine as one of 30 "high tech hot shots to watch" (Pandiscio, 1999, p. 150).

The Influence of Teachers

Eric's teachers in public schools and other art classes influenced his art making both positively and negatively. He felt his elementary school environment supported his interests, but his teachers did not make any deep impressions. He did not attend art classes when he was a freshman or sophomore in high school, but enrolled as a junior in an advanced drawing class. He remembered his teacher as neither creative nor supportive. A painting teacher in a course he took at Indiana University that same year did influence him positively. At this time, he felt he was struggling to reach some goal, and the struggle was accompanied by what he described as

a real kind of frustration. I knew something was out there but I didn't know what it was. I was extremely dissatisfied. Then I was working on a drawing of a model and she corrected it, ruining it by drawing on it with a palette knife. I was furious; she had violated my drawing. I started painting just to spite her, exaggerating what she suggested by making the drawing more geometric. Suddenly an immense feeling unfolded. I remember thinking that if I became an artist it would be because of this experience. (Zimmerman, 1995, p. 142)

Until this time, Eric had not been aware that art making required planning, working through problems, or finding solutions, all of which require cognitive ability as well as technical facility. After having this break-through experience, he felt returning to high school art classes would be entering his high school art teacher's "cave of clichés." His English teacher, however, employed an intellectual and creative approach to learning and encouraged visual responses to assignments. This is evident in a visual narrative he created from Shakespeare's *Macbeth*. Eric remembered this teacher as one "who taught him how to write and read critically."

In his senior year, Eric was able to study half a day in the Fine Arts Department at Indiana University and did not have any trouble fitting into the classes. He remembered one fine arts faculty member as an outstanding mentor who challenged students to think about space in sophisticated ways and encouraged them to find their own directions. This teacher helped Eric see that there were no absolute solutions to art problems and that criticism is always subject to interpretation. Eric was eager for instruction and open to any assistance his teach-

Plate 3.6 A visual narrative of a specific act and scene from *Macbeth*

ers could provide. He admired their technical competence and ability to communicate and carry on a critical dialogue about their students' artworks.

School Projects

When Eric was attending elementary school, innovative teaching strategies and individualized curriculum models dominated the practices in his school. Students' individual projects usually were related to specific themes. In second grade, Eric incorporated ideas about combat into his artwork, and a theme of whales dominated his third-grade schoolwork and his spontaneous artwork done at home. In elementary school, Eric often chose to do visual interpretations rather than written book reports: In fourth grade, Eric made cutouts illuminating scenes for each of five books in a series; he made characters for each scene who had to age from one scene to another. These books were fantasy tales, and his report was "a filmic kind of thing, a kind of epic in scope."

Eric had many opportunities to use his imagination in response to social studies assignments. In fifth grade, he created a travel brochure that advertised life in a fantasy kingdom called Sanctuary, described as "the armpit of an empire." Such reports were evidence of Eric's interest in visual narratives and his ability to plan an assignment, organize different elements, employ humor and puns, and create a product that was engaging. For an eighth-grade science class, Eric created a number of visuals, including a poster that explained a wind-powered machine he had created, an illustration for a solar energy report that included superheroes in combat scenes, and a detailed drawing of a dissected rat. In high school, classes were more compartmentalized and the flexibility of doing artwork along with written reports for class assignments was no longer an option.

Games

Another category of school projects that elicited Eric's interest and response to school assignments was games. Since he was in first grade, he displayed a keen interest in games and the processes of gaming; this interest continued through college and

Plate 3.7 A drawing a group of whales created in the third grade

persists into his present work. In fifth grade, Eric created The Digestive Game that combined scientific curiosity, humor, writing, research skills, and his ability to depict ideas graphically. It was a teaching tool about how the body digests foods, and the object was for foods to leave the body as waste. Also during fifth grade, when Eric studied with a private teacher who was an artist and published his own comic book stories. Under his guidance, Eric made a board game that featured a battle between two medieval fantasy armies; it was very complex visually and conceptually and was influenced by Eric's interest in the game *Dungeons and Dragons*, which he had begun to play at this time.

Visual Narratives

Eric also spent a great amount of time doing spontaneous narratives with very complex story lines. These were a favorite drawing mode, and movement and action were depicted as taking place over time in many scenes. The visual narratives he created demonstrated his growing ability to depict figures and animals in action, as well as his conceptual ability to combine many different visual elements in coherent scenes. A visual narrative, created when he was five, included spaceships that displayed his interest in flight, and he would often erase spaceships that were destroyed when he told the story. When he was in the third and fourth grades, Eric's visual narratives were principally about space wars; this interest was evident in the Epic and Sagas class he took at the Summer Arts Institute after sixth grade. Creating games and drawing visual narratives with superheroes were also dominant themes during Eric's junior high school years and in the first year of high school. A Prince Parthan series was a visual narrative with a very complex story line and many characters who represented good and evil.

Subjects in Artwork

Subject matter in Eric's artwork varied according to his interests and specific assignments given by teachers. When he was quite young, subjects

Plate 3.8 A book report in the form of cut-out figures

frequently included animals, members of his immediate family, houses, trees, mazes, trucks, submarines, self-portraits, ghosts, and monsters. New subjects were added through the sixth grade, such as war themes, whales, spaceships, Star Wars figures, superheroes, and medieval fantasies. When he took art classes in high school, his subjects were still lifes, self-portraits, and family members. Subjects he created at the Interlochen National Music Camp were more challenging. In a ceramics class, he constructed a chess set with royal figures, and a monster head derived from many drawings. Student dancers and musicians performing for visual arts classes and a number of landscapes were themes in his drawings and paintings. When Eric was a senior in high school and attending art classes at Indiana University in the afternoons, he worked mostly from models and painted landscapes. At this time his interest changed from an emphasis on imaginative and fantastic subject matter to aesthetics, with a focus on what Eric later expressed as "not

emotion or psychology, but upon what art is and how it is created and perceived."

Self-Confidence and Competitiveness

Eric always set high standards and was very competitive, both with himself and the achievements of others. By the time he was in junior high school, Eric remembered, he "looked for an opportunity to demonstrate [his] rendering ability, but this showing off grew thin after a year." When he first went to Interlochen, he was concerned that he would be "shown up"; however, he received the highest visual art award given that summer. He was very involved in his art work and always confident that the high goals he set could be achieved.

At the same time, Eric felt he was advancing as an artist, quickly making progress in his own work. He reported that he enjoyed watching his own progress, realizing he had taken leaps forward, and was exploring multiple possibilities and solutions

Plate 3.9 A visual narrative of Nukeman from the Epics and Sagas class at the IU Summer ARTS Institute

to problems. Attending college classes while he was in high school helped him maximize his learning experiences. When he was in university art classes, he was "focused, had limitless energy, and was continually challenged."

Issues About Art Making

Eric remembered it was always important for him to "get the details right." The inclusion of many elements in his drawings when he was four was evidence of his keen observation of the world, and his renderings of whales in the fourth and fifth grades received the same attention to detail that he gave his later, more mature, paintings of people and landscapes.

Technical challenges of making art often frustrated Eric, and he remembered that at age five he was not able to depict the complexity of interlocking branches when drawing a tree, or how leaves were attached to branches, or how to mix colors to make the tree look realistic. In elementary school, he would get so involved in the process of rendering forms that he often neglected to worry about neatness, correct proportions, or perspective. In his junior year in high school he was experimenting and developing a style that continued into college. He simplified forms into flat, thick lines that gave an abstract, graphic quality to his works. Filmmaking influenced Eric's drawings in his senior year of high school in respect to the idea of carving forms. As Eric said later, "a viewer could roam

Plate 3.10 A painting of a young woman that received a National Scholastic Award

about the drawing and move through time and space." He described artworks done at this time as "filmmaking ideas about drawing" that contained seeds of what were to germinate into his current interests in technology and multimedia.

Eric's discussions about copying involved issues of plagiarism, reproducing and reinterpreting art works by artists, and using images from popular media. Modeling his own images after images by others was a salient factor in Eric's development. From first to fifth grade, Eric adapted Ed Emberly's images; creating those drawings gave him confidence and helped develop his skills. From fourth grade through junior high school, Eric copied from comic, fantasy, and science fiction images and learned to draw people from popular culture. He reported he still doesn't mind reinterpreting someone else's work.

Culture and Conceptual Issues

Eric's art making was greatly influenced by the middle-class culture and academic environment in which he developed his interests and motivation. Commencing at fourth grade and continuing throughout high school, established popular cul-

Plate 3.11 A picnic scene that reflects interest in carving out space through a complex linear composition

ture forms, including fantasy and science fiction, had a great impact on his artworks. A number of popular influences became important, including books about dinosaurs and spaceships, Micronauts and Shogun warrior figures, and the Star Wars movies. When he was in elementary school, movie and television monsters influenced the themes and styles of his work. Movies, books, and fantasy games were other popular sources. In junior high school, illustrated books, comic books, rock groups, magazines, movies, and video games influenced Eric's art talent development.

Three salient issues surfaced throughout conversations with Eric: the influence of academic training, formalism versus expressionism, and the role of the viewer in respect to an artwork. Eric believed that any paradigm taught as the truth may be dangerous, and he often rejected academic ways of teaching art. Implicit relationships among the act of painting, the viewer, and a subject became of primary importance to Eric when he studied at Indiana University. He remembered he was "sizing

up the viewer as if painting it, but it's a portrait of me wearing yellow gloves and a mask. I was grappling with relationships between an artist, viewer, and subject."

Eric's Reflections on This Study

When Eric was 24, he read this case study and reflected on the interviews and his mother's interpretations. He reported that the enriched and accelerated education opportunities he received supplied him with experiences that enabled his works to change and mature. He enjoys confronting viewers with culturally constructed dichotomies between high and popular art. The contemporary expression, "the canvas is dead," summarizes Eric's disenchantment with drawing and painting and his current interest in using new technologies. He concluded, "I'm finally making my own art, combining diverse interests in theory, games, visual art, performance art, storytelling, and social reconstruction of art. This is my critical

Plate 3.12 A self-portrait with gloves

self-consciousness, nurtured by institutional education and home life."

Discussion and Conclusions of the Study

In this study Eric made many positive references to the benefits of accelerated and enriched opportunities for study in the visual arts that have been expressed by others (VanTassel-Baska, 1986, 1987, 1998). There is concern, however, that acceleration may have detrimental effects on students' social development, although research has failed to justify these concerns. D. H. Feldman (1980) and Feldman and Goldmith (1986a) studied precocious children in many areas and were convinced that all progress is the result of intensive and prolonged instruction. Successful teachers of highly able stu-

dents, knowledgeable about subject matter and able to communicate effectively, can lead their students to attain high levels of achievement. Talent does not develop without an enormous amount of work, practice, and study, coupled with direct assistance, guidance, and encouragement. The conclusion that an individual's talent involves interplay of many forces, including culture and education, has great relevance for the education of artistically talented students.

Teachers whom Eric viewed positively possessed important characteristics, including an emphasis on art skills, general art knowledge, empathy, ability to make classes challenging, willingness to help students, and an expectation that students should examine their reasons for making art. Eric also was fortunate because most of his elementary and junior high school teachers were flexible, taught theme-oriented classes, and allowed students to complete assignments with both visual and verbal problem solving. These curriculum adaptations allowed Eric to express his skills, abilities, values, and understandings in a variety of discursive and nondiscursive contexts.

Eric described a number of transformational experiences that allowed him to view himself as a young artist achieving his own goals, rather than being a student creating art in isolation from others. Today he is using technologies to solve some of the problems he grappled with as a talented adolescent. Artistic development, therefore, is not an automatic consequence of maturation; it is, instead, a learned set of complex abilities that to a large extent are greatly influenced by an artist's culture and educational opportunities available within that culture.

RECOMMENDATIONS FOR EDUCATING ARTISTICALLY TALENTED STUDENTS BASED ON STUDENT CHARACTERISTICS

Based on our research about student characteristics and art talent development, we offer the following recommendations about the education of artistically talented students. These recommendations are based on findings from others' research and our own research about artistically talented

Plate 3.13 A self-portrait created at Interlochen Art Academy

students' characteristics and appropriate educational opportunities.

Recommendation 1. Art talent development should not be understood only as a single-minded quest for depicting the world realistically. Students' artworks should be considered in terms of perceptual qualities, expression and skills with media, and conceptual qualities, including themes, puns, paradoxes, and metaphors. These qualities may have more relevance for planning learning activities than projects that simply have depicting the world realistically as outcomes. Development of self-expression and acquisition of culturally approved graphic models and conventions, including skills and techniques, cannot simply be understood as the acquisition of skills of visual reproduction.

Recommendation 2. The myth that artistically talented students learn best when left to their own devices, if provided with a wide variety of materials, is still prevalent in many art classes across the United States. We have presented a number of studies that challenge this notion. The impact of educational opportunities, educational settings, and the role of art teachers on the development of artistically talented students is important in developing art talent. In the studies we reported, most students were found to be aware of their talents, interested in improving their abilities, and introspective about the role of the arts in their lives. All progress is the result of intensive and prolonged instruction; talent does not develop without a substantial amount of practice and study, along with assistance, guidance, and encouragement. The conclusion that an individual's talent involves interplay of many forces, including culture and education, has a great relevance for the education of artistically talented students. Art talent development is a learned set of complex abilities and not an automatic consequence of maturation. Such development is greatly influenced by the culture and educational opportunities accessible within that culture.

Recommendation 3. Visual art talent development should be focused on students' backgrounds, personalities, gender orientations, skill development, cognitive and affective abilities, local cultural contexts, and global popular culture. Learned sets of abilities are greatly influenced by cultures in which students live, study, and work. Multiple criteria that are sensitive to the communities in which students learn need to be developed and studied in terms of their effectiveness in a variety of settings. Teachers should be aware of cultural stereotyping in their choices of subject matter and media when developing learning activities for students from a variety of cultural backgrounds. Gender differences also should also be considered when planning curricula to support art talent development. To help build self-esteem and confidence, role models for girls can be very productive if women artists and artists of color are included in art programs for artistically talented students. Girls also should be encouraged to develop skills and realistic expectations for anticipated careers as artists.

Recommendation 4. Labeling students as gifted or talented does not appear to have negative consequences in schools. Students think that hard work, not native ability, leads to success and they want their gifts and talents to be recognized as the result of effort, rather than being a gift that does not demand time and a great amount of effort to develop. Most artistically talented students enjoy working at a high level of difficulty when grouped with others of similar ability.

Recommendation 5. Artistically talented students in middle and high school enjoy being part of the world of art rather than being viewed simply as students in art classes. Students described transformational experiences that allowed them to view themselves as young artists achieving their own goals, rather than being students isolated from contact with the art world. Trips to artists' studios, art museums, local galleries, and workshops producing locally made crafts, as well as speaking to and hearing lectures from artists and art historians, can greatly contribute to students motivation and identification with the world of art on a professional level.

Recommendation 6. The importance of family support and belonging to a social community in school should be recognized as salient issues in art talent development. Encouragement by students' families or other significant adults plays a vital role in helping them maintain their interests and development in art. Parents and others should be welcomed into art classes; they should be informed about their children's art activities and invited to attend school art exhibitions. Parents and others should be encouraged to support and assist their daughters' and sons' interests in the visual arts. School also should offer a social community where students who have interests and abilities in the arts can interact and share ideas and interests with others with similar concerns.

Recommendation 7. There is a myth that artistically talented students often do not excel academically. Our studies indicate consistently that high-ability art students have positive reactions to schooling and are excellent students in most subjects. Artistically talented students perceive their need to be challenged and taught at higher ability levels that would improve their art talent development. They need to be challenged both ideationally and visually and encouraged to use their discursive and nondiscursive aptitudes to find problems and solve them at levels that challenge their abilities.

Recommendation 8. Certain teacher characteristics seemed to match the needs and characteristics of most artistically talented students. Successful teachers are viewed as supporting and encouraging, rather than demanding conformity and adherence to rules. They also provide theme-oriented, accelerated and enriched opportunities for art study. These teachers are flexible and allow students to pursue personal interests, placing emphasis on art skills, having general art knowledge, and empathy with students. These teachers of highly able students are able to communicate effectively and can lead their students to attain high levels of achievement.

4 Teacher Characteristics and Teaching Strategies

Plate 4.1 An etching by an eighth-grade student at the IU Summer Arts Institute that demonstrates skillful technical ability

In the education of artistically talented students, teacher characteristics and teaching strategies play an important role in art talent development. In this chapter characteristics and teaching strategies of two art teachers of artistically talented teenagers are contrasted and compared in order to determine what is successful in the classroom. Next, approaches to teacher-guided discussions about art, in particular Clark's Looking At and Talking About

Art approach, are discussed with an emphasis on teacher strategies. Then research on developing leadership abilities of teachers of artistically talented students is discussed and a special focus on voice—how these teachers can use their personal and professional voices to effect change—is included. Along with the research on voice, a model for developing effective leadership for teachers of artistically talented students also is presented. Finally, recommendations for teachers of artistically talented students are given.

CHARACTERISTICS OF TEACHERS OF ARTISTICALLY TALENTED STUDENTS

Descriptions of ideal teachers for gifted and talented students have been generated by a number of authors (e.g. Tomlinson et al., 2002; VanTassel-Baska, 1998). These generally are unrealistic because they are either unattainable or fail to differentiate between good teachers for all students and good teachers for students with high abilities (Gallagher & Gallagher, 1994). Although there are a few qualitative studies about teachers of academically talented students, there is a paucity of studies about teachers of artistically talented students. Case studies about art teaching, however, have been reported in general education literature (e.g., N. Johnson, 1985; Stokrocki, 1990, 1995).

A Study of Two Art Teachers

Two case studies by Zimmerman (1991, 1992b) were conducted to describe and analyze characteristics of teachers of artistically talented, 13- to 16-year-old students, in a 2-week painting course at the Indiana University Summer Arts Institute. Her purpose was to discover salient characteristics of art teachers in determining successful classroom practice for teaching artistically talented students.

Methodology, Data Collection, and Analysis

As a director of the institute, and with both teachers' permission and cooperation, Zimmerman was able to observe two painting classes for their entire duration. She used case study methodology and collected data by means of notes; audiotapes of class sessions; slides of classroom activities and student artwork; audiotapes of student, teacher, and group interviews; students' registration forms; and five adult observers' journals. In addition, she used Stokrocki's (1986) time-sampling method to collect data and organize categories for reporting and comparing her studies. Categories for time

sampling of instruction were managerial (teacher organization of tools, materials, and space), substantive (related to teaching subject matter), and appraisal (concerning teachers responses and judgments). Data were analyzed by content, comparison, and time-sampling analyses and were concurrently verified from journals and conversations with observers and teachers.

The advanced painting classes met during 2 consecutive summers for 11 instructional days. During the first year, there were 24 students who would be entering Grades 8 through 11 in the fall. During the second year, there were 20 students in the painting class and two-thirds as many were entering Grades 9 and 10. Of the total number of students in both classes, most were from Indiana, two were from other states, and four were from Singapore. About two-thirds of the students came from rural communities, and nearly half received scholarships. The painting room for both classes was a large studio space used during the academic year for college students. The room had the typical ambience of paint-encrusted walls, with large standing easels; storage spaces where paintings could be placed vertically to dry; small tables that held pallets; brushes, and tubes of paint; large windows that allowed bright light to filter into the classroom; and sinks that provided a place to socialize and to clean acrylic paint from brushes and palettes.

Results of the Study

The Teachers' Philosophies. Mark taught the painting class the first year and Laura taught the second year [these names are fictitious]. Both were faculty members who taught fine arts to undergraduates. They were physically very different; Mark was a large man, about 6'5" tall, and Laura was a small woman, about 5'2". Both were in their middle thirties and dressed casually to accommodate the warm weather.

Mark spoke in a booming voice that projected over all other conversations and amplified his presence. Teaching a painting class for Mark was about relating to people, and what students created was secondary. He said, "Students can burn you up easily; they can be excited one minute and bored the next." To capture their attention, "a teacher needs to be dynamic to keep them interested and challenged." When teaching, Mark tried to identify and concentrate on leaders of the group because, he claimed, they could set the mood and interest for all the others.

Laura taught by repetition; she believed that if she repeated the same instructions several times her students would eventually understand what she expected them to do. She often told students to try to make their paintings as realistic as possible. For example, she asked one student what color the model's eyes were. When the student replied, "Blue-green," she said, "Then paint them that way." She did not appear to care how much noise students made in her class. She explained, "I try to talk to them as equals and not as an adult to a child." At the beginning, she told an observer she did not think the students were especially talented, but on the third day of class she changed her mind and expressed surprise that they were progressing so quickly through her lessons.

In conversations with Mark and Laura, they both considered themselves artists who teach. Mark's principle focus was on helping students understand the frustrations, sources of inspiration, and intense personal involvement of being an artist as well as technical skills such as drawing in correct proportion, mixing and applying paint to a surface, and balancing a composition. For Mark, teaching was "about relating to people," and what students actually created was secondary. He believed the teacher's role was very important and that teachers were responsible for helping students learn both about themselves and their artwork.

Laura's principal focus was on developing art-making skills, and she did not believe it was important to build personal relationships with students. She viewed herself as an artist who had a responsibility to teach a painting class and critique her students' artwork. Laura's overall teaching emphasis was on having students make their images as realistic as possible.

Curriculum Concerns. As required, Mark outlined what he expected to teach, although he "needed to get a sense of them and what they were capable of doing" before he finalized his program. He said they would begin by painting simple spheres and "big eyes, big lips, and big noses," and progress to "interpretations of portraits by artists, and then complete self-portraits." During the final critique, Mark stressed two important things: first, that he wanted to help them understand what it was like to be an artist (described as "intense feelings of something starting to happen with intense frustrations as major energy shifts"), and, second, that he wanted to have them paint adequate self-portraits.

At first, Laura attempted to adapt her curriculum for students by condensing a semester's college course. During the second week she became more flexible and adjusted her teaching to the students' interests and abilities, as well as to the brief 10-day schedule. She began by having students make color wheels and value scales with neutral grays to get the students "warmed up" for their final still life paintings. On several occasions, she told students their obligation was to complete the projects she assigned. When giving directions for creating still life paintings, she told them if they started at 1:30 they should be finished at 3:30. All of Laura's curricular concerns centered around developing art-making skills with emphases on color mixing, creating solid shapes, and depicting realistic images.

Teaching Content. Mark typically spent 32 percent of his class time on substantive instruction. Along with his sense of humor and ability to empathize with his students, Mark assumed roles as teacher-artist and teacher-storyteller. As an artist who teaches, Mark shared "secrets of shading" and "doing self-portraits" and the mystery of "learning to draw realistically." He described these techniques as "secrets that are not shared in art schools where you are supposed to let your feelings show." He told students that he had had to master these systems by himself, but he was sharing these secrets with them.

Mark also told his students not to worry about being creative; "Your pictures feel personal, like particular worlds, and your creativity will come out automatically." Only when their portraits were in progress did Mark address problems of self-expression or interpretation. He compared reproductions of an early Rembrandt portrait and another Rembrandt created in old age. In the latter, Mark explained, "he is actually living a life instead of living a role."

Mark invited his students to visit his painting studio to share how he works as an artist, his tools

Plate 4.2 An interpretive artwork created in Mark's class that is based on a Renaissance painting

and materials, the content of his drawings and paintings, and his own frustrations. For Mark, teaching is not a one-dimensional activity: "A teacher is responsible for influencing all aspects of students' lives." While students painted, he stood in the middle of the room or strolled around and told stories. Students had no trouble concentrating on their work and listening to him. Not all stories related to class content, but they often carried a moral message or dealt with ethical and political issues not discussed in most classrooms. He built conceptual bridges between art works and popular culture heroes. Topics included Alexander the Great (how he was able to conquer worlds), why old masters did not show teeth in their paintings (dentistry was at very early stages), an old Zen tale (about seeking something and not finding it), Amazon women (their power and dedication to ideals), parents' preoccupations with their teenage children, the value of not smoking, and adolescents' worries about what roles they will play in life. Art works by Durer, Rembrandt, Raphael, Botticelli, Kollwitz, Hals, Corinth, Freud, and Renoir were related to posters or videos by Jimi Hendrix, Jim Morrison, Michael Jackson, Rambo, Prince, Cher, Grace Jones, or Roger Rabbit. His comparisons,

Plate 4.3 A still-life painting completed in Laura's class

such as "this Botticelli looks like a yuppie" or "this Renoir lady looks like Cher" captured the students' attention.

Mark often was concerned about how well he was getting his message across and whether students were responding. He frequently asked if they were getting bored and would tell a joke or do something outrageous to capture their attention. He constantly reassured them that he knew they would experience "boredom, frustration, and rage. Paint anyhow. In five minutes, it will go away." He

told them, "Talent is not all you need to be successful. Students need interest, drive, and ambition."

Laura typically spent 19 percent of her class time on substantive instruction. Her approach to teaching involved viewing herself as a technician who imparts information. Her principle method was to lecture and repeat the same information numbers of times to both the entire class and to individual students. She spoke from the middle of the room and students often could not hear her over their chatter and noise. She showed slides of college stu-

Plate 4.4 A self-portrait produced in Mark's class

dents' work from previous classes, drew charts, wrote terms on the chalkboard, and held up successful student work in progress for students to view. When she showed other students' artwork, she emphasized technical properties: "In this one there are four values," or "This one is drawn well," or "This one took a week to complete." Laura did show slides of her own artwork to engage them in a dialogue and enable them to observe how she worked. She told them about how she created her paintings. "I had a little trouble with this one. Now I do all the preliminary painting first. . . . When I finish it, I put it away for a couple of months. Then I pull it out again. . . . You're more objective then

and not so ego-involved." She revealed how she had once painted an entire room in order to create a painting: "I actually painted the checkerboard pattern on the floor. I *really* painted what I saw."

Laura's directions always involved discussions about how to do a specific exercise: "You have to do a black, white, and gray painting. Decide on your composition and sketch it quickly." Realism was the yardstick by which all work was measured: "This one does not have outlines around the objects. It looks more real."

Individual and Group Critiques. Mark and Laura both spent about half of their class time critiquing

Plate 4.5 A still-life painting created in Laura's class

in-progress and finished student products. Mark spent 86 percent of this time engaged in individual critiques and 14 percent in critiques directed to the entire class. Laura spent almost 100 percent of this time conducting individual critiques; she conducted only one brief group critique.

Mark's critique strategy was to tell students what he thought they could do to improve. To make corrections, he often painted on the side of a canvas, on the back of a canvas, or directly on a work in progress. His comments generally included summarizing and reinforcing concepts taught in class: "You did a psychological portrait. It's a realistic distortion." "People can see better than cameras." "Don't worry about realism." "Look at your real eye, figure out how eyelashes are made." "The mouth needs to be lowered; it is too near the nose." Praise statements such as "going great," "looks much better," and "looking fine," always preceded suggestions for improvement. Conversations with students having trouble evidenced his ability to empathize: "Get yourself together. You have a strong will; you are indulging yourself by thinking you can't do things." "You have a lot of strength . . . you will be great someday." "Your sense of panic won't go away unless you do things; it's not that serious." "One day you will discover your strength—you're more capable than a great many people. You're tired, but you can do it." In large group critiques, Mark's intent was to encourage feelings of accomplishment.

He would begin by complimenting the class and his group critiques always proceeded from positive comments and suggestions: "You guys did extremely well for 10 days," or "You're doing very well, better than my undergraduate class."

Laura employed individual critiques to inform students about what they should be doing or ask what they might do to improve their paintings. In a few instances, she praised the work of the entire group positively. Commenting about the students' work, she said, "I think everybody is going along fine. Go ahead and finish off. I think everybody has the idea." In 192 out of 194 recorded interactions, Laura's conversations pertained only to technical properties. She usually began an individual critique by praising the students, and then suggested changes. She began with remarks such as "looks good," "there you go," "much better," "real good so far," and "pretty amazing." Then she usually made suggestions for improvement such as "squint more to see the darkest values," "a bit too reddish," and "if you don't like the way you did it, paint it again." When students were frustrated and could not paint, she treated their inability to proceed as a technical problem they had to overcome. When one student lamented, "This looks terrible, I can't do it," Laura replied, "Use the viewfinder. Decide what you want to do. Don't worry if it isn't perfect. Just paint." When a student said he was finished and did not want to work further, she told him, "An artist who works like this and does not finish will not make a living."

Laura and Mark's approaches to each student were positive. Praise statements usually preceded corrections and suggestions for improvement. Both teachers' comments generally included summarizing and reinforcing concepts that were taught in class. Another strategy was to compliment the entire group orally. Laura did this when most students completed a project, and Mark did it before he began a group critique. In Laura's class, humor was evident in only one recorded teacher-student exchange; she told a student about his painting of a model, "If you put more white on her skin, she will look as if she is dead."

Classroom Management. Mark spent 15 percent and Laura spent 20 percent of total class time distributing and collecting tools and materials and physically organizing their environments. Mark al-ways greeted students at the door, told them what supplies they needed, and directed them to where the supplies were located. Whenever the noise level began to rise, Mark would tell a story or organize a group critique. Having taught at the institute the previous year, Mark stressed the need for explicit cleanup directions. Laura told the students about supplies, how to set up their palettes, clean their brushes, what colors and how much paint they would need, where to store their works, and where to get and return their art supplies. She did not make an effort to get students to clean up and abdicated this responsibility to other adults who were observing in the classroom.

Student Responses. Students were unanimous in their approval of Mark. They "liked his class," thought "he was fun," "entertaining," "a great teacher," and an "expressive person." They believed they learned more in Mark's class than in their usual art classes. Fifty-eight percent explained that the art teachers in their schools rarely spoke to them individually and didn't know much about painting concepts or techniques. Sixty-five percent mentioned Mark's direct instructional methods as helping them learn to paint, look at things differently, and understand basic structures. Two students cited group critiques as means to learn "from our own mistakes" and noted that Mark always had "something good and something bad" to say about everyone. Forty percent of the students liked Mark's sense of humor and the relaxed atmosphere he created. One said, "Laughter is really good to break the tension when you are concentrating." Ninety percent claimed his stories were informative, introduced history, humor, or facts, and kept students alert. Mark's sentiments about students working when they are frustrated impressed another, who noted "when you are down and really feel bored, he pushed you through it. It's really best to paint when you're frustrated. You see the light at the end of the tunnel."

Seventy-five percent of the students expressed a fondness for Laura, felt she was a good teacher, and said they enjoyed her class: "I like the way she treats people," or "If something is wrong, she'll tell you and give you suggestions about what to do." Students felt she was patient, listened, gave them individual attention, and was cheerful and had a positive attitude. Two students, however, thought

Laura was "fair" although "she's used to teaching college kids and when we get noisy she just keeps talking and we don't hear anything." One said, "She doesn't force you to change and she hints that you can do it if you want to." Two students felt they developed their first understanding of how to paint while in her class.

Adult Observer Responses. Art classes at the institute also served as field sites for art teachers enrolled in a practicum experience in our Artistically Talented Program (see Introduction). Every day, two of these observers were in Mark's room and three were in Laura's room. Mark did not mind the observers, although he said they could only observe and not interfere with his teaching. One observer thought "he was a terrific teacher" although "he could influence students who were vulnerable and under his spell." Another noted that Mark was "charismatic, he is his own person in every way" and he "loved the way Mark introduced history, criticism, and aesthetics in his classes."

Laura did not mind observers in her room and encouraged them to help students with their work. Unfortunately, an observer noted, "she was definitely an artist and less a teacher and didn't know much about managing young people." The consensus was that students learned skills and techniques and the paintings the students created "were outstanding." Her three observers concluded that Laura was not comfortable teaching her students: "She never connected with them. There was no close bonding." Laura's teaching in individual critiques was praised, however: "She worked very well on a one-on-one basis, but it was the 24 with whom she had trouble."

Discussion and Conclusions of the Study

It is evident that both teachers met the goals they set for their classes. Mark's emphasis on both cognitive and affective skills was evident throughout his teaching. He wanted his students to understand what it was like to be an artist and to paint adequate self-portraits. Sometimes boredom or frustration prevented students from learning and Mark was able to recognize they were not performing adequately and helped them reach their potential. Laura's goal for her students to paint realistically was accomplished.

Her emphases were on developing skills and techniques and giving individual attention to her students. She did not, however, attend to class control, preparation, organization, or anticipating students' problems.

The data from these two case studies suggest that preparation of professional artists before they enter a secondary-level classroom environment is of paramount importance. If Laura had not had help from the adult observers, her classes may have been chaotic, with less time available for teaching her students. It would appear that art teachers of talented students, therefore, should be knowledgeable about pedagogy as well as possess art-making skills; moreover, they should be able to relate this knowledge about teaching to their knowledge about the art world.

If outsiders were to measure the success of Mark's or Laura's classes, they would arrive at very positive conclusions. Both teachers stressed acquiring skills and techniques through teaching.

Mark, however, was able to be critically reflective about his role as a teacher and presented his students with learning experiences that emphasized feelings of competence and shared behaviors, promoted goal-seeking and goal-achieving behaviors, encouraged searches for novelty and complexity, and provided feelings of belonging. It can be concluded that artists who teach talented students should be aware that their students will need knowledge and understandings that include awareness of contexts in which they create art, examine their reasons for creating art, and become intensely involved in issues beyond the acquisition of skills or techniques. It is suggested that teachers of talented students understand each student's sensibilities, teach proactively, present mediated learning experiences, and reflect critically about their teaching practices. They also should have preparatory experiences in learning how to organize art classes for young students.

TEACHER-GUIDED DISCUSSIONS ABOUT ART

Not only are teacher characteristics and strategies significant in helping enhance students' art talent development, but teaching strategies that

Plate 4.6 An imaginative self-portrait completed in Mark's class

relate to art appreciation inquiry also are important for developing perceptual skills and understandings about art history, art criticism, and aesthetics, which have direct application to studio art activities. Clark's Looking At and Talking About Art (LATA) method can offer unique opportunities for introducing all students to discussing works of art, developing higher order thinking skills, appreciating and understanding works of art, and developing their ease when discussing artworks.

Students' learned abilities to read images, for example, are evidenced when a group of them collectively discuss and analyze an image such as George Tooker's *Government Bureau* and realize the image represents a group of people frustrated by having to go from one office to another and deal with impersonal clerks who can't or won't help them. These students have perceived pictorial clues, analyzed their meanings, and used problem-solving and critical-thinking skills to give meaning to what they perceived in the image.

Clark developed Looking At and Talking About Art activities to teach students about how to engage in dialogue about artworks and the work of artists (Wilson & Clark, 2000). His approach has been useful as an introduction to more advanced methods advocated by other art educators, such as Anderson (1995); Broudy (1972, 1987), Efland, Freedman, & Stuhr (1996); and E. B. Feldman (1973, 1981). Clark sees LATA activities as introductory because they encourage open, interpretive dialogue without requiring a specialized art vocabulary. Their primary purpose is to offer students opportunities to engage in dialogue, shape their perceptions, and express ideas about specific attributes of works of art.

In the past, research about discussions of works of art with public school students was limited to one or two approaches to art criticism. Hamblen (1984, 1985) analyzed 16 articles about processes used by teachers and found that most programs were based on E. B. Feldman's *critical performance* or Broudy's *aesthetic scanning* procedures. For the past 3 decades, Feldman's (1973, 1981) writings have influenced art criticism methods used across the country. He advocated a structured approach to art criticism through stages of description, analysis, interpretation, and judgment that is commonly used by art teachers. Feldman described question-answer dialogue as a desirable strategy for teachers to use in art criticism activities, but he did not offer specific guidelines for conducting such activities with students. Broudy (1972, 1987) devised aesthetic scanning to help students become aware of the content and form in works of art. His method involved developing students' skills of discerning and discussing sensory, formal, technical, expressive, and extra-aesthetic properties of works of art.

Mittler (1980, 1985) described another approach to criticism and history, for use in secondary-level art classes. He equated art criticism with looking for internal cues and art history with looking for external cues when discussing art works. Barrett (1990) advocated conducting art criticism through describing, interpreting, and analyzing photographs and theorizing about photography. He also edited a compilation of lessons (1995) that contains a variety of approaches teachers can use for engaging students thoughtfully with art objects. Anderson (1992), writing about values that can be achieved by studying works of art, claimed that making students aware of visual, conceptual, and emotional expressions can give students access to meanings, directions, and structures that can inform their own works.

Although art educators have advocated a variety of strategies for development of image-analysis skills, few have written about the teacher's role in such discussions. Clark found that students often are not familiar with discussion of art as a classroom activity and are reluctant to contribute to such discussions. Clark emphasized classroom interchanges in which students

1. Learn how and what questions to ask about works of art
2. Become aware of nonobvious aspects of works of art
3. Increase their curiosity about the visual arts
4. Become comfortable talking about art and artists

During Looking At and Talking About Art activities, a teacher leads students through discussion of one or more works of art in order to help them become more aware of design and composition, styles of art, artists, content themes and meanings, and other concepts. During these discussions, students use their own conceptions to build knowledgeable perceptions and informed opinions about art, form emotive responses to artworks, and develop insights about conceptual and social themes encountered in works of art. Individualized guidance and development of each student's responses and higher order thinking skills are vital to implementation of LATA activities.

A Study of the Looking and Talking About Art Approach

The purpose of this study was to observe Clark's Looking and Talking About Art (LATA) method and describe it as a series of complex classroom interactions. No formal analysis of Clark's method had existed prior to this study, and this research may be useful to teachers who want to introduce discussion of artworks into their classrooms. Clark developed the LATA approach over several decades of working with groups of students in college classes, in elementary and middle schools, in a summer program for talented art students, and in in-service staff development classes.

Methodology

Students in this study were attending a middle school in a medium-sized community. They were 12 to 15 years old and enrolled in either a required seventh-grade art class or an advanced elective eighth-grade art class. Few of these students had any experience with art appreciation. Large-sized art prints were selected with easily recognizable images of landscapes and portraits in many styles.

Data Collection and Analysis

Each of the two classes was video- and audio-taped during six sessions. A camera at the back of the room provided a clear view of the prints and the teacher, and a camera at the front of the room captured details of students' interactions. Two audiotape recorders also were used for voice recordings in classes and for interviews with students and the teacher. Following each day's classes, Clark was interviewed and tape-recorded by Trudy Wilson, the primary researcher for this study. Content and comparative analyses began by unitizing teacher and student data that were grouped onto cards and, subsequently, into thematic categories.

Results of the Study

The LATA approach is focused on problem-solving and self-expression experiences to help students develop individual capacities and abilities as responders to works of art. Their interactions and social and emotional responses are vitally important because a LATA goal is to have students become aware of their cognitive abilities and emotive reactions to works of art. It is important that the teacher respond positively to as many students' answers as possible during LATA activities to encourage all students to respond. In the LATA study, Clark used various types of questioning strategies to encourage responses. He often deliberately withheld artists' names or titles of images to encourage students to share their insights without being influenced by that information. He opened each session with questions or directions, such as "What do you see in this image?" or "Tell us what you first noticed in this image." These questions gave students opportunities to originate topics for discussion because all dialogue was based on students' responses.

In an attempt to graphically represent the makeup of LATA activities, Wilson created a cognitive map that included all the findings from the study (see Figure 4.1). The diamond in the center represents the four primary elements of an activity. The *pre-activity* element includes general and specific preparations, such as selecting works of art. *Review* refers to orientation activities. The *nonartwork related* element includes introductory and closing statements and behavior management strategies. *Pedagogical strategies* includes the different kinds of discussion strategies used in a LATA activity.

Pedagogical Strategies. These strategies demonstrate general interaction patterns that contributed to the flow of each LATA session. (All student names in the examples given are fictious). Using *instructional strategies*, Clark invariably asked an initiating question and received responses. This pattern was used to begin each session, change the topic of a discussion, or maintain a discussion. He also encouraged several responses to each question asked. Occasionally, he created a string of simple questions and answers, such as "George, how does painting #2 differ from painting #5?" or "Emily, what do you see in this painting?" From responses by students, Clark also built initiating questions, either immediately after a response or later.

Using *discusson-flow strategies*, Clark often made students' questions or statements the basis for another question. "Henry, why did you say the people are all alike? Why did you say you didn't like it?" or "Ernie, you liked this image, then found out it was a photograph, and then you didn't like it. Why?" He used summaries of students' responses to form the basis for another question, review responses and interactions, or summarize responses as a statement. These summaries often led to new questions. In response to looking at an Impressionist painting, for example, he said, "It's not that clear and starts getting ambiguous when you look at it closely. What do you see?" or "Does it look realistic? How would you compare that with the realistic photograph we just looked at?" Contextual information often was not given. Clark used statements about some aspect to form another question, enrich discussion within responses, or conclude. For example, when viewing a Mexican mural from the 1930s, Clark asked, "They had a war much like we had in terms of becoming an independent nation. What do you see that tells us more about this situation?"

Within sets of interactions with students, Clark used *individual-interaction strategies* for handling responses. He expressed open acceptance of all students' early responses in order to encourage their

Figure 4.1. Cognitive Map of Looking and Talking About Art Activities

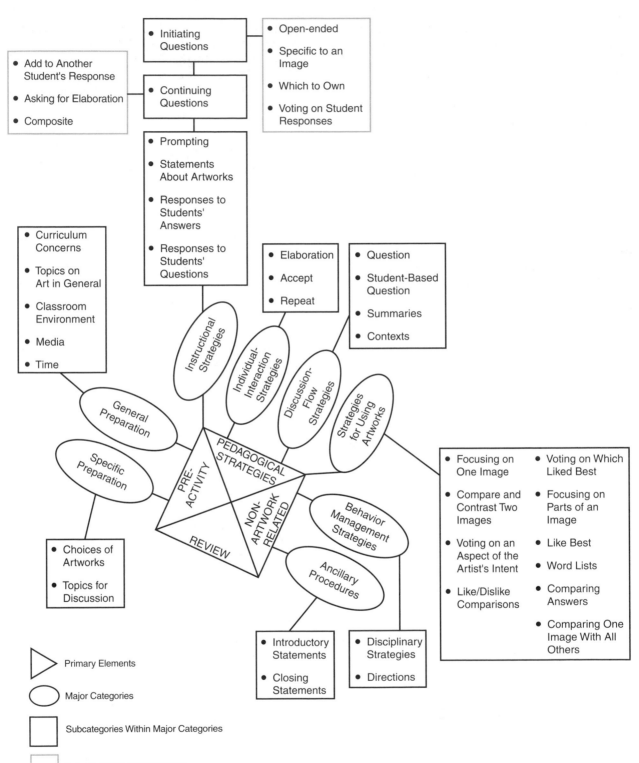

continuing participation. Clark often repeated a response because he felt that a teacher should restate responses for students who may not have heard or to check what was said for accuracy. One of Clark's most important strategies was to ask for elaboration of a previous answer or response. This gave students opportunities to think beyond first responses and give more information, thus building the knowledge base of both the individual responding and of other students in the class.

Clark had many *strategies for using artworks* to maintain students' interest and participation. These included:

1. Focusing discussion on one image
2. Comparing and contrasting two images
3. Eliminating images students wanted excluded
4. Eliciting like and dislike comparisons
5. Focusing discussion on one part of an image
6. Asking for a list of descriptive words
7. Comparing one image with others
8. Comparing answers by two or more students

Discussion and Conclusions of the Study

Conducting LATA activities involves a complex set of pedagogical strategies, planning, and management. During observations, Clark revealed an approach to teaching about artworks that included a rationale, preparation, techniques for leading in and out of discussions, how to handle inappropriate behaviors, and how to give directions (see Figure 4.1). In order to sustain classroom dialogue during LATA activities, Clark respected each student's responses, encouraged participation in shared experiences, and valued each student's contributions. To help students speak knowledgeably about works of art, a teacher must spend considerable effort building an engaging and inviting environment.

In interviews, Clark provided the following guide for others interested in conducting beginning-level LATA activities:

General preparation: Select images or objects and specific objectives for discussions.
Specific preparation: Select artworks for each session and establish familiarity with information about images.

During each session: Provide a review of previous activities and set introductory statements and plan closing statements. Provide directions for taking part in all discussions and ask students to approach each image being discussed and point out aspects to encourage familiarity with works of art. Use a variety of strategies as stimuli for discussions and summaries and always plan positive reinforcements for participants.

LATA activities help students build their knowledge bases and bolster their confidence in voicing their own opinions and analyses, as was demonstrated by the increasing interactions of students during these discussions. The ability of students to

Plate 4.7 An IU Summer Arts Institute student calls attention to characteristics of a painting during a visit to the IU Art Museum

talk about every aspect of art, including formal attributes, techniques, meanings, emotions, meanings, and subject matters was important to the purposes of Looking At and Talking About Art activities. It was clear that students bore major responsibilities for the direction of these teacher-guided activities. The LATA process, therefore, provided students with opportunities to become aware of the variety of responses they might have and encouraged them to express their own reactions and opinions about works of art. The primary intention of LATA activities with high-ability art students is that they become empowered by teachers who listen to their perceptions and build a discussion that leads to skills of awareness, problem solving, and critical thinking. With these understandings, students can go on to full and meaningful discussions of diverse aspects of images in relation to each artwork shown. The value of these activities is that they provide effective strategies for involving students in discussions about art that focus on respect for each student's thinking. This engenders students' confidence in their own abilities, increases their interest in art, and increases their ability to discuss artworks.

LEADERSHIP ROLES FOR TEACHERS OF TALENTED ART STUDENTS

In an era of cuts in school funding, art classes sometimes are eliminated or poorly funded and programs focused on developing art talent often are the most vulnerable. It therefore is of primary concern to develop leadership abilities in teachers of artistically talented students to help them become empowered as informed teachers and advocates for their students.

Zimmerman has been involved in researching leadership issues in art teacher education for the past decade, along with her colleague Frances Thurber, who teaches at the University of Nebraska in Omaha. Their goal is to educate teachers to become empowered and take leadership roles in a variety of educational contexts (Thurber & Zimmerman, 1997; Zimmerman, 1997d, 1997f). Recently, an in-service teacher gave Zimmerman a sheet of paper with the words NO GIRLS ALOUD printed in bold letters in a childish hand. In this teacher's third-grade art class, one group of boys had isolated themselves in a corner of

the art room and posted that sign. What an apt metaphor this was for both isolation and silencing that so many teachers face when confronting established hierarchies in public schools in the United States.

Most teachers in the United States are women, except in higher education, and it is important to discover means to help empower them to become leaders and take actions to improve programs for all students. Maeroff (1988) concluded that intense summer institutes, with educational programs throughout a school year, are most successful in building leadership skills that enable teachers to create networks with other teachers.

Study of Developing Teacher Leadership Roles in Art Education

Although research about in-service art teachers has been increasing in recent years, there still is little inquiry about staff development aimed at developing leadership roles in art education. Motivated by an interest in discovering whether in-service teachers were able to build community relationships through networking, take initiatives to change their classroom practice, engage actively in the content of their disciplines, and eventually become leaders in their schools, communities, and beyond, Zimmerman conducted two research studies: One involved focus groups of the 18 participants in the Artistically Talented Program (ATP) in 1994, and the other involved a survey sent to all teachers who had participated in ATP from 1990 to 1994.

Methodology, Data Collection, and Analysis

All 18 art teachers who attended the 1994 ATP met in three focus groups during the summer to discuss issues relevant to the ATP. Information gathered from their applications indicated that this was a highly motivated group of teachers who had taken some leadership initiatives in their schools. These teachers, like prior groups at ATP, represented a wide range of ages, experiences, teaching situations, grade levels, and cultural, ethnic, and racial backgrounds. Except for one man, their commonality was that they were all women art teachers.

Zimmerman also surveyed all 54 past participants of ATP from 1990 to 1994, including those in the 1994 focus groups, to determine whether they were able to become empowered and maintain leadership positions in their communities. There were 46 (90%) responses. The vast majority were white women (three were men), with an equal number of elementary and secondary teachers. The majority were teaching in small, rural towns in the midwestern United States.

All 18 of the teachers at the ATP in 1994 participated in one of three focus groups; two groups consisted of new ATP participants and one was comprised of returning participants. The survey form sent to all ATP alumni consisted of 11 questions that focused on their leadership roles, funding applied for, role changes in schools, opportunities created for their artistically talented students, published writings, initiatives in organizing high-ability art classes, their present positions, and effects of attending ATP. Content analysis was used to analyze data of transcriptions of group discussions and results of the survey (Zimmerman, 1997d, 1997f).

Results of the Study

ATP alumni experienced many role changes, such as serving as department chairs or establishing districtwide art programs. They also networked with other ATP alumni, changed how they taught and constructed curricula, gained self-confidence, and continued their formal education and received advanced degrees.

Their students received many scholarships and awards, won art competitions, and became willing to take risks. ATP alumni also received support from other ATP alumni to pursue meaningful practice, gain self-esteem, become enthusiastic about teaching, and procure outside funding for their art programs. Personal accomplishments included experiencing self-renewal, receiving awards for teaching, and receiving increased support from administrators.

Discussion and Conclusions of the Study

It appears most objectives set by the ATP were met by an overwhelming majority of participants,

evidenced by focus group and survey responses; this experience helped them find their own voices. Many held leadership positions at local and state levels; received scholarships, awards, and grants; created new programs for their art students; published articles, reports, or other writings; and differentiated curricula. The majority gained knowledge about art content, achieved feelings of self-esteem, collaborated with others, and became caring and empowered leaders who made positive changes in their classrooms, communities, and schools, as well as at the state level and beyond.

Instruction at ATP focused on content, teaching strategies, and future empowerment for in-service art teachers with interest and motivation to become leaders in educating artistically talented students. A framework emerged from data in the focus group study and survey results. It appears that increasing knowledge of subject matter and pedagogy, building self-esteem, and allowing choices may lead teachers eventually to collaborate with others in respect to making changes in their private and professional lives. This results in communities of caring and educated teachers able to assume new leadership roles in their schools, communities, and state organizations.

Collaborative Research About Voice and Leadership

Voice in literature about contemporary feminist pedagogy has become a metaphor for oppressing and silencing women in education and other professional contexts. A number of contemporary writers include, or allude to, voice in titles of books they have written: *Without a Word: Teaching Beyond Women's Silence* (Lewis, 1993); *In A Different Voice: Psychological Theory and Women's Development* (Gilligan, 1982); *Women's Ways of Knowing: The Development of Self, Voice, and Mind* (Belenky, Clinchy, Goldberger, & Tarule, 1986); and *Voicing Today's Visions: Writing by Contemporary Women Artists* (Witzling, 1994).

Zimmerman and Thurber collaborated on a conceptual model for developing in-service art teachers' voices. The model begins with an interchange of teachers' own voices and those of their students. This is necessary for them to develop their private voices through self-reflection, validate their own experiences, collaborate on combining their voices with others, and develop a public voice to effect change as a transformational and political act, alone or in chorus with others. Their emphases on teaching in-service teachers was to encourage them to be reflective practitioners who are able to enter discourses about their disciplines, participate in interpretation and critique in a community of teachers and students, and present these analyses in public forums. Once teachers become empowered, they can speak publicly, assume leadership roles, and seek opportunities to share their voices with others.

An important aspect of this process is collaborative conversation. Teachers should become part of a group and break away from feelings of isolation. Within groups, they can share responses with one another in a reflective mode. They can develop confidence in their own voices through a community of supportive peers and engage in discourse about theory and practice. The end result can be in-service teachers developing their professional voices by restructuring their classrooms so that diversity is respected and everyone's voice can be heard. Maeroff (1988) found in-service education to be a powerful tool to empower teachers by breaking down isolation and building networks, bolstering teacher confidence, increasing knowledge of subject matter and pedagogy, and promoting learning that involves teachers' access to decision making. Darling-Hammond (1993) suggested that school reform would not be effective unless administration and professional in-service programs provide opportunities for teachers to exercise their collective voices and strive for feelings of accomplishment as they participate in school reform. These efforts then are linked to promotion of equity and social justice.

Methodology, Data Collection, and Analysis

Zimmerman described her experiences in respect to conducting voice-to-voice dialogue with ATP participants through empowering them to find their personal voices, develop collaborative voices with others, and form public voices that seek to transform their local community environments and beyond. The role that voice played in the ATP is evident when data from survey results, focus group discussions, and class evaluations were examined with emphasis on in-service teachers' emerging feelings of empowerment through their private, public, and collaborative voices. (See preceding study for information on the survey and focus groups.)

Results of the Research

Private Voices. Developing their own reflective voices and having conviction to voice their opinions were important issues for ATP participants. One spoke of gaining confidence in her accomplishments and, in turn, receiving respect from parents, teachers, administrators, and community members: "Reflecting on my own teaching practice gave me a new voice and a purpose to pursue meaningful projects for my students and provide them with community support." Not all found it easy to make their voices heard and acknowledged. According to many ATP participants, the process of discovering one's own voice began with self-reflection: "Then I felt what I had to say was valued."

Some ATP alumni felt personally empowered and able to be heard in their schools. One said, "I have a plan and it will be carried out. Art is noticed in my school." Another explained, "I am no longer an institutionalized babysitter, as many teachers have been viewed; I've seen changes in attitudes and support for my art teacher role." Several ATP alumni found themselves constantly seeking new challenges. One explained about meeting obstacles and overcoming them: "I feel I found a fence; I am over that fence and am ready to go over the next. It is going to be bigger and I have to push hard."

Collaborative Voices. Once ATP alumni discovered their voices, they found networking with other ATP alumni could help them become more effective. Feelings of isolation and despair, before they became ATP participants, were expressed by a number of teachers: "In my school, I have sat in the corner, thinking I am inferior because no one cares. Then I get with all these other people and it is possible to be a dynamic, powerful teacher." The value of exchanging ideas with other art teachers reverberated throughout the focus groups and on the survey responses. One teacher discovered that "there was an atmosphere that promoted sharing, growing, opportunities for creative investigations, and a safe place to voice my own thoughts and ideas." Another explained, "My experience was a reawakening. Although I had attended workshops and read articles, it was not like living and talking with others who were happy to share new and exciting ideas."

What one teacher described as "the important element of the human connection" was acknowledged, and resulting feelings of empowerment and self-confidence were apparent. Some representative remarks were: "The collegiality has given me and others courage to keep growing. Knowing there are colleagues who support you is a great confidence builder." and "We learned from each other, listened, shared ideas, and exchanged information. All class members were accepted and no one was more important than another." Another teacher's comment summarized the power of working with others and developing collaborative voices: "Now, so much more seems possible."

Public Voices. Going beyond the classroom to make their voices heard in public was a theme that many expressed: "I think it is absolutely imperative to involve the arts with a community focus, knowing the artists, knowing how city government works, and documenting everything through access to public venues." Comments also indicated that some ATP participants were going to take action and effect change in their schools: "I feel I am going to stir up a lot of trouble when I go back to teaching. I am trying to think of ways to effect change without alienating others."

Discussion and Conclusions of the Research: Voice for Art Education

As a result of Thurber and Zimmerman's inquiries and teaching experiences, they constructed a conceptual framework for aspects of voice they believe may have great relevance for in-service art teachers (see Figure 4.2). Girls definitely were *allowed*, and could speak *aloud*, as they focused on professional growth of teacher-leaders in in-service programs.

In the model, private voice (Personal Self section) depicts how teachers begin to experience personal voice and empowerment when they become reflective practitioners who are valued for their personal and professional experiences as teachers. Self-knowledge and autonomy are key outcomes of this process in professional development. Creating a collaborative voice (Professional Self section) with peers and in-service program leaders provides opportunities for teachers to speak and exchange ideas with others. This transition moves beyond personal empowerment and autonomy to increased knowledge of content and pedagogy, to a context where individuals' professional experiences are validated and possibilities for shared communication and collaborative professional vision are possible. Some teacher-leaders are empowered to move into an active and public arena and begin to reform education. Then a public voice (Social Action Self section) becomes possible, when these teachers become agents for change in a shifting paradigm of educational reform. Individually or collectively, teacher-leaders should seek to empower others through their public, ethical, moral, and social actions. Manifestations might include assuming leadership of regional or national organizations, publishing innovative research, or organizing community efforts for worthwhile educational projects reaching underserved members in their communities. Thurber and Zimmerman have continued their collaborative dialogue to gain better understanding of the power of personal, professional, and public voices for in-service teachers of talented art students who feel confident to use their personal and professional voices to affect educational changes in their schools, school districts, communities, and beyond.

RECOMMENDATIONS FOR TEACHERS OF ARTISTICALLY TALENTED STUDENTS

Based on literature in the field, studies we have conducted, and our own practical experiences with teacher characteristics and teaching strategies, we would like to make the following recommendations for teachers of artistically talented students.

Recommendation 1. Although teaching students about art skills and techniques is crucial for art talent development, teachers of artistically talented students also should focus on each student's talents and develop strategies to meet

Figure 4.2. Development of a Voice in In-Service Education

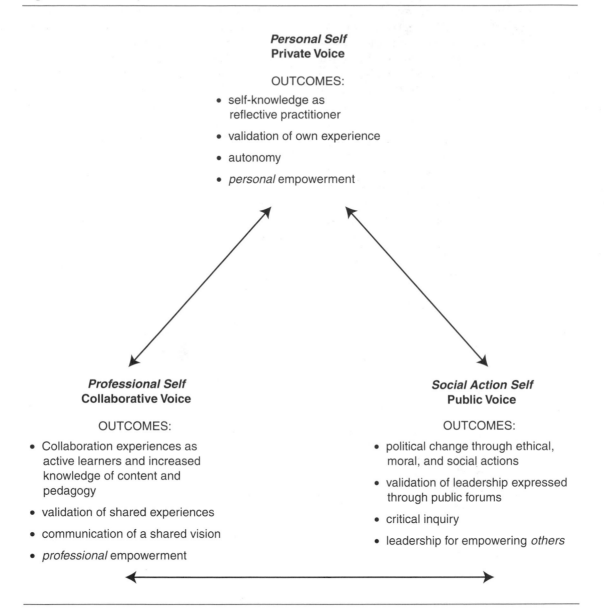

individual needs. It is important for teachers to be able to critically reflect about their teaching responsibilities and encourage their students to develop feelings of competence, set goals at a high level, and search for a variety of means for self-expression. These teachers should encourage their students to reflect on why they are creating art and the contexts in which they are engaged in art inquiry and production.

Recommendation 2. Teachers of artistically talented students should develop strategies so that their students can feel confident when engaging in Looking and Talking About Art activities and learning about the worlds of art. Students should be encouraged to initiate questions and discuss issues and concerns raised by viewing and interacting with those who create objects within a visual culture and with the objects they create. Through art appreciation activities that include critical inquiry, students can develop problem-solving skills and become aware of what has and is happening in art worlds both locally and globally.

Recommendation 3. Empowering teachers to develop their private, collaborative, and public voices can have larger outcomes than promoting art talent development in each teacher's local community. As a group, these teachers have potential to become powerful advocates for social action that can result in excellent and equitable education for all students. Developing teaching strategies to meet the needs of artistically talented students should be a high priority in any gifted and talented program at any level.

5 Curriculum

Plate 5.1 A linoleum-cut print by a seventh-grade IU Summer Arts Institute student created after a visit to the IU Greenhouse

The Marland Report (1972), the United States Office of Education, and federal legislation relative to gifted and talented children call for special educational programs appropriate to the needs of children identified as possessing superior abilities in intellectual aptitude, creativity, specific academic subjects, leadership, and the visual and performing arts. Such programs "require services or activities not ordinarily provided by the schools" (Gifted and Talented Children's Act, 1978). In the visual arts, providing special services and activities is particularly difficult because most art programs in schools are wholly idiosyncratic. When develop-

ing programs that support art talent development, it is necessary to establish a philosophy, purposes, goals, and structure that will guide all program decisions and define the special offering of services or activities not ordinarily provided by the schools. In order to do this, it is necessary to identify a program framework from which unique services and activities can be derived.

In this chapter, several curriculum frameworks and practical applications are outlined that are appropriate for educating artistically talented students. A program structure for educating artistically talented students and curricula are suggested as necessary for formulating content for fostering art talent development. Issues related to differentiating curricula to meet the unique needs of talented art students also are discussed. Several models are introduced that can aid in the differentiation process and a number of curriculum applications are outlined. A curriculum model and framework, influenced by the culture in which artistically talented students live and are educated, offers a structure for curriculum content based on adaptations of professional art roles. Then, descriptions of community-based art curricula for artistically talented students based on these curriculum concepts are introduced. Finally, recommendations for developing curricula for art talent development are summarized.

A PROGRAM STRUCTURE FOR EDUCATING ARTISTICALLY TALENTED STUDENTS

In 1983, we outlined a basic program structure for visual arts education that encompasses several curricular orientations (society-centered, child-centered, subject matter–centered) and curricular components (student, teacher, content, and settings). Each of the components of student, teacher, content, and setting require adaptation from regular school programs to special services and activities appropriate for special programs for artistically talented students.

In a *society-centered program*, emphasis is on meeting a community's social needs through learning social values and content derived from broad, societal problems; learning activities evolve as outcomes of group needs and interests. The major role of the teacher is that of coordinator and mediator of learning, guiding students in their efforts to meet a community's social needs. In an art program, emphasis would be upon helping students understand the role of art in society and the expression of social values through the arts. Artistically talented students also can learn to take a social activist position to change practices that they do not think are appropriate for their schools and/or communities, such as advocating about lack of inclusion of student artwork in local community events, having students write letters to local officials about

the need for special programs for art talent development in communities where these programs have been eliminated, and engaging in community action programs protesting visually inappropriate and distracting signage that compromises aesthetic values and a community's ecological concerns.

In a *child-centered program*, expressed interests and needs of students determine content and structure for the curriculum; individual problem solving and self-expression are the dominant methods. The major role of the teacher is to act as a facilitator for each student's need for expression and as a mentor for each student's instruction. In an art program, emphasis would be upon helping each student express his or her personal needs and develop his or her capacities and abilities in art.

In a *subject matter–centered program*, emphasis is based upon classified and organized disciplines of knowledge; learning activities emphasize methods, techniques, and findings within separate subject disciplines. The major role of the teacher is that of programmer of content and instructor of knowledge, understandings, and skills. In an art program, emphasis would be upon perceptual-conceptual inquiry that would develop student capacities for skillful art production, criticism, and appreciation.

School program planning has been viewed traditionally as representing these three different orientations in schooling. Many theorists have discussed how curricula differ as a result of their focus upon society-centered, child-centered, or subject matter–centered orientations (Chapman, 1978; Clark & Zimmerman, 1984; Efland, 1970; Eisner, 1972). Emphasizing one orientation and one set of goals does not preclude concern with the educational goals of other orientations. Improving society, helping each person achieve personal fulfillment, and transmitting the cultural heritage are generally recognized as goals that must be taught in order to create an enlightened citizenry (Chapman, 1978). In a democratic society, all these goals and orientations must be given attention in adequate art education programs.

We define *general curriculum* as a planned sequence of learning experiences based on a particular content that includes student and teacher tasks and outcomes and that takes place in a specified educational setting. We define *art curriculum* as a planned sequence of learning experiences about art content that includes student and teacher tasks and outcomes and that takes place in an environment designed for art learning. To construct an adequate art program based upon this definition, a complex of planned relationships among art content, student and teacher tasks and outcomes about art, and an educational setting that supports art learning must be specified.

We established in other writings that the important content to be learned in a complete art program should include knowledge, understandings, and skills about art history, art criticism, art production, and aesthetics (Clark & Zimmerman, 1978a, 1978b, 1984, 1986, 1988a). Art programs should also be concerned with students' readiness for art learning and level of development, students' art tasks and outcomes, and teachers' roles and methodologies related to appropriate learning experiences in art. An educational setting should be specified as an environment for art learning in the classroom, school, community, and society that includes administrative climate, support mechanisms of the environment, and the immediate physical environment. The setting is also defined by additional factors of materials, equipment, other resources, and time available to teachers and students. Components for a complete art program in all three curricular orientations are shown in Figure 5.1. We believe that all decisions about these components should be meaningfully interrelated in order to facilitate successful learning experiences about art.

We originally presented this program structure as a basis for arguing that a good school art program would include all of the orientation/component intersections and would, therefore, be complete. This argument also applies to unique programs for artistically talented students. It is important for all students to study various aspects of art that would contribute to improving society, achieving personal fulfillment, and knowing and understanding their cultural heritage.

Adaptations of the program structure just presented need to be made in planning and implementing a program for artistically talented students. The identification of this unique group needs to be guided by decisions of program philosophy and goals. Their educational programs, like those of other students, need to accommodate to their

unique readiness for art learning and levels of development in art, and provide appropriate tasks and outcomes about art. Teachers of artistically talented students should be aware that a program's philosophy and goals guide decisions about their roles and strategies appropriate to various aspects of an educational program. The content to be learned in a program for artistically talented students should be defined as accelerated and enriched learning experiences. Settings for special programs may be in schools, museums, community agencies, or other places supportive to the education of artistically talented students. Curriculum content, to be appropriate for students with high interests and abilities in the visual arts, needs to be created in ways that take into consideration their capabilities as similar to, but at the same time different from, expectations for other students. Means to differentiate curriculum for artistically talented students therefore will be discussed next.

Differentiating Curricula for Developing Art Talent

Differentiated instruction is an important concept in curriculum planning for developing art talent. Differentiated instruction focuses on learning strategies that are more qualitative than quantitative; adding more of the same content is not equal to learning experiences that are qualitatively different from those offered to most students. In these kinds of experiences a variety of approaches to content, process, product, learning environments, and assessments are promoted through both individual and whole-class instruction. Curricula that are differentiated for artistically talented students should differ from curricula that may be appropriate for whole-school enrichment. If all students are expected to succeed in a differentiated program, then the program is not to be considered as appropriate for talented art students (Clark & Zimmerman, 2001a).

Two models that influenced curriculum development in our Artistically Talented Program (ATP) and Project ARTS were the School-Wide Enrichment Triad Model (Renzulli & Reis, 1994) and Revolving Door Identification Model (Renzulli, Reis, & Smith, 1981). The School-Wide Enrichment Triad Model is a product of 15 years of research and field-testing that combined the Enrichment Triad

Figure 5.1. A Program Structure for Educating Artistically Talented Students

	Student Component	Teacher Component	Content Component	Setting Component
Society-Centered Orientation	Readiness and motivation for participation in art activities that result in social development and attainment of knowledge, understandings, and skills about art	Role as art coordinator and mediator based on a social interaction model Strategies for social interaction toward attainment of knowledge about art though society	Social orientation to selection of art content from art history, art criticism, art production, and aesthetics	Administrative arrangements, materials, and environments that facilitate social development and knowledge and skills about art
Child-Centered Orientation	Readiness and motivation for participation in art activities that result in personal development and attainment of knowledge, understandings, and skills about art	Role as art facilitator and mentor based on a personal sources model Strategies for personal growth toward attainment of knowledge about art through the self	Personal orientation to selection of art content from art history, art criticism, art production, and aesthetics	Administrative arrangements, materials, and environments that facilitate personal development and knowledge and skills about art
Subject Matter–Centered Orientation	Readiness and motivation for participating in art activities that result in conceptual-perceptual development and attainment of knowledge, understandings, and skills about art	Role as art programmer and instructor based on an information processing model Strategies for conceptual-perceptual inquiry toward attainment of knowledge, skills, and understandings about art through study of art disciplines and cultural heritages	Information processing orientation to selection of art content from art history, art criticism, art production, and aesthetics	Administrative arrangements, materials, and environments that facilitate conceptual-perceptual development and knowledge and skills about art

Model (Renzulli, 1977) and Revolving Door Identification Model. The Enrichment Triad Model offers three types of enrichment. In Type I, exploratory experiences are offered to all students, including field trips, speakers, museum programs, art performances, and learning centers that expose students to new topics and ideas that are not part of the regular school curriculum. Type II enrichment activities are designed to provide opportunities for organizing thinking and feeling processes that are essential for learning. Students are encouraged to learn advanced reference and research skills, engage in activities that develop inquiry processes such as research design and interpretation of data, participate in planning, decision making, and forecasting results of their research, and participate in advanced computer programming and graphic production minicourses and other venues to learn specific technical skills. Type III activities focus on individual and small-group investigations

of real-life problems by high-ability talented students. In Type III activities, teachers identify and focus student interest, find appropriate outlets for student projects, provide methodological assistance, and help students make their inquiries public for appropriate audiences. For arts students, creating a body of artwork and displaying it publicly, writing and utilizing a computer graphics program to present information, or publishing an article in a local newspaper are examples of Type III activities. The Revolving Door Identification Model allows students to enter and exit talent development programs according to their interests and abilities. Students, therefore, can study for three months about a specific topic, such as architectural preservation, and exit a program when another topic is introduced that may not interest them or that does not match their art abilities.

These models often provided structures for ATP and Project ARTS teachers as they developed programs for artistically talented students in their home communities. Units of instruction focusing on particular themes with related art forms and art-making processes were developed as students were exposed to new concepts and interests. Some students went on to explore advanced levels of thinking, use advanced research skills, and become engaged in in-depth inquiry and art production related to a specific theme.

In addition, other suggestions from educators about developing art talent were used to help ATP and Project ARTS teachers develop curriculum units. These units employed problem finding and problem solving and structured and unstructured tasks, a combination of discursive and nondiscursive tasks, independent units of study, integration of art with other subjects, and a wide range of tasks that challenged their artistically talented students. Maker's (1982) and Tomlinson's (1995) models for curriculum development suggested how content, process, product, learning environment, and assessment modifications could be used to differentiate curricula for art talent development that differed from usual student work. In respect to content modification of ideas, concepts, and facts, focus was on abstractness, complexity, and variety; themes and key issues; study of methods of disciplines in art; understanding rather than memorizing; and relationships of themes to students' lives. In respect to process modifications, concern was with how materials, activities, and questions were presented. Focus was on higher levels of thinking, open-ended learning activities in which there were no obvious answers, self-motivated inquiry where students were free to choose their own topics to explore, relating new information to previous understandings, engaging in group interactions and simulations where students could develop leadership skills, and changing pace to adapt to a variety of learning situations. Product modifications of reports, artworks, and performances that resembled the work of professionals were based on real problems, presented to real audiences (such as city council members), and displayed in public arenas. Students were encouraged to blend multiple sources of information and develop timelines for checking in with the teacher and completing work. Learning environment modifications included a student-centered approach and allowed choices of problems to study, openness and flexibility for change, and freedom for students to leave the classroom to do their research and complete projects. Assessment modifications included use of formative and summative evaluations and clearly explained success criteria developed by the students and teachers.

Curricular Examples From the Artistically Talented Program

Each summer for 4 years, we codirected a 2-week Artistically Talented Program (ATP) for inservice visual art teachers at Indiana University funded by the Indiana Department of Education, Office of Gifted and Talented Programs. Thematic units of instruction developed by the teachers were based on the Renzulli and Reis, Maker, and Tomlinson models, Feldman's Universal to Unique Continuum, and our Structure for Learning Experiences in the Visual Arts and Expanded Structure for Learning Experiences in the Visual Arts (the last three models are presented in the next two sections of this chapter). Thematic teaching was used to increase complexity and in-depth content related to the study of art and integration with other subjects. In these ways, students were encouraged to examine interrelationships among facts, rules, and concepts. Examples of broad overarching themes that were converted into curriculum units included change, conflict, patterns, power, heroism, extinction, adaptation, and cooperation.

One of the thematic units of instruction that ATP teachers developed was *More Than Meets the Eye: Architectural Preservation Awareness*, a unit designed for fourth- and fifth-grade students that involved studying the architecture in their local community (Cole, 1993). In this unit students contrasted and compared values and philosophies that shaped buildings. These students investigated how space was used, what value conflicts existed within their communities, and the importance of using aesthetic criteria to evaluate building design. Drawing skills were taught using a variety of techniques. To develop understanding about the work of contemporary architects, after studying local historically significant, endangered buildings, each student chose one building and designed a new use for it, combining freehand drawings and computer-generated images.

Another unit for fourth- and fifth-grade students, *How Impressionism Reflected Social Impact of the 1880s*, involved studying about Impressionists and how they were impacted by social and historical concerns (R. Johnson, 1993). Students learned that artists in the late 1800s were affected by many changes happening in the world about them and that these changes were reflected in their artworks. Students conducted research about photography, which created new conditions, and other inventions like the collapsible paint tube, which made it possible for artists to paint out of doors more easily. Each student then collected photographs related to an outdoor scene they intended to portray. Using these photographs, they did several sketches and created a composition that represented an impression of their scene at a particular time of day.

Other units of instruction were developed and taught at the junior high school level. *Social Problems and Art: How Artists Can Use Their Talents to Help*

Their Communities used the AIDS issue as an example (Grube, 1993). Students studied ways artists use their work to expose and confront social problems in their communities. This unit required problem solving; decision making; looking, talking, and writing about art and artists in the students' local communities; art making; and marketing of art works.

Boxes: Private/Public Spaces, created for high school students, focused on the theme of "the box"—from embryo to coffin—as a metaphor for life (Andrews, 1994). Juxtaposition of themes of space, time, and energy provided new ways for students to create art. Students researched psychology of space, explored construction techniques, and found solutions to atypical space and shape relationships. Students also investigated objects and their sources, analyzed integral features, and linked their own art making to personal experiences. As a result of the unit, one student designed a small

Plate 5.2 An Impressionist-like sketch of an outdoor scene by a seventh grade IU Summer ARTS Institute student that was later rendered as a painting

Japanese meditative garden in a shadow box. She wrote, "The experience of creating this garden helped me understand that visual experiences depend on the perspective of the viewer and that some artworks are constantly changing."

Students identified as artistically talented need to have differentiated curricula developed for them that address appropriate content, processes, products, learning environments, and assessments. Teachers, curriculum coordinators, administrators, and community advisors should select a curriculum design that takes into account the backgrounds of the students and the values of the communities in which they live; competencies of teachers responsible for creating art talent development programs; and local, state, and national standards. Several curriculum models have been presented for helping develop and design differentiated curricula, yet there are many other models that may also be applied to this task. In the following section, we will present and discuss a model we initiated for all art students and have used in programs for developing curriculum for art talent development.

A CURRICULUM STRUCTURE FOR LEARNING EXPERIENCES IN THE VISUAL ARTS

Study of the visual arts is essential in an education program for all students that aims to develop personal, social, and cognitive skills that are necessary for participation in a democratic society. As part of a general curriculum, appropriate art experiences should promote students' personal, social, perceptual, and conceptual growth through directed study of the arts. The visual arts should be studied to help students understand and appreciate the feelings, ideas, and values that major arts traditions communicate. Without art as both a separate discipline, and also part of general curricula, students' learning experiences are incomplete.

We believe that all students possess art talent to some degree the way they also possess academic abilities and intelligence. It is commonly agreed that an individual who has been carefully tested with an achievement or intelligence test will have a score somewhere on a broad scale of normally distributed scores. Some students will receive a low score, the majority will receive an average score, and some will receive a high score. Achievement and intelligence are constructs that include many deviations above or below a mean and are sensitive to cultural and societal values. What is valued in a particular setting influences how students score on standardized tests, and it should be noted that such tests have been criticized as being biased for some student populations.

As result of our research, we believe art talent, like other abilities, is normally distributed in the world population. Some people, therefore, will demonstrate low abilities, most people will demonstrate average abilities, and some people will demonstrate high abilities in the visual arts. Art abilities, although subject to natural capacities, also are influenced by educational interventions; all students, therefore, can develop understandings, skills, and abilities about the arts.

In most elementary, junior high, and high school art classes there is a broad continuum ranging from students with beginning or naive talent to those with grade-level or average abilities, to those with advanced, somewhat sophisticated talents. Availability of an educational structure with content that encompasses teaching art to below average, average, above average, and high-ability students would be useful for art teachers who want to accommodate all of their students' needs and abilities. Opportunities for remedial, general, and accelerated art activities are predicated on content structures that accommodate a variety of levels of achievement.

Professional Role Models

Activities of visual arts professionals suggest sources for designing outcomes for visual arts curricula that address complex contemporary issues, such as the role of the visual arts in a variety of cultures, environmental and social concerns, art talent development, and increasing creativity. Professional practices of artists are sources for content and design of related educational activities unique to the visual arts. Clearly, children may never function as arts professionals although they certainly can experience tasks and outcomes that are derived and adapted for school-age students from these roles. It is possible to identify and define content and learning experiences appropriate to professional roles, while maintaining awareness that each role is not discrete and should be integrated with others in classroom practices (Clark, Day, & Greer, 1987; Clark & Zimmerman, 1978a, 1978b, 1981, 2000).

This is not a new idea; science, mathematics, music, and other major disciplines and academic programs for the gifted and talented have long taught advanced students to perform tasks similar to the work of professionals in their fields. What, however, do practitioners in these roles actually do? What knowledge, skills, and understandings must they possess? Answers to these questions are essential to establishing content and structure for art education curricula and programs. Artists create works of art. Art critics analyze, interpret, and criticize works of art. Art historians place artworks in regional, stylistic, and historical contexts. Aestheticians generate theories about art and aesthetics and develop criteria by which works of art are judged and meanings are determined. All these professionals consider societal implications about contexts where art is created. Art, as we define it, encompasses a variety of works including overlapping categories such as folk art, outsider art, women's art, craftwork, artwork from non-Western cultures, visual culture, popular art, tourist art, computer graphics, industrial design, architecture, and advertising art. Like other programs, content of visual arts curricula would need to be ordered in developmental sequences appropriate to the needs of learners. Any structure for learning experiences in the visual arts should rest on the important supposition that all learners need planned teacher interventions and sequenced learning activities. It is also important to realize that content found in the structure needs to be closely aligned with state and national standards found in both art education and gifted and talented initiatives for both students and teachers.

We have designed a Structure for Learning Experiences in the Visual Arts that is divided into a number of categories (see Figure 5.2). The structure contains seven successive stages beginning with an Entering or Naive Stage and ending with an Exiting or Sophisticated Stage. Between the Entering and Exiting Stages are five Stages of Teacher Interventions and Learning Experiences (Introductory, Rudimentary, Intermediate, Advanced, and Mastery Stages). Naive learners at the Entering Stage have not been exposed to teaching interventions, and those at the Exiting Stage, who may be becoming professionals in the arts, usually are beyond needing formal teacher interventions. Naive learners will produce unskilled artworks and subjective reactions and psychological reports about works of art. They also will exhibit uninformed judgments and preference statements that are not expressed publicly, and their art making and art understandings are naive and evidence a lack of awareness of artworks in a historical context. Sophisticated learners demonstrate professional understandings about qualitative, exemplary works produced by artists, art critics, art historians, aestheticians, and other arts professionals. These learners will report subjective and objective reactions and interpretive understandings about works of art. They display skills, knowledge, and personal preferences along with objectified judgments expressed both privately and publicly that are subject to external criticism.

In this structure, learners move horizontally from a Naive Stage to an Introductory Stage that encompasses beginning experiences that prepare them for further teacher interventions. At the Rudimentary Stage, learners' decreased naivete and emerging sophistication provide a background for more difficult learning tasks. At the Intermediate and Advanced Stages, teacher interventions and educational encounters decrease naivete to the point where learners reach higher stages of skills and understandings. Further attainment of understandings, knowledge, and skills moves learners, with teacher contributions, to a Mastery Stage where their abilities are demonstrated at a near-mastery level. Even professional adults rarely attain the ideal end stage.

We advocate that a focus on one role should not dominate instruction or learner experiences nor should one role be studied exclusively at any time. All roles should be integrated in classroom practice and integrated with other studies. In programs based on this model, learners would be instructed in tasks related to all professional roles in the arts and instruction would be cycled in ordered sequences of increasing difficulty. The content for the empty boxes in Figure 5.2 will be explained

Figure 5.2. A Structure for Learning Experiences in the Visual Arts

Entering Stage	Teacher Interventions and Stages of Learning Experiences					Exiting Stage
Naive Stage	*Introductory* → *Stage*	*Rudimentary* → *Stage*	*Intermediate* → *Stage*	*Advanced* → *Stage*	*Mastery* → *Stage*	*Sophisticated* → *Stage*
Art Making Strand Unskilled maker of art						**Artist:** creator of works of art confirmed by a community of experts
Art Criticism Strand Producer of purely subjective reports and uninformed judgments about a work of art						**Art Critic:** producer of public statements about works of art that are interpretations and judgments based upon objective criteria
Art History Strand Producer of reports that demonstrate lack of awareness of works of art in historical context						**Art Historian:** producer of public statements about historical relations and cultural contexts of works of art that may be confirmed or denied by a community of experts
Aesthetics Strands Producer of purely subjective reports and uninformed preference statements about works of art.						**Aesthetician:** producer of public writings about the nature of art, art theory, and artistic standards that may be confirmed or denied by a community of experts

and applied to the structure with a few examples that demonstrate how the model can be applied in practice.

Strands for Learning Experiences in the Visual Arts

Sequences of content are focused on important skills and understandings, with discrete learning activities. In the first column shown in Figure 5.2 under the Naive Stage are four separate content strands: Art Making, Art Criticism, Art History, and Aesthetics. Also within each strand there are four or more substrands. The contents of these strands do not exhaust all possible parameters, although they do focus on basically important tasks and

understandings related to each strand. Each strand presents an accumulated progression of closely related constructs. These are ordered horizontally and shown sequentially from Introductory to Rudimentary, to Intermediate, to Advanced, to Mastery Stages for learners. Each of the stages is dependent on teacher interventions with planned educational encounters. For the empty boxes found in the structure in Figure 5.2, suggestions for content appropriate for learners' art development for each of four strands from Introductory through Mastery Stages will be outlined below. For example, in the Art Making Strand there are four substrands: Media and Skills, Concepts and Knowledge, Critique of Learners' Artworks, and Personal Style in Learners' Artworks. Each substrand contains teacher interventions and learning experiences described from Introductory through Mastery Stages.

Art Making Strand

Media and Skills are developed from introductory, exploratory experiences leading to more skill demanding rudimentary, intermediate, and advanced experiences in which limitations and possibilities of specific media are explored. These lead to mastery-level uses of media and skills in the creation of works of art.

Concepts and Knowledge about making art in a culture begin with introductory, exploratory experiences with concepts. Increasingly difficult tasks that relate skillful uses of media to applications of concepts and knowledge are required at the rudimentary, intermediate, and advanced levels. At the mastery level, understanding of concepts and knowledge are demonstrated in the creation of relatively mature works of art.

Critique of Learners' Artwork begins after students have had manipulative experiences with media and exploratory experiences with concepts. Appropriate skills are developed at rudimentary, intermediate, and advanced levels. At the mastery level, learners qualitatively critique their own works in progress or when completed.

Personal Style in Learners' Artwork emerges only at an advanced level of development, derived from previous learning experiences and familiarity with a variety of artists' styles. It culminates in demonstration of a mature, personal style at the mastery level.

Art Criticism Strand

Vocabulary and Categories of Description are developed from introductory experiences in which learners begin with a basic vocabulary and end with the ability to categorize works of art through description and analysis at the mastery level.

Contextual Criticism begins with simple familiarity with works of art. Directed description and analysis experiences, emphasizing observable qualities in works of art, lead to more advanced and mastery-level descriptions, analyses, interpretations, and mastery judgments. At advanced levels, contexts

and environments within which works of art are created are also studied, leading to both phenomenological and contextual criticism.

Understanding the Work of Art Critics is developed as learning experiences that begin with undifferentiated discussion of works of art and are developed through many directed oral discussions of specific works of art. At advanced levels, learners read, study, and analyze art criticism to understand the work of art critics.

Writing Criticism of Specific Works of Art begins with subjective, undifferentiated judgments. These lead to successive learning experiences that clarify differences between subjective and objective criteria and judgments and personal interpretations of works of art.

Meta-Criticism provides advanced-level opportunities for students to analyze and critique works by art critics.

Art History Strand

Art History Research begins with exposure to specific works of art with an emphasis on cultural artifacts. Teachers direct experiences with rudimentary technical descriptions and classifications of works of art that lead to selected classification systems of placement. Students will engage in identification, authentication, and attribution of unique works of art conducted at the mastery level.

Sociocultural Interpretation starts with general awareness of social and cultural influences on works of art. Then learners become involved in tasks that develop greater understanding of the influence of society and cultures on artists and their works. At the mastery level, students write sociocultural interpretations of works of art as public reports.

Writing Art History begins with simple awareness of a time continuum in respect to works of art. Learners at the rudimentary level are introduced to study and applications of general historical inquiry. With this background, at intermediate and advanced levels, teachers have students study specific art history research methodologies. At the mastery level, students generate art historical research as written reports subject to public criticism.

Meta-Art History is taught at advanced and mastery levels. In the advanced level, teacher-directed study involves diverse and congruent art history methodologies and theories. At the mastery level, students critique writings by art historians and generate theories of art in relation to cultural history and criticism of the writings of art historians.

Aesthetics Strand

Vocabulary and Categories of Description, at the introductory level, involve untutored discussions of works of art. Higher level learning experiences involve use of increasingly appropriate vocabulary and categorization skills. At the mastery level, students use refined vocabulary and categorization skills when discussing works of art.

Standards of Quality begin from commonsense criteria used when discussing works of art. As students progress, they use increasingly advanced sources of aesthetic criteria applied to works of art. Advanced students justify their statements by aesthetic criteria based on standards of quality related to works of art.

Preferences Through Aesthetic Criteria are developed from rudimentary to advanced exercises in describing, analyzing, and interpreting qualities in works of art based on aesthetic criteria, philosophical methods, and awareness of different aesthetic preferences in a variety of contexts. Experiencing and valuing works of art aesthetically, at the mastery level, results in refined preferences and taste.

Essays About Aesthetics would be read at intermediate and advanced levels and students would produce essays about aesthetics subject to public criticism.

Theorizing About Art would be studied only at advanced or mastery levels and students would generate theories about art and aesthetic issues.

It should be noted that the art critic and aesthetician roles tend to have similar tasks and become differentiated only at very high levels. Because aestheticians perform only at the meta-level, educational tasks are rarely the same as professional work of the aesthetician.

Acceleration and Enrichment Opportunities

We have outlined educationally sound sequences of concepts with utility for curricula and program design in visual arts education and appli-

cability to the needs of artistically talented students. In Chapter 4, Clark's use of Looking At and Talking About Art (LATA) strategies involved students at many ability levels and he had to adapt his responses and questions to a variety of student responses. Many of the tasks he employed were at the Rudimentary or Intermediate Stage in the Structure for Learning Experiences in the Visual Arts. This was due to their lack of exposure to teacher-guided discussions with works of art.

Acceleration in visual arts curricula could mean attainment of increased precision of meaning and understanding of specific aspects of producing, conceptualizing, and talking and writing about works of art. The Structure for Learning Experiences in the Visual Arts takes into account students at all ability levels and in several areas in the visual arts. More talented and able students can move from naive stages to more advanced stages at a faster pace than average or lower ability arts students in the same class.

Although new programs have proliferated in the visual arts, many of these have been designed and implemented on pragmatic bases without references to theory. Major reasons are that theory generation and research are largely lacking and local programs often are created in response to immediate political pressures or economic resources. In order to educate artistically talented students effectively, a beginning point would be to identify models having theoretical foundations that can be extended to meet the unique educational needs of such students. In the next section, we will discuss how we included concepts found in a developmental education model and integrated them with the Structure for Learning in the Visual Arts that we just described.

AN EXPANDED CURRICULUM STRUCTURE FOR EDUCATING ARTISTICALLY TALENTED STUDENTS

It is generally agreed upon in most art education literature on art development in the Western world, that children usually pass through three general stages (Hurwitz & Day, 2001). These three stages are usually referred to as the manipulative stage (ages 2 through 5), the symbol-making stage (ages 6 through 9), and the preadolescent stage (ages 10 through 13). In the first stage, children explore and manipulate materials; later in this stage children give titles to their marks. During the second stage, children develop a series of symbols that stand for objects that they experience and are related to a context within their graphic designs. In the third stage, children become critical of their artwork and express themselves in a less-spontaneous manner than before with much more self-consciousness about their art products. These stages are found in the artwork of most children; however, each child's work contains unique qualities that are only associated with that particular child.

Grounded in these stages of children's graphic development, Gardner and Winner (1982) designed a general model of art development in which they proposed that for all children there is a period in early childhood (5–7 years) when they produce artworks with many qualities similar to those attributed to modern artists. By late childhood (8–9 years), however, children's graphic artwork becomes lifeless and lacks the spontaneous quality of their earlier work. For those few who evidence interests and abilities in the visual arts, their artwork regains potency by midadolescence. This pattern of initial aesthetic response, then loss of this response, to regaining beginning aesthetic characteristics has been referred to as the *U-curved trajectory* in graphic development. Davis's (1997a, 1997b) research supported the existence of this U-curve and suggested it should be accepted universally. Pariser & van den Berg (1997a, 1997b) in another study concluded that a U-curved sorting pattern was more dependent upon judges' educational, cultural, and artistic backgrounds than on the form and content of children's drawings. Kindler (2000) and Kindler, Pariser, van den Berg, and Lui (2001) found in their research in respect to the universality of the U-curve that only some judges who have training and education in the fine arts create a U-shaped ordering of the drawings.

Traditionally in art talent development studies, researchers advocate a path of development that culminates in the acquisition of drawing skills by which realistic images are produced and a mastery of perspective is evident. Recently, a number of researchers have proposed that there are a number of other pathways for children to develop their

art abilities, and realism is only one of these routes (Kindler & Darras, 1998; N. Smith, 1998; Willats, 1997; Wolf & Perry, 1988). Kindler and Darras's (1998) model of art development includes many routes beginning with experiments and achievement of skills and abilities that are not from realism but resemble those of professional artists. Although the notion of stage development is not rejected, it should be modified to accommodate a number of contemporary conceptions about art talent development, such as Feldman's powerful construct, the Universal to Unique Continuum.

The writings of David Henry Feldman (1982, 1983, 1985) present a theory for educating artistically talented students that offers new insights taken from child development theory. Feldman asserts that child development stages are

1. Found in specific domains of knowledge, rather than in a child's mind
2. Continuous and process based, rather than trait based
3. The direct result of educational encounters, rather than simple maturation
4. Controlled by specialized environments in which children may or may not operate, rather than spontaneously generated

Another source for theory construction is our Structure for Learning Experiences in the Visual Arts. We have used it to guide identification and education of artistically talented students, evaluations of educational materials, and outlining of research problems about educating artistically talented students. Although Feldman's writings describe educational aspects of teaching, student development, and the role of contexts and environments for learning, they do not prescribe content for an education program. Our structure specifically addresses art content and prescribes its organization as an educational construct. By integrating Feldman's continuum with our structure, a more complete basis for curricula can be created to guide the design of education programs for artistically talented students.

Feldman's Unique to Universal Continuum

Feldman's *Universal to Unique Continuum* (UU) describes cognitive development through a series of continuous stages or domains. It is based upon Piaget's child development theory, but differs in several aspects. Domains are viewed as continuous rather than distinct, and are seen as a gradual progression that represents them as existing primarily in a body of knowledge. Domains, therefore, are not seen as structured wholes, but as levels of achievement within specific bodies of knowledge. Feldman's theory does not represent domains as beng restricted to universal cognitive development, and he views domains as sequential and hierarchically integrated and influenced by culture and education. No domain is lost as a child moves in the sequence, but they are integrated into each successive domain through transition processes.

The Universal to Unique Continuum is composed of five developmental domains:

1. Universal
2. Cultural
3. Discipline-based
4. Idiosyncratic
5. Unique

Movement is horizontal from the universal to the unique and dependent upon a number of conditions that lead to different levels of achievement. Each of the domains is attained by increasingly smaller numbers of people. The *universal domain* consists of knowledge generally achieved by all individuals, such as mastering essentials of a language and acquiring numerous cognitive operations. Universal knowledge occurs independently and prior to more specific knowledge that requires instruction. Not all universal knowledge needs to be acquired before cultural learnings also take place. All individuals in a culture are expected to acquire certain aspects of knowledge and these are found in the *cultural domain*. Examples of cultural domains include being able to read, write, and do computations. The *discipline-based domain* involves mastery of a particular discipline and generally takes place in schools. Fewer people are able or interested in learning in discipline-based domains than in cultural ones. The *idiosyncratic domain* is usually represented by subdomains of a discipline or craft and is characterized by a person's specialty, such as programming computers for graphic rep-

resentation at a professional level. In the *unique domain* achievements are made by only a small number of people and represent new forms of knowledge or organization within a domain that typically have never been accomplished in quite the same way, such as Einstein's theory of relativity. Feldman believes only some unique achievements are creative in the sense that they become incorporated into larger bodies of knowledge and change the ways of thinking in particular fields.

Achievement by individuals in each of these domains is dependent upon supportive environmental conditions, instruction, invariant progression through the stages described, and access to the required knowledge. Students can be prepared to move from any domain to the next, but will not achieve this transition if supportive conditions are not available. The talents of a child with the potential to become a successful artist would languish without access to effective and supportive teachers, opportunities to view and create art, and access to learning materials that would communicate the required knowledge to develop the child's potential. According to Feldman, students do not progress along the continuum without directive and intentional instruction. All new knowledge is generated originally in the unique domain. Over time, unique understandings become accessible to more and more people and begin to become available to people in previous domains. Knowledge useful to all people eventually extends to the universal domain and knowledge used only by specialists remains in the idiosyncratic or unique domains.

Applications to Art Talent Development

Many ideas contained in Feldman's writings have direct relevance for art educators and for art talent development. His domains can be used to clarify and inform questions that art educators have asked about students, teaching art, and environments for art education. Early scribbles and drawings of "tadpole" people exemplify universal performance in art. Although children's first scribbles and figures are almost entirely determined by universal forces, very little time passes before the influence of culture begins to interact with natural forces. The culture domain impinges on children and they begin to develop imagery based on what they understand their culture values or encompasses. An example would be the recent proliferation of superhero figures influenced by Japanese comic books (*manga*) and science imagery in drawings of elementary and secondary school students. Most aspects of the cultural domain and all aspects of the discipline-based domain are the result of adult interventions and educational activities. When students begin to learn specific techniques related to a particular medium, such as foreshortening in drawing, they are performing in the discipline-based region. Students who are interested and talented master knowledge in the discipline-based region and move on to various levels in the idiosyncratic region. A student who has mastered elements of drawing and computer graphics at a professional level has entered the idiosyncratic region. The unique region is only achieved by a few adult individuals, such as Julie Taymor who has changed the way costume and stage design are conceived and executed in the Western world. This kind of contribution, once made, becomes adapted by other artists and is no longer considered a unique contribution.

According to Feldman, all children attempt to draw, but their activities are not the same as those involved in development of an artist. He observed that almost all student art begins during the cultural domain and develops into the discipline-based domain. Only motivated students who are talented in the arts, however, would be producing or performing in the idiosyncratic domain. In teacher interventions, cultural aspects of art traditions from many sources should be studied to enable all students to understand their own and others' art heritages and traditions.

Integration of the Feldman Model and the Clark and Zimmerman Structure

The structure we proposed to guide decisions about content choices for learning experiences in the visual arts at various stages of development was based on the assumption that learners would enter studies of the visual arts in a naive and uninformed state and would exit, ideally, in a sophisticated state

as a primary result of teacher interventions and educational activities (see above and Figure 5.2). Enrichment for artistically talented students would mean the attainment of a greater depth of knowledge, skills, and values at any place on the structure than that achieved by most students.

The integration of the Unique to Universal Continuum with our Structure for Learning Experiences in the Visual Arts has the power to provide an expanded art education framework for all students at all levels of achievement, as well as for artistically talented students. Both the continuum and our structure are predicated upon an ordered sequence of concepts with increasing complexity for learners in which horizontal movement demands instructional interventions. Those who pursue education are smaller in number at each successive stage in both constructs. Before educational interventions, all individuals have universal and some cultural awareness about the visual arts but may be described as predominantly naive.

When students enter school or begin their education, universal or cultural awareness about art predominates. Without deliberate educational experiences, most students will remain at this level. Introductory and rudimentary learning experiences, however, should provide a background for most students that may lead to advanced learning about art. Some students will have opportunities for intermediate and advanced learning and will increase their knowledge, skills, and values beyond those of most others. Many operating at the mastery or sophisticated levels will eventually choose careers in art after they have completed their education. A few artistically talented students, with advanced abilities, will operate at the idiosyncratic level. Of these, only a small number will go on to the unique domain and possibly make creative contributions as adults to the world of the visual arts.

Applications of the Expanded Structure

We have used this integrated structure, the Expanded Structure for Learning Experiences in the Visual Arts, to help teachers of artistically talented students plan theme-based units of instruction as well as entire art programs. We will discuss two of these units in detail below. Both units were sensitive to local community-based issues and concerns, which was one reason they were successful.

Benton's Murals Unit (Indiana). The unit, Issues Surrounding Thomas Hart Benton's Indiana Murals, was created for a fourth-grade art class that included students at all levels of ability (Sandberg, 2003). This unit employs the expanded structure and complies with the National Art Standards. The Benton murals in Bloomington, Indiana, are a local resource that can be used to develop concepts and art learning experiences at the Rudimentary and Intermediate Stages of the expanded structure that involve many teacher interventions in respect to teaching strategies and differentiated curriculum. The classes for which this unit was developed included a number of artistically talented students who were engaged in learning experiences at the Intermediate Stage as well as students who were operating at Introductory and Rudimentary stages.

This unit provides an in-depth examination about the artist Thomas Hart Benton, the history of the creation and relocation of the murals, Benton's methods and techniques of painting, and the controversy about the mural's content and worth as public art. Students also are given opportunities to research Indiana history and can then create a new mural for public display that depicts Indiana history from 1933 to the present. The unit consisted of eight one-hour art lessons, beginning with a video introduction about the artist and the creation of the murals, accompanied by quizzes about the video's content for students at different learning stages. The next part involved a closer look at the 22 panels that comprise the mural, a depiction of the social history of Indiana painted by Benton for the 1933 Chicago World's Fair. Students took a field trip to see the murals and wrote open-ended responses to questions about the panels. A few examples of the questions follow:

1. Are the people in the paintings depicted realistically? Please explain your answer.
2. Explain what the land or geography of Indiana is like in the painting.
3. What symbols can you find in the paintings and what do they represent?

The unit continued with students making egg tempera paints and experimenting with this media.

At the same time, students researched Indiana history from 1933 to the present in their history classes. This research was then translated into sketches focusing on symbols that were later incorporated into a school mural. The students' images were enlarged by using a grid method Benton had used when creating his murals. Students in the class who demonstrated art abilities and interest in the project became group leaders who helped other students include their ideas in final preparation for painting. At the same time, students studied about messages found in murals that were created at various time periods and in different venues.

Depiction of the Ku Klux Klan in one of the Benton mural panels, located in a classroom on the Indiana University campus, inspired a public debate about whether this mural panel depicted hatred or history. Several fourth-grade students conducted research and interviewed several people on campus who were involved in the debate. Later, these students were able to lead heated debates in their art classes about the mural's content. At the unit's culmination, students studied elements and principles of design and incorporated knowledge from their art history, art criticism, and aesthetic experiences into their art-making experiences and completed their own Indiana history mural for display at the school. Students were assessed at each phase of the unit, conducted class critiques, and answered a form on which they were able to evaluate the teacher's planning and execution of the unit.

This unit included content related to Art Making, Art Criticism, Art History, and Aesthetic Strands at the Rudimentary and Intermediate Stages and concepts related to the Cultural and Disciplined-Based Domains in Feldman's model. Content and concepts included exploratory and more skillful use of art media, knowledge about Benton's creation of works of art, engagement in description and analysis experiences with the murals, and study of newspaper and other popular media's discussion of the mural controversy. Students wrote objective critiques about the Benton and other murals, were exposed to and conducted research about Indiana history and the history of the Benton murals, studied social and cultural influences on past and present interpretation of the Benton and other murals, and engaged in debate at beginning stages about the content of public art and the reactions to it by local citizens.

Contemporary Art Unit (*Hong Kong*). Another example of the expanded structure was one that we used when the Hong Kong Department of Education asked us to help them create a pilot program for the development of students talented in the visual arts (Clark & Zimmerman, 2003). General goals for the project were to develop a range of reference tools for identifying students who are recognized to be talented or have potential in the visual arts, and to offer selected teachers some programs to help them construct curricula and assessments for their identified students.

We recommend that, in workshop settings, teachers learn to encourage independent thought, spontaneity, and originality in their artistically talented students through differentiated and enriched curricula. We therefore suggested that teachers develop local, theme-oriented units of instruction. We also recommended that open-ended assignments be used that include a variety of tasks designed to emphasize both verbal and visual problem-finding and problem-solving skills, integrate art with other subjects, use socially relevant subject matter, and modify and differentiate art content to create enriched curricula for art talent development. We also advocated use of a variety of authentic assessment instruments, designed by local consultants in collaboration with participating teachers.

Two primary and three secondary schools in Hong Kong were selected to participate in this project. We conducted workshops about differentiated curriculum construction and program assessment for artistically talented students. All teachers and consultants participating in the program, as well as some of their colleagues, attended these workshops. We will focus on one secondary school in the project to demonstrate how the expanded structure was used to create a theme-based curriculum.

The focus of this thematic unit was ideas and self-development through the study of contemporary art. As a role model of a professional artist, the teacher presented his own photographs and explained how he generates ideas. Students then used digital cameras to record their collections of favorite objects. Next, they created plaster molds of these objects and critiqued them as a group. In small groups, they studied books and visuals related to contemporary art and photography. A local guest artist showed the students a variety of artworks and reference books and then related them to the technical and expressive needs of each student. A journalism student shared his viewpoints about the students' artworks to stimulate their creativity from a different point of view. The teacher then encouraged differentiated outcomes of student planning and execution of their artwork.

The students produced and critiqued their paintings as final products based on their own interests and self-development that was reflected in the research they conducted prior to the final execution of their artwork. Some themes of the paintings students created were a layered spatial image containing a box in the center with personal letters that the student never mailed; a three panel image about women's issues with the last depicting a woman tied with ropes; and a local legend about a monster who kills fishes with one hand and saves fishes with the other.

In this unit students were working at the Discipline-Based Stage and included content found in Art Making, Art Criticism, Art History, and Aesthetic Strands. Intermediate skills, and some advanced skills, in the use of media and development of art-making concepts and self-criticism were used when they created their paintings. They used intermediate and some advanced terminology and concepts to describe and critique other students' and artists' works and researched contemporary criticism of some of the artwork presented in class. They learned about cultural influences on imagery that artists created in the past that provided a foundation for their projects. The students also learned about contemporary art in respect to an expanding definition about what is included in the art world today.

ART CURRICULA FOR RURAL, ARTISTICALLY TALENTED STUDENTS

Projects ARTS was a 3-year research and development program designed to serve the needs of students with high interest and abilities in the visual and performing arts who attended rural elementary schools in three states. The process of designing and implementing differentiated curricula was guided by a concern for meeting the needs of culturally diverse, artistically talented students (Clark & Zimmerman, 2001b; Marché, 1997). We were influenced by Sleeter and Grant's (1987) and Banks' (1993) approaches to multicultural education in which cultural pluralism, cultural diversity, and social equity for all students is emphasized. Contributions from a variety of groups with diverse cultural values are integrated as important parts of multicultural education. Goals for this approach include celebrating diversity, emphasizing respect for a variety of life styles and human rights, and empowering all members of participating groups. We used these explanations about multicultural programs to help students from different racial and/or ethnic backgrounds retain their cultural heritages and, at the same time, adapt practices considered necessary to function in society as a whole.

Curriculum Writing and Implementation

We established that all Project ARTS initiatives would be locally generated and that we would avoid intervening directly or establishing policies that influenced the climate and organization of any of the cooperating sites or schools. Teachers, staffs, and advisory committee members were encouraged to focus on their school populations and communities when making recommendations about implementing curricula. At each school, staffs built their art curricula around greater understanding of the local community. Emphases were placed on each community's unique members and their histories, local festivals and holiday celebrations, and arts traditions. Studying arts and crafts, musical and oral traditions, and skills of artists and artisans is an obvious vehicle for further study of arts in local communities.

Rural arts students from diverse cultures often possess traits, folkways, and learning styles that differ from those of the dominant culture. Celebration of important holidays and local customs through the arts is a common characteristic of many rural cultures. The staff of Project ARTS emphasized a multiethnic approach to teaching art students by helping them understand and appreciate different categories of objects (e.g., crafts, folk arts, popular arts, women's arts, vernacular art) because these would enable them to appreciate

their own cultural traditions, those of their families, and those of other cultures. As a result, we encouraged teachers at each participating school to form parent and community-based advisory groups to identify and bring local cultural resources into their art curricula.

In this way, Project ARTS programs met Maker's (1982) recommendations to create qualitatively different and justifiable curricula and to take into account what is unique when creating programs for rural, artistically talented students. We initiated teacher development workshops at all sites throughout the course of the project. Along with inclusion of local cultural resources, other areas of concern included differentiating curricula for artistically talented students and nonstudio approaches to art education.

Curriculum differentiation workshops for teachers stressed the need for modification of art programs to feature resources, materials, and opportunities not generally offered in the schools. Ideas included making content, process, product, and learning environments so they were more advanced and sophisticated than in most art curricula (Gross, MacLeod, Dummond, & Merrick, 2001; Gross, Sleap, & Pretorius, 1999; Tomlinson et al, 2002; VanTassel-Baska, 1998). Content modification was explored that would result in differing degrees of abstractness, complexity, variety, and organization, and differing uses of resource materials. Process modifications stressed the potential of developing higher levels of thinking, providing greater evidence of reasoning, and allowing greater freedom of choice than are found in typical art programs. These processes increased group interactions and learning through discovery at a fast and varied pace. Focus was on art products, based on real problems and addressing real audiences, that were to be evaluated and displayed in public arenas. Physical and psychological learning environments were discussed that were student-centered and stressed independence for students engaged with complex ideas and resources.

Additional workshops presenting nonstudio approaches to art education were needed because of the disparities in the experiences teachers brought to this project. While most teachers were reasonably familiar with art making, information about objectives, processes, and resources for doing art-related inquiry often were lacking. Workshops emphasized looking, talking, and writing about art and provided practice and examples for classroom applications (for more information about these processes see Chapter 4).

Variations in level and kinds of in-service instruction for teachers revealed sensitivity to variations in context, culture, and preexisting conditions across sites. When each site initiated Project ARTS programs, participants entered from different starting points and brought individual strengths, problems, and solutions that persisted throughout the 3-year course of the project. Schools in New Mexico began with a general arts program with no specialized art teachers. Schools in South Carolina had well-developed art and music programs, but no provision for gifted or talented students. Schools in Indiana had well-established arts, music, and gifted and talented programs. In each school district, however, existing curricula and programs, based on state guidelines, largely ignored the unique historical and cultural backgrounds of the students who comprised the majority populations in these schools.

Curriculum Units in Indiana

Two Indiana schools, located about 60 miles apart in two different counties, participated in Project ARTS and developed separate arts curricula. In one school, eight units based on local cultures and using art media and processes were developed. Students explored and recorded their homes, community, and environment using still and video cameras. In *Photography: Through Hoosier Eyes*, students analyzed photographs and learned darkroom techniques. *Video Production: An Indiana Cultural Perspective* involved research, script writing, camera handling, and editing skills. Other units, such as *Indiana Landscape Painting: Story of the Land*; *Drawing: Hoosier Farming and Its Traditions*; and *Indiana Mural Painting: Walls Tell a Story* were based on art media and processes and linked to local history and traditions. Research for these units was carried into music classes, where it became the foundation for public performances at local museums and meetings of community organizations. Unit outcomes included a photo scrapbook of students' families and home environments; videotapes; an illustrated recipe book; and an Indiana treasure box that in-

cluded artifacts, craft items, natural objects, and printed information. At the other school, four curriculum units were developed. These included *Architecture in Art* (a survey of architectural styles), *Architecture Reflected in Movement* (creative movement interpreting architectural forms), *History of Stinesville* (history of the community), and *Folk Songs* and *Dances* (pioneer songs and dances with similarities to architectural elements). Student research played a central role throughout and made extensive use of local historians, artists, and community members.

Curriculum Units in New Mexico

The two participating schools in New Mexico were in the same school district. One was a pueblo school administered by the district with oversight provided by a tribal council. Curricula in both schools

Plate 5.3 A drawing by a fourth-grade Project ARTS student of the bandstand in his local community that appears on the cover of a booklet students wrote about Orleans, Indiana

were developed and implemented by special education and gifted and talented teachers who had minimal to moderate knowledge of art education. One notable exception was a pueblo member with an extensive background in fine arts. As a result of participation in this project, he began teaching art on a regular basis to Project ARTS students and to all students at the school. This was unusual because there were almost no specialist art teachers at elementary schools in New Mexico at that time. During Project ARTS, New Mexico teachers met periodically for workshops on basic art education and curriculum writing, and interested parents and local artists often joined these meetings.

At the other school, three thematic curriculum units based on local history were developed and taught. Each featured specific areas of integration with language arts, math, science, and social studies. A curriculum for the year was titled *A Historical and Cultural Journey of Our Community: A Walk Down Main Street*. Subunits included Map Making (drawing, reading, city planning, and topography) and Mural Painting (a mural depicting community history from prehistoric to modern times). Teachers developed curriculum guidelines based on historical, social, and cultural histories of the local community. Their goal was to develop a sense of community history, with its ties to the Spanish culture, through exploration and research about architecture and growth of local businesses and a local church. A wide variety of artists and artisans who live and work in the community came to share their artistry with students and links between the school and community became very strong.

One starting point for creating the art curriculum was a Catholic church, the community's most important gathering place. Restoration of the old church included reconstruction of the exterior and a new fresco painted by muralists from Santa Fe, New Mexico. The fresco was a highlight of the experiences offered; students were able to walk to the church daily to observe, videotape, and photograph the creation of the fresco. They conducted historical research and interviewed adults to discover how the church was constructed, what tools were used, and what were the origins of the materials used.

Students created a timeline showing the stages of their local Main Street as it was developed and

Plate 5.4 An observational drawing by a third-grade Project ARTS student of a religious figure found in a local church that was being renovated

built. They interviewed community members who remembered various stages of community development or whose families were among the founders of the community. Further research examined genealogies of families and how the city and its streets were planned and developed. Students also were engaged in multifaceted research about both local and world architecture, noting how styles changed over the years. Drawing skills were developed using freehand drawing, mechanical tools, and computer programs. In addition, oral histories about grandparents and elders in the community were video-

and audiotaped. Students learned interviewing techniques from a local newspaper reporter and how to use video- and tape-recording equipment, and made illustrations of memorable scenes from stories collected in their interviews. These were combined with transcriptions of oral histories and bound into handmade books for their exhibit called A Journey Down Main Street.

At the Pueblo, traditional art forms include beadwork, jewelry, and the pueblo's famed shell inlay work. The traditional pottery style, passed down through generations, is widely recognized and valued. Painting and drawing in the school are subject to some limitations about symbols that are sacred to the people. Because of the community members' deep respect for these symbols, these are not suitable for drawings or paintings produced in art classes. Landscapes, still lifes, houses, animals, and people, however, were acceptable and popular for student artwork. Teachers framed their curriculum around a series of four media- and process-based units fo-

cused on the theme, Traditions of Art in the Pueblo Culture. Local pueblo life, history, and arts traditions were integrated into all unit lessons. Most lessons featured instruction in Keres, the native language of the pueblo. Art produced in units called *Lines, Shapes, and Patterns in Design* and *Stimulating Creative Thinking* were drawn from traditional motifs. Work on *Exploring Architecture and Three Dimensional Space* began with a study of adobe construction and included suggestions for extensions and visuals for teachers. Local artists and artisans came into classrooms to present their artworks, and parent groups were active in consultation during curriculum development and program advocacy throughout Project ARTS. The coordinating teacher at Santo Domingo School wrote in her journal: "As we have developed and presented activities, we have experienced a special joy that links us. Children have used their native language and English to express their ideas and interests in art and have been encouraged to produce art that emphasizes their cultural environment."

Plate 5.5 A drawing by a third-grade Project ARTS student that is inspired by a Native American shield

Curriculum Units in South Carolina

Project ARTS teachers in all three South Carolina schools worked to write a common curriculum based on the theme, Gullah Life and Culture. Field trips to artists' studios, local historic and cultural sites, and visits by artists to the schools comprised a large segment of the curriculum. In a storytelling unit, students studied the popular role of storytelling in the Gullah culture and learned the importance of storytelling in other cultures. They listened to local storytellers and wrote, illustrated, and videotaped their own stories. Units about family structures and rituals, work, leisure, and celebrations also were developed. In the family structure unit, students researched family roles, food and meals, education, religion, and beliefs that integrated art with other subjects. Study of work and leisure involved students in making games and toys, growing indigo plants to use in creating dyes, and learning to make baskets. Students took many field trips to local historical sites, art galleries, local performances, and artists' studios, and displayed their art work at the Gullah Heritage Days festival and a number of local galleries.

Curriculum Outcomes at All Sites

During the third year, differentiated curricula were extended to include music and dance, and packaged sets of artifacts and print materials were assembled at each site and sent to students and teachers in other states. In addition, recipe books created by students, student-made videotapes, and student-to-student correspondence were exchanged between all Project ARTS schools. In this way, the arts of other cultures were included, compared, and contrasted with local arts traditions. Programs at all sites featured exhibitions and performances of student work in a variety of public arenas. In New Mexico, a local art gallery, the town hall, and the public library were sites for exhibits and presentations of student work. In South Carolina, a working relationship was forged with the historic Penn Center, dedicated to preserving Gullah culture. Students displayed artworks and performed songs, dances, and drumming during the Penn Center's annual Gullah Heritage Days festival. Similarly, Indiana schools forged new relationships with a historical museum, resulting in a

Plate 5.6 A collage produced by a group of fifth-grade Project ARTS students at Beaufort Elementary School as part of a multi-image, illustrated, Gullah story

three-month exhibit of student works and a public performance of music, drama, and dance created to tell local history and folklore.

While all of the schools experienced benefits from these relationships, their communities also profited. Community members validated their history and culture and were encouraged by students' excitement and interest. Students were encouraged to value art in their own cultures as a bridge to understanding art created in a variety of contexts. Exchanges of student-produced videotapes from each school provided understanding of the history and culture of each community that often was engaging, but sometimes disturbing; one student in South Carolina claimed the video from Indiana was "scary" because all the children were white. This led to a valuable discussion about similarities between students in the two schools. Three-way video teleconferencing helped establish a sense of community among the sites. Expecting to find each other strange and different, students were pleased to discover they shared many common interests.

Conclusions of the Study

Teachers are the key to successful outcomes for any large-scale project. It has been demonstrated in rural schools that proposals to make changes often are viewed as threats to community values and stability. Teachers who have taught for many years often are skeptical of change and have witnessed programs that were initiated but soon vanished in their schools. In rural communities, it is clear that time is required to gain teachers' trust and willingness to participate. Teachers also should be aware of different groups of people existing in the communities in which they teach, what these groups value about art, and how they express their values. There has been an influx of students from non-Western cultures into the United States who bring a rich history of art making that should be honored in their new settings. There also are groups, such as Native Americans, Hispanic Americans, African Americans, and those of Appalachian and European descent, whose art legacies date back many generations. Some art traditions of these groups are not compatible with Western fine art aesthetic expectations and, unfortunately, they generally are excluded from art education curricula

in the schools. Although these sites received advisory support from a variety of sources, successful outcomes of the project suggest ways all art teachers in rural communities might enrich and assess their curricula. The diversity of approaches adopted across project sites could be implemented in almost any community.

RECOMMENDATIONS FOR CURRICULA FOR ART TALENT DEVELOPMENT

Several aspects of developing and implementing curricula for art talent development have been presented in this chapter. In particular, the need for a program structure was emphasized. Following are recommendations based on these ideas and issues.

Recommendation 1. When constructing curricula for artistically talented students, a structure for learning experiences in the visual arts should be established, and we believe this structure should explicate educationally sound sequences of concepts. These should have utility for curriculum and program design in visual arts education and applicability to the needs of artistically talented students at all levels. We believe the Expanded Structure for Learning Experiences in the Visual Arts is one such structure that is valuable because it identifies a holistic direction for visual arts education. Its content identifies aspects of the unique contribution that the visual arts can make to all students' education. We also believe a valid visual arts program based on this curriculum model can lead naive students toward a more sophisticated, knowledgeable understanding of, and participation in, the world of the visual arts.

Recommendation 2. In order to create an educational program that goes beyond those ordinarily provided by schools, programs for artistically talented students should develop more advanced learning activities and present content in greater depth and breadth than is typical for any grade level.

Recommendation 3. All aspects of art development are dependent upon conditions that should be considered when constructing curriculum for art talent development. These conditions should include joint efforts among students, a developed subject matter, supportive individuals, levels of support in a culture, and other factors. The degree to which these conditions interact determines the ability of any school art program to educate artistically talented students to their full potential.

Recommendation 4. Deliberately and carefully constructed curricula are essential if artistically talented students are to be able to demonstrate acquisition of skills, knowledge, and understandings about the visual arts. Such achievement is not possible without intensive instruction and specialized resources for art learning. If talented art students are to advance rapidly through all aspects of a visual arts education, teachers and administrators need to realize such progress is dependent upon deliberate instruction. For artistically talented students to achieve mastery levels of learning, they must be led through coherent educational experiences and recognize the relatedness and contributory aspects of each stage. If art is stressed only in terms of untutored self-expression, most individuals will simply attain universal or cultural (or naive to rudimentary) knowledge, skills, and understandings about art.

Recommendation 5. Schools should stress art as a respected body of knowledge and abilities that are necessary so that talented students are able to achieve discipline-based, idiosyncratic, and eventually mastery levels of learning. Where learning about art is highly valued, more students will achieve at higher levels of learning. In the future, there is a strong possibility that these students will continue to support the arts,

appreciate the arts in their lives, and help develop supportive communities for the arts in society.

Recommendation 6. Teachers and staff should determine their own project goals and activities as an important community-building task. Self-identification with their local communities can give art teachers motivation to work toward community-based program goals. Art teachers who want to integrate understanding of their local communities into their curricula for artistically talented students need to involve and build support from a wide base of community members.

Recommendation 7. Focus on local culture in any school should require participation of communities of interested parents, local craftspeople, and historians. These groups should be encouraged to create favorable prospects for continuation of their communities. Public presentations of artistically talented student work should take place locally so student learning can be enhanced. Through such participatory presentations, artistically talented students and teachers can share benefits of their projects. When students' own artistic heritages and those of their local communities are celebrated and incorporated into art curricula, students, parents, teachers, and community members can learn to value the traditions of others and their own heritages. They can begin to take actions to ensure that curricula in local schools are responsive to concepts expressed in their cultures and understand what art is and why it is made, the differences in human experiences, and the variety of contexts in which art has been made and continues to be created.

6 Programming and Assessment

Plate 6.1 A written and illustrated narrative drawing by a seventh-grade student at the IU Summer Arts Institute

A variety of programming opportunities and authentic assessments are available for use in the education of artistically talented students. Although authentic assessment places additional demands on teachers, students, and resources, the final results are well worth the effort. In this chapter, we describe alternatives in educational planning that have been proven to be appropriate for talented art students. Next, a number of locally developed authentic assessment measures are included that have relevance for evaluation of other programs for artistically talented students that emphasize community-based art education. Then examples of a variety of program assessments are offered to determine student and teacher progress and achievements. Finally, recommendations for conducting authentic assessments are given.

PROGRAMMING OPPORTUNITIES FOR ARTISTICALLY TALENTED STUDENTS

There have been few studies, and no large-scale or longitudinal studies, directed toward evaluating the effectiveness of programs developed to meet the needs of artistically talented students. Little research is available, therefore, to direct decision making about programming opportunities for such students. Some of the best sources of information at this time are directed toward intellectually and academically talented students. Some art educators, however, questioned the assumption that all research directed specifically toward the needs of academically gifted students applies directly to artistically talented visual arts students. Several writers have questioned the singular focus of professionals in gifted and talented education on traditional subjects and intellectual or academic aspects of giftedness. Gardner, for example, said, "I was surprised when I got into academic psychology that the arts were almost entirely excluded, as if it would be embarrassing to study them in a cognitive way" (Quoted in Buescher, 1985, p. 182). "Administrators, teachers and parents," Wenner stated, "often find it difficult to accept talent in the arts as being equal in importance to talent in the academic fields" (1985, p. 221). Artistically talented students do need differentiated curricula and programming opportunities designed specifically to serve their unique characteristics and abilities. However, many aspects of programs designed for academically talented students are also applicable for those who are identified as artistically talented. In fact these two groups of students often overlap in their skills and abilities.

There are many definition and semantic problems in relation to terms used to describe appropriate programming opportunities for artistically talented students in the visual arts that should be clarified. Different categories and definitions have been offered for programming opportunities in gifted and talented programs throughout the United States. Based upon review of the literature of gifted and talented education and art education, the following outline contains the most popular programming opportunities and options for gifted and talented students in both general studies and the visual arts (Clark & Zimmerman, 1994).

I. Mixed-ability Grouping
   A. In-class enrichment (e.g., horizontal and vertical enrichment, cooperative learning)
   B. Individualized instruction (e.g., self-study units and mentoring)
II. Ability Grouping
   A. Specialized schools (e.g., magnet schools)
   B. Special classes in regular schools for all of the school day (e.g., classes recruited from one school or classes recruited from several schools)
   C. Special grouping for part of the school day (e.g., pull-out programs, special courses, released time, clubs, artists in residence)
   D. Grouping for school-related activities (e.g., field trips, school/museum visits)
III. Acceleration
   A. Grade skipping
   B. Early admissions
   C. Rapid progress (e.g., accelerated progress, advanced placement, credit by examination)

In the following discussion, programming opportunities and options will be defined and discussed based on most commonly used practices. Alternative points of view will be set forth as they relate to the education of students who are talented in both academics and in the arts as school subjects.

Mixed-Ability Grouping

The most common adaptation of students' abilities has been for teachers to create two or three differentiated ability groups in reading, language arts, science, or other subjects. All students know immediately, however, which group is composed of low, grade-level, or high-ability students.

In-class enrichment has been used to provide highly able students with a variety of learning situations, materials, and activities that provide learning experiences with depth and breadth beyond those offered in regular school programs. Horizontal enrichment consists of nonaccelerated learning activities that maintain students' age and grade groupings, while broadening their interests and introducing them to new subject matters. In vertical enrichment, students are taught sequentially with activities and materials appropriate to their capacities or ability levels, regardless of their ages or grade levels.

Rogers (1991) claimed that full-time enrichment programs produce substantial gains in general achievement, critical thinking, and creativity for gifted students and found that in-class grouping produces substantial academic gains if curricula are differentiated. An advantage of enrichment is that it provides a means for differentiated education for high-ability students in schools and school districts that are not large enough to offer specialized classes. It is inexpensive and demands few changes in a classroom or the general school setting. In art education, enrichment has come to mean providing small-group or individualized instruction to high-ability students who remain in mixed-ability or heterogeneous classes with their age peers. General visual arts classes have been characterized as offering enrichment for all students, but such claims deny the value of appropriate learning activities at various ability levels and do not attend to the abilities and needs of artistically talented students.

There is an ongoing debate in the field of gifted and talented education about the effects of mixed-ability or cooperative learning on the education of high-ability students. Slavin (1980), defined *cooperative learning* as "classroom techniques in which students work on learning activities in small groups and receive rewards or recognition based on their group's performance" (p. 315). Despite the popularity of cooperative learning programs, some educators have challenged claims of its success in regard to high-ability students. Based on her analyses of cooperative learning research, Robinson (1991) recommended that cooperative learning should not be substituted for specialized services for gifted and talented students. At this time, applicability of cooperative learning in the visual arts needs to be further investigated to determine its value for art talent development.

A unit about Japanese art was taught by an art teacher to a fourth-grade class in Fort Wayne, In-

diana (Kruse, 1991). This school had a yearlong emphasis on multicultural education integrated into the regular school curriculum. To highlight each culture, students created a play or presentation offered to the rest of the school. This fourth-grade class was taught a unit about Japanese art and culture, and students were encouraged to work together to share ideas, plans, and materials. Three artistically talented students emerged as group leaders and helped others with ideas and construction problems. One artistically talented boy became interested in origami (paper folding) and became so proficient he began inventing his own origami models.

Khatena (1992) described two models of individualized instruction as methods for accommodating the needs of gifted and talented students. One is "educator-controlled learning" in which individualized education programs are managed by a teacher. Another is "self-directed learning" in which students manage their own learning programs. Many secondary school art teachers individualize their curricula; they assign project standards and expectations without specifying working processes or project characteristics. Students with more highly developed art skills and knowledge may be more comfortable and are more likely to perform well with open-ended learning opportunities and when confronted with problems that stretch their knowledge, skills, and abilities.

There are many commercial instructional resources available to schools that can be used in support of visual arts education as individualized or self-study units. These learning resources often are expensive and are not advertised commonly in art education or general education publications. Teachers who may want to have high-ability students work with self-study units often do not have time to assume responsibility for designing such units for their students, although they can adapt many slide sets available from museums, internet resources, and other materials for this purpose. Learning centers that promote independent study also can be used to guide artistically talented students in regular classrooms by allowing them to select their own content areas or design their own research projects to meet their individual needs.

Self-study units were developed by upper-elementary-level teachers in Worcester, Massachusetts (Hurwitz, 1983). Forty-five schools and 350 students participated in this self-study program with its goal of providing an art program for students without having them leave their regular classes. Students worked on self-study units after they completed their normal workload. Five thematic units of instruction were designed so that written materials, art resources, tools, and media were combined in a series of packets.

Khatena (1992) viewed a *mentor* as anyone in a professional community who evidences success in a particular area and also works with and guides students with an interest in that professional community. Mentorship programs offer viable options for talented visual arts students considering vocational choices such as commercial design, landscape architecture, computer graphics, or sign painting. Art students who are interested in studying areas of art such as painting, printmaking, local crafts, art history, or art criticism also might be engaged with mentors who are experts in these professions.

Ability Grouping

Kulik (1992) defined *ability grouping* as "the separation of same-grade school children into groups or classes that differ markedly in school aptitude" (p. ix). Ability grouping can take many forms, including special schools for gifted students, special class periods when gifted students leave their regular classroom for part of their work, or ability groups within the regular classroom. More contemporary sources include cross-grade grouping, within-class grouping, accelerated classes, and special enriched classes. Ability grouping often is described by different terms, such as *multilevel grouping, multitrack programs, pull-out programs, honors programs, homogeneous grouping*, or *cluster classes*.

Advantages of ability grouping include a reduced range of individual differences, benefiting both teachers and students. Talented students in ability groups are more likely to explore and exchange ideas with greater group acceptance and can pursue more advanced study in selected areas than other student groups. They also are more likely to show significant gain scores on achievement measures (Kulik, 1992). A disadvantage of ability grouping is its cost, since specialized teachers, materials, and extra classrooms may be re-

quired. Ability grouping requires sufficient numbers of students with similar ability levels to justify forming the appropriate groups. An often-voiced concern is that ability grouping may remove students from classrooms who teachers believe are important to include in mixed-ability groups.

In gifted and talented art education, ability grouping has taken many forms, from specialized schools (arts magnet schools) to part-time pull-out programs as part of a school's gifted and talented program. In some elementary and secondary schools, artistically talented students are offered some form of art club as a regular part of the school calendar. More frequently, cluster groups have been formed for specialized, art-related activities, such as field trips to an accessible art museum, visits to an artist's studio, or attendance at an exhibition.

Nonresidential arts schools include arts schools, such as magnet schools, that offer specialized programs for students talented in the visual arts who reside within the sponsoring school district. These schools, at the middle and high school level, usually are focused on strong academic programs as well as intensive, preprofessional instruction in the arts.

Residential arts schools include privately supported boarding schools for the arts and some state-supported schools. Attendance is often selective and not confined to school districts. Rigorous academic and specialized art curricula characterize this kind of school. Founded over 70 years ago, the Interlochen Arts Academy is a private, year-round, secondary, college-preparatory school that offers programs in creative writing, dance, music, theater, theater design and production, and the visual arts.

The most common type of ability grouping for artistically talented students is residential arts programs held during the summer months on college or university campuses. These usually are intensive programs that meet the entire day and require students to become deeply involved in what they are studying. They draw from district, state, national, or international sources. The Interlochen Arts Academy, for example, also offers a summer residential program in music and the visual arts for upper elementary through high school students.

Many communities offer extra-school, nonresidential arts centers that meet for all or part of the academic year and offer programs for artistically talented students. These programs may be offered at school sites, museums, community centers, or other local facilities with a specialized staff. Students often take academic courses in their regular schools and also travel to an extra-school center for specialized arts classes.

In a special in-school program for 15 artistically talented students in rural Modoc, Indiana, students studied about the Serpent Mound in southwestern Ohio (Mullins, 1993). Students learned about characteristics of the Serpent Mound and postulated the significance of the serpent symbol and its relationship to surrounding geographic features. They took a field trip to the Serpent Mound, created a geographic map of that mound, and visited another mound being excavated by a local geologist. They discussed implications of the intentions of the mound builders in relation to time and direction. Then analyses of contemporary earthworks were used as comparative studies of motifs in structures to help make connections between past and contemporary cultures.

A number of arts programs are also provided for artistically talented students by various community agencies with special time schedules. The education staff at the Huntington Art Gallery in Austin, Texas, offered a program as a series of monthly museum visits and carefully constructed preparation and follow-up experiences for students. Preparation materials and previsit lessons enabled teachers to motivate students' interests in specific visits. This enrichment program was focused on understanding major ideas and techniques related to the world of art.

Acceleration

A frequently cited definition of *acceleration* is progress through an education program at a faster rate or a younger age than the norm. Slavin (1990) described three kinds of acceleration: high school advanced placement courses, middle and senior high school advanced courses with differentiated curricula, and elementary school programs in which students stay in one grade and go to other grades for advanced education. Khatena (1992) listed several administrative arrangements for acceleration: early entrance into school, early exit from school, skipping grades, taking senior-level courses in earlier grades, completing 2 or more years of study in 1 year, using mentors, obtaining course credit by examination, taking college-level correspondence courses, and attending private schools.

Decades of writers about acceleration programs for gifted and talented students have warned about social, emotional, and other adjustment problems, although many educators have concluded that such anticipated social and emotional problems are unfounded. Claims about acceleration programs creating skill gaps in core areas of a curriculum also have not been verified by research. VanTassel-Baska (1986, 1992) contended that acceleration is a highly effective technique that improves motivation, confidence, and scholarship; prevents habits of laziness; allows for earlier completion of professional education; and reduces the costs of a student's education. Stanley (1977) added that acceleration programs reduce egotism and arrogance, provide more time to explore careers, create better preparation for advanced study in college, and benefit society by providing more years in a chosen profession and creating better citizens with better education.

An advantage of acceleration is that it requires a minimum of expenditures and can be accommodated in most school settings. Most acceleration of art students occurs in nongraded groupings or out-of-school programs. Such programs in schools are not common because they are dependent upon graded, sequential, articulated curricula. An exception is the Advanced Placement (AP) art program for high school students. Any school in the United States can participate in *Advanced Placement Programs* (1993) in art history, general art studio, and drawing courses. These programs provide experiences at college and professional art school levels for high school students. Advanced placement programs conducted in public and private high schools reflect several administrative arrangements: informal tutoring between one or two students and a teacher, selected grouping within regular art classes, special classes that meet as a distinct group, and programs created in conjunction with museums.

A high school in Winnetka, Illinois, offers gifted and talented students special classes in many subjects based upon Advanced Placement courses. This program allows students to pursue one art discipline for 3 years and to enroll in an AP Studio Art course. Students take field trips to art galleries and other local art events and maintain a sketchbook and journal that includes reviews of exhibits, photographs, notes, and drawings.

Another accelerated program is the International Baccalaureate (IB) program. In this program, students take courses and examinations in six subject areas including art. Candidates take a course in the theory of knowledge and are required to complete an extended essay, based on a research project; they also participate in some form of creative or social services project. In the United States, the IB is offered as an honors curriculum and students can receive college credit for their courses. Artistically talented students can take accelerated IB art courses and move ahead to demanding experiences that require problem solving and complex and abstract thinking.

Summary and Conclusions About Programming Opportunities

There are many alternatives in educational planning that have proven to be appropriate for artistically talented students. Administrators of school-based programs for highly talented art students should create a climate in which flexibility and alternatives in program planning are encouraged. As students progress to higher levels of achievement in the visual arts, if at all possible, they should be encouraged to attend advanced classes and/or study with mentor-artists. They can be offered options that include

1. Attending college or university for advanced art courses
2. Taking part in Advanced Placement art courses
3. Enrolling in correspondence courses with advanced art content
4. Using opportunities to bypass course prerequisites
5. Studying with a mentor for part of the school day
6. Earning full credit for courses by examination

In addition, they need appropriate workspaces so their knowledge, skills, and abilities are developed beyond what normally would be possible at elementary or high school levels in regular art classes. Once programming initiatives are established and implemented for developing art talent, these programs should be evaluated so that students' progress and achievements are assessed appropriately and equitably.

AUTHENTIC ASSESSMENTS AND ART TALENT DEVELOPMENT

There has been an active interest for educators to use authentic assessment methods that more adequately assess student progress and achievements across a wide variety of disciplines (Zimmerman, 1997c). Such assessments involve examination of processes as well as products of learning. Students are given opportunities to engage in learning activities that are integrated, complex, and challenging. Most standardized tests contain multiple-choice items and are based on recall of factual knowledge, isolated skills, and memorization of procedures. They do not require judgment, analysis, reflection, or higher level skills needed for generating arguments and constructing solutions to problems. Standardized tests, however, are easy to administer and score, take a short time to complete, and carry credibility due to their popularity and long history of use.

Standardized testing is viewed by some educators as a political necessity and can be used to report how students achieve in terms of general aspects of education. Assessment instruments that approximate real-life situations and involve integrated, complex, and challenging tasks also can be used to assess individual achievement and higher level thinking skills (Zimmerman, 1997a, 1997b). According to Worthen and Spandel (1991), standardized tests should represent only a small part of assessing learning, whereas teacher-centered assessment should play the greatest role.

Authentic assessment can be viewed as a process in which students are actively engaged in learning and instruction is an integral part of determining their achievements. Most successful authentic assessment programs require collaboration between teachers and students, although the extent of such collaboration will depend upon the educational setting, nature and diversity of students, the teacher's philosophy and teaching strategies, and local directives in respect to program content. Authentic assessments in classrooms should be designed to support instruction, require tasks with instructional value, and be informal, teacher-initiated, adapted to local contexts, sensitive to changes in learning, meaningful to students, and capable of supplying immediately, detailed feedback. Such assessments also should consider that learners differ in their cultural backgrounds, interests, cognitive styles, rates of learning, patterns of development, abilities, work habits, past experiences, and temperaments (Zimmerman, 1992d).

Authentic Assessment in Project ARTS

In Project ARTS, artistically talented students were active participants in creating and constructing their own responses to tasks and demonstrating processes used for solving problems to audiences in public arenas. High-ability rural arts students from diverse backgrounds come to school possessing unique characteristics that should be taken into consideration when evaluation measures are being developed. They can be evaluated more equitably than through the use of standardized tests if flexible and personally constructed criteria are selected to assess their progress and achievement. Evaluation procedures used in Project ARTS had the potential to improve teaching and learning; teachers were educated to use authentic and appropriate evaluation procedures to meet the needs of their rural artistically talented students (Marché & Zimmerman, 2000; Zimmerman, 1997a).

A number of researchers suggest that authentic assessments should employ a variety of measures over time to assess students' use of multiple strategies over a wide range of educational tasks (Herman, Aschbacher, & Winters, 1992; Zimmerman, 1992a). In fact, Schavelson, Baxter, and Pine (1992) recommended that about 10 tasks are needed to assess a student's understanding of a particular subject and caution should be used about relying on portfolio work alone to make judgments about a student's progress and achievements in art. In assessing Project ARTS, many different measures were used to determine student and teacher progress and achievements. Sources for assessment of students' developing understandings, skills, and techniques about the visual arts included

1. Portfolios of unfinished work
2. Peer critiques, self-evaluations, contracts, diary notes, and student journals

3. Journal notes produced by the teacher
4. Video interviews
5. Work produced by students
6. Teacher, student, and parent assessments
7. Group presentations and public art exhibitions

(See Figure 6.1 for a list of assessment procedures broken down by state.)

In addition to evidence of learning in creation of studio art projects, projects that emphasized other arts aspects also were assessed authentically. It was one of the goals of Project ARTS to have students present their artwork publicly in local contexts to community members and other interested audiences. An important aspect of Project ARTS was that parents and community members were involved in assessment programs in their local schools and communities.

Authentic assessment measures that were used were sensitive to pluralistic issues and reinforced academic achievements and self-esteem of students whose backgrounds did not reflect dominant cultures. It was recognized that far greater numbers of students could be viewed as having potential art talent if a variety of assessment tasks and measures were used. Recently, an emphasis on creating art curricula and assessments responsive to local needs of students, families, and communities has been referred to as a community-based orientation to art education (Blandy & Hoffman, 1993). Relationships to historical, social, or religious and spiritual contexts in which students live also were taken into consideration in planning Project ARTS assessments (Sullivan, 1993).

Local Assessment Measures

Unique assessment measures and activities were developed at each site, although all students participating in Project ARTS were videotaped describing selected artworks they created in their schools. This common measure was used to assess student growth throughout their participation. Project ARTS teachers kept reflective journals about their experiences associated with the project, and all the schools created public exhibitions, displaying works in progress and finished products. During the first, second, and third years of the project, local evaluators used interviews and observations with teachers and students to assess progress and achievement

Figure 6.1. Assessment Procedures Used in Project ARTS Programs in Indiana (IN), New Mexico (NM), and South Carolina (SC)

	IN	NM	SC
Student project assessments	√	√	√
Teacher project assessments	√	√	√
Regular teacher assessments		√	
In-process portfolios		√	
Video portfolios	√	√	√
Group critiques	√	√	√
Teacher journals	√	√	√
Teacher interviews	√	√	√
Videotaped interviews with students	√	√	√
Videotaped interviews with teacher and administrator		√	
Student journals	√		√
Videotaped class sessions		√	√
Videoconferences	√	√	√
Art exhibitions	√	√	√
Musical performances	√		√
Reports in newspapers	√	√	√
Student research reports	√	√	√
Final teacher assessments	√	√	√
Final student assessments	√	√	√

of project goals. An outside evaluator conducted surveys and interviews with students, teachers, administrators, parents, community members, and project staff members and used a variety of written materials and artwork produced at each site as parts of a general program assessment. In all three states students kept reflective journals in which teachers provided constructive criticisms. They developed portfolios of work in progress and completed self-evaluation forms and checklists, wrote and published articles about their activities, and had public showings of paintings, films, and other products they created.

Following are a variety of authentic assessment procedures that appear to have been successful in gathering information about student progress and achievement in respect to Project ARTS' goals and objectives.

Indiana Assessments. Assessment of student artworks was based on task commitment, critical and creative thinking, social development, and research skills (see Figure 6.2). Students were rated as exhibiting strengths, performing as required, or needing improvement in various areas of the curriculum. Students also filled out evaluation forms and rated and described their favorite and least favorite activities (see Figure 6.3).

End-of-project self-evaluation forms asked students to comment on various aspects of the particular classes they had taken (see Figure 6.4). Students made a number of suggestions, such as using various graphic programs and new techniques to "learn how they shoot movies in Hollywood." Students also were asked about guest speakers and field trips, what project they enjoyed most, what they learned, and what they would change. Learning how to

Figure 6.2. Project ARTS (IN): Teacher Evaluation Form

Name: _____   Grade: _____   Date: _____

> **S** = exhibits strength in this area
>
> ✓ = performs task as required
>
> **N** = needs to improve in this area

This evaluation is based on your student's performance as exhibited during gifted and talented sessions.

*If blank, student was not evaluated in that category during this grading period.

Task Commitment	Critical/Creative Thinking
_____ Sets own goals	_____ Understands basic concepts
_____ Works independently	_____ Applies concepts to new situations
_____ Completes work on time	_____ Generates/shares new ideas
_____ Uses time effectively	_____ Enjoys a challenge, tries new things
_____ Finishes work accurately	_____ Adds details or combines ideas
_____ Is responsible, brings materials to sessions	
Social Development	**Research Skills**
_____ Is considerate to others	_____ Plans, prepares materials effectively
_____ Seems to enjoy Project ARTS	_____ Organizes information skillfully
_____ Participates in discussions	_____ Completes required assignment
_____ Accepts other ideas	_____ Shares finished product
_____ Shows leadership in decision making	

Number of missed assignments during 9 weeks: _____

Comments: _____

_____

_____

_____

express themselves and doing things on their own was important for several students: "One thing I learned was that you can always try and eventually you will succeed." The whole project received very positive comments, and many students commented that they enjoyed seeing their work displayed in a variety of public places.

The art teacher wrote in her journal about what she considered strengths in Project ARTS policies and practices:

Project ARTS put my students in touch with community resources, made them aware of vocational possibilities in the arts, and helped

Figure 6.3. Project ARTS (IN): Student Assessment Form

Name: _____ Date: _____

Please think carefully about each of the following items. Rate each one with appropriate number, using this scale:

1 = like very much	2 = like	3 = OK	4 = dislike	5 = did not like at all

    1. Practicing for the program.   _____
    2. Doing artwork for the various projects.   _____
    3. Learning the dulcimer.   _____
    4. Performing the program.   _____
    5. Doing research for my part in the program.   _____
    6. Taking field trips for my part in the program.   _____
    7. Listening to guest speakers for Project ARTS.   _____
    8. Writing to pen pals.   _____
    9. Learning the songs and music for the program.   _____
  10. Reading the literature for diversity study.   _____
  11. Using the computer in the art room.   _____
  12. Working with Project ARTS students.   _____
  13. Working with teachers.   _____

Now, use the same scale above, but instead of sharing your feelings for the various items, indicate with the number how much you think you learned from each.

1 = like very much	2 = like	3 = OK	4 = dislike	5 = did not like at all

    1. Practicing for the program.   _____
    2. Doing artwork for the various projects.   _____
    3. Learning the dulcimer.   _____
    4. Performing the program.   _____
    5. Doing research for my part in the program.   _____
    6. Taking field trips for my part in the program.   _____
    7. Listening to guest speakers for Project ARTS.   _____
    8. Writing to pen pals.   _____
    9. Learning the songs and music for the program.   _____
  10. Reading the literature for diversity study.   _____
  11. Using the computer in the art room.   _____
  12. Working with Project ARTS students.   _____
  13. Working with teachers.   _____

Just write in the answers to the following:

1.   What was your favorite activity this year with Project ARTS? Why?

2.   Which was your least favorite activity this year with Project ARTS? Why?

3.   Which activity do you feel you learned the most from? Why?

4.   What has Project ARTS taught you about yourself?

Figure 6.4. Project ARTS (IN): Final Student Evaluation Form

Name _____ Age _____ Grade _____

Project ARTS groups: _____

What group or project did you enjoy most, and why?

What were your impressions of the special speakers and guests?

Did you attend the Project ARTS day at the Monroe County Museum?

Comments:

What was one thing you learned or gained through participation in Project ARTS?

What would you change?

Comments about Project ARTS:

them learn about a variety of methods so they could do more effective artwork. Students were given opportunities to become aware of the history of the surrounding community, and the visibility of the performance and art show at the end made these experiences particularly rewarding.

The gifted and talented coordinator also was the Project ARTS art teacher and she wrote:

During this project, my students interacted with students from the Gullah culture in South Carolina and from the Hispanic and Pueblo cultures in New Mexico. As a part of our program, we exchanged lesson plans and curricula, studied our own local cul-

tures, made and exchanged videos and photos, exchanged pen pal cards, and talked to one another through video conferences. Through these exchanges, students learned that others were much like themselves, even though they may be from different backgrounds.

New Mexico Assessments. Teachers kept personal notebooks during the duration of Project ARTS and documented lesson effectiveness and student attitudes toward lessons. Each student kept a working portfolio of developing ideas, mastering new ideas, and experiments with new media and techniques. Students were involved in the assessment process and asked to explain their ideas, choices of materials, and use of design elements and principles.

Comparing and contrasting their own works over time helped students see their own achievements. During the second year, the art teacher evaluated student progress and achievement based on written forms and interviews with students (see Figure 6.5). Students were awarded points based upon motivation and enthusiasm in class work, their art talent and desire to work, completing assignments and projects, interest in outside activities, and completing sketchbooks and other tasks. During the final year, the art teacher assessed students with the following criteria: sketchbooks demonstrating techniques taught in classes; portfolios of works in progress and completed; attending classes regularly; contributing art work to newsletters, contests, and bulletin boards; and sharing artwork and techniques with fellow students and family members.

A special education teacher indicated students were evaluated on an ongoing basis, using students' work on murals and in their portfolios. Work on the murals and other projects helped students grow artistically and had impact on their classroom work and their feelings of self-esteem. The principal stated her overwhelming support for Project ARTS: "Students are more aware of art and efforts of the community. We were able to get a lot of artwork by local artists; several artists loaned works to be hung around the school. Awareness of art has been heightened, and there is no vandalism."

South Carolina Assessments. One teacher used individual project evaluation forms and a summary of student achievements to assess individual projects, overall progress, and self-evaluations (see Figure 6.6). Students' comments addressed personal satisfaction with completed products and noted their pleasure in being in the program. Parent surveys included open-ended items and all students reported they were excited about learning about Gullah culture. One parent commented: "She really liked Gullah culture because it was close to her home. She never knew all that was just out her back door." The biggest benefits children received from the program included exposure to different cultures, growth in self-esteem, growing interest in art, dancing and drumming in public performances, and participating in a variety of art projects and experiences based on different cultures.

Students filled out evaluation forms about their individual projects (see Figure 6.7). One was a trip to a local art gallery to view a local artist's works. Students explained what they thought the artworks were about and reported themes present in the artworks. Student responses in their journals indicated progress from early in the program and reflections of their progress. One student commented, "I looked at my work and compared it with work I did last year, and I was impressed by how my work had changed."

Students filled out final assessment forms and addressed their favorite projects, what they learned, what being in the program meant to them, whether the entrance test was fair, whether the right students were chosen, and what they would change. Students' comments included: "I learned I can do whatever I want, if I put my mind to it," and "I learned how creative I can be." Teacher evaluation forms included a checklist and a measurement scale. Four items addressed art skills and achievements and other art behaviors. Teacher comments addressed a student who evidenced high levels of achievement and one who did not:

He was always dependable and ready to try any task asked of him, but rarely put himself forward the first months. Over the two years, his artwork matured and his eagerness to help has continued. His enthusiasm and willingness to cooperate in class and his eagerness to try new or unfamiliar tasks helps motivate his peers. He is able to apply new information to his work and to process criticism and apply it to new situations.

She can accomplish the goals she wants, however, she preferred the glamour and importance of being in the project to the actual challenge of mastering new skills in her artwork. She quickly looses interest, frequently doesn't finish her work, and does not respond well to criticism.

The local site consultant in South Carolina commented:

Everyone involved in Project ARTS gained from the experience. The training and materi-

Figure 6.5. Project ARTS (NM): Native American Student Creativity Behavioral Checklist

Student's Name: _____ Age: _____

School: _____ Grade: _____

Note: Behaviors listed may or may not be observed in a classroom environment. Panelists stated that a Native American student would be more likely to display some of the behaviors among other Native Americans, at social gatherings or at home, and that some students may not necessarily express creative behaviors verbally.

Directions: Circle the number that best describes this student as you know him/her:

1 = never	2 = rarely	3 = sometimes	4 = frequently	5 = always

1. Displays intellectual playfulness; fantasizes; imagines; manipulates ideas by elaboration or modification   1   2   3   4   5
2. Is a high risk taker; is adventurous and speculative   1   2   3   4   5
3. Has a different criteria for success   1   2   3   4   5
4. Displays a keen sense of humor reflective of own cultural background   1   2   3   4   5
5. Is individualistic; does not fear being different   1   2   3   4   5
6. Predicts from present information   1   2   3   4   5
7. Displays curiosity about many things; has many interests   1   2   3   4   5
8. Generates large number of ideas or solutions to problems/questions   1   2   3   4   5
9. Demonstrates exceptional ability in written expression; creates stories, poems, etc.   1   2   3   4   5
10. Is sensitive to color, design, arrangement, and other qualities of artistic appreciation and understanding   1   2   3   4   5
11. Is sensitive to melody, rhythm, form, tone, mood, and other qualities of music appreciation   1   2   3   4   5
12. Demonstrates exceptional ability/potential in one of the fine arts (depending on experience and nurturance)   1   2   3   4   5
13. Demonstrates unusual ability in one of the practical arts (wood, handicrafts, metal, mechanics, etc.)   1   2   3   4   5
14. Demonstrates exceptional skill and ability in physical coordination activities   1   2   3   4   5
15. Shows interest in unconventional careers   1   2   3   4   5
16. Improvises with commonplace materials   1   2   3   4   5
17. Is emotionally responsive (may not overtly respond in classroom environment)   1   2   3   4   5
18. Demonstrates ability in oral expression (may not be orally expressive in classroom environment)   1   2   3   4   5
19. Is aware of own impulses and open to the irrational in self   1   2   3   4   5

Plate 6.2 An abstracted bird image created by a student at Santo Domingo Elementary School

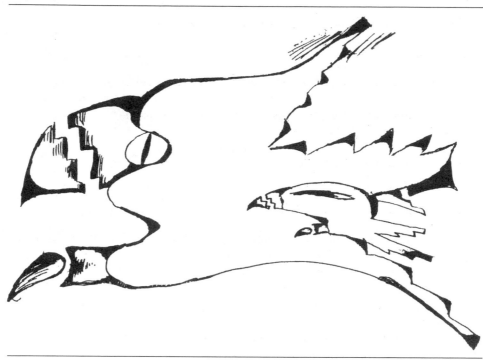

als provided established a sound basis to begin our work. Visitations with other states, ethnic groups, and schools brought different perspectives and a richness to the diversity reflected in their art. The program also offered many professional development activities with direct bearing on classes to help preservice and in-service teachers identify students, create curricula, and devise authentic assessments.

In her journal, an art teacher wrote: "Project ARTS has been a learning experience for me in so many ways. I am going to change the way I teach because of it."

Conclusions About Assessment in Project ARTS

A final report on Project ARTS was delivered to the federal government that incorporated all findings from internal evaluators' reports, the external evaluator's report, and feedback from administrators, teachers, site directors, artists, and community members. It was claimed, in the internal report, that numerous decisions made in the structure of the proposal added greatly to the probability for lasting success of project goals (Zimmerman, 1999). First was the decision to emphasize community-based determination of project activities and outcomes. Teachers and on-site staff were empowered to assess their own situations, select their own directions, and plan their own means to achieve ends, all within the general framework of the project. By not insisting on uniformity across sites, the project directors acknowledged local conditions, needs, and appropriate methods for meeting those needs. At every site, there were connections to community arts and artists and opportunities were created for parents and community members to become involved with and appreciate student's accomplishments.

Several aspects of authentic assessments hold particular significance for artistically talented students from diverse populations. Authentic assessments require sharing that actively involves learners and their teachers in determining the means, methods, criteria, and areas to be assessed. Because teachers

Figure 6.6. Project ARTS (SC): Student Assessment Form

Project: _____

Student's Name: _____ Grade: _____

Circle the most suitable number to respond to the following questions:

	Excellent	Fair	Poor
1. Did the student exhibit appropriate listening qualities?	1	2	3
2. Was the student an active participant in the discussion?	1	2	3
3. Does the student present creativity and originality in artwork?	1	2	3
4. Was the student productive in his/her work?	1	2	3
5. Is the student's work pleasing to the eye?	1	2	3
6. Was the student following directions for the lesson?	1	2	3
7. Did the student's work successfully communicate his/her ideas?	1	2	3
8. Did the student's work show improvement over time?	1	2	3

Comments: _____

_____

_____

and students were involved in authentic assessments, their socially and culturally constructed understandings, individual goals, and unique strengths became integral to the assessment process. Such assessments help students become reflective about their learning, cultivate skills of self-assessment, and result in an internal focus of control or empowerment.

Authentic Assessment at the Indiana University Summer Arts Institute

Authentic assessment procedures at the Indiana University Summer Arts Institute (IUSAI) served to help select students for entrance into the institute, provided feedback about teaching/learning processes, demonstrated to what extent students and teachers had met their objectives, informed students and their parents about student progress and achievements and where improvements were necessary, and encouraged changes in the current program.

An advanced painting class at IUSAI will be described as an example of how authentic assessment was conducted at the classroom level (Zimmerman, 1992a, 1997b). This class met for 11 instructional days from 10:00 am to 12:00 noon and was the most advanced of three painting classes offered during the summer of 1988. The 20 students in this class were to enter Grades 8 through 11 the following fall. Because this was a special summer program, students received no high school credit for their participation and no formal grades were given.

We decided to use a variety of assessment measures to evaluate students' progress and achievements during the 2-week session they attended this program. We followed Schavelson et al.'s (1992) suggestion that about 10 tasks are needed to assess a student's understanding of a particular subject area. In assessing the painting class, 12 different measures were used to determine student and teacher progress and achievements.

Figure 6.7. Project ARTS: Final Student Evaluation Form

Student's Name: _____ Grade: _____ Teacher: _____

	Seldom	*Occasionally*	*Frequently*	*Always*
Arrives to class on time				
Attends class meetings				
Draws in sketchbook				
Brings sketchbook to class				
Is quiet and listens when asked				
Participates in class discussions				
Uses time well				
Puts effort into his/her artwork				
Is self-motivated, self-stimulated to make art				
Uses his/her own ideas to make original art				
Creates skillful, well-organized compositions				
Uses media effectively				
Works on art projects until they are finished				
Demonstrates desire to improve own art work				

Screening Procedures

As part of an application packet submitted to the Summer Arts Institute, students were asked to tell why they desired to attend this summer program. They were given an entire page to respond and no specific guidelines to follow. Because desire and interest are important factors in identifying high-ability students, this open-ended question provided valuable information about the values and interests of students applying to attend the institute. One of our objectives was not only to identify students with recognized talent, but also those with potential talent who had high interest in the visual arts and a persistence of expressive effort.

Criteria used for selection were:

1. Highly interested in one or more of the visual arts
2. Experienced and participating in one or more of the visual arts
3. Highly motivated and self-confident in one or more of the arts

4. Having achievement test scores at least two grades higher than the student's present grade
5. Having intelligence measured above average intelligence
6. Presently placed in a local gifted and talented program.

Students had to meet at least three of the six requirements to be considered for acceptance into the IUSAI. We did this to throw a wide net and capture students with both potential and demonstrated talent in the visual arts. We also did not want to privilege students who were economically advantaged and could afford extra lessons or other enriched art experiences.

Students were asked to reply to this statement on the nomination form: "Tell us why you would like to attend the Summer Arts Institute and describe your previous art experiences." Responses of the students who later attended the advanced painting class varied in length and content and differed according to their backgrounds and previous art experiences. Most of the students at the insti-

Plate 6.3 A linoleum print of her family made by a third grade student at J.J. Davis Elementary School

tute came from rural towns in Indiana, and half received scholarship aid to help defray costs. The following are short excerpts from one girl's application form that typify the kinds of responses we received. Included with this student's responses are statements by her mother, principal, and art teacher. These nominations provided ample evidence that this student had the interest and ability to have a successful institute experience.

Student's response:
    I have always loved art and am especially interested in drawing. In my free time I like to draw sketches of people and landscapes. I like to create people from my own imagination. I also am interested in photography and although I have only had limited experience in this art form, I have a strong interest in it. I presently am considering a career in art.

Principal's recommendation:
    She is a good student who is self-motivated, intuitive, and creative and is multitalented and has excellent relationships with teachers and peers.

Art teacher's recommendation:
> She is highly creative and does excep-
> tional art work. She has an outgoing
> personality and fine wit and will enjoy
> attending the institute.

Parent's comments:
> She has been interested in drawing since
> age 4 and draws and doodles whenever
> possible. She loves to do artwork and has
> won the following awards [which were
> listed].

Class Assessment

As part of a larger research study, Zimmerman observed every class meeting and interviewed the teacher of the advanced painting class (for a detailed description of this painting teacher, Mark, see Chapter 4 in this book). Information was collected by means of notes; tapes of five teaching sessions that included individual and group critiques by the painting teacher; slides of classroom activities; and student portfolios containing sketches, related resources, artwork in process and completed pieces; students' sketchbook journals; taped teacher interviews; and two art teacher–observer journals. In addition, three focus group meetings were held with six to eight students in each group, and two doctoral students individually interviewed all 20 students in the class in respect to their reflections about their artwork, experiences in the painting class, and the institute in general. After the institute concluded, observations of the final exhibition of student work and evaluations were collected from students, teachers, and parents.

Teacher Observer Responses

The painting class served as a field site for two art teachers enrolled in a practicum experience in a class taught in conjunction with the institute at the Artistically Talented Program (ATP). These teachers were observers for all sessions of the painting class and kept journals with their observations and reflections about the class. Their journals were based on their observation notes in which they raised questions and concerns and described dilem-

mas and how these problems were resolved. In addition, they were required to write summary reflections after each class observation and a final summary about their entire practicum experience.

One of the two observers noted that Mark, the art teacher, focused on problem-solving skills and introduced other art disciplines into his curriculum:

> He noticed that some of the kids were acting
> bored with their paintings and he pointed
> out that the reason people get bored when
> they paint is that they are not convinced
> that their work is "real." He brought up that
> painting involved problem solving and the
> students had to use analysis to figure out
> what the problem was in their own work. He
> said not to assume the whole painting is
> "wrong" and told them to analyze exactly
> where the problem lies. I thought this was a
> great way to introduce critical-thinking
> skills.

She also wrote

> I love the way he introduces art history, art
> criticism, and aesthetics into a studio class! It
> is a perfect example how this can be done
> informally and not in a lecture situation."
> This observer also noted one problem she had
> with the teacher's strategies: "This man has a
> lot of power and these children could easily
> fall under his spell and take some of his
> remarks literally, when what he really wants
> to do is make them think."

The other observer noted that when a student was frustrated, the teacher told her to solve her painting problems and "don't just dump the work. Stand back and coolly analyze. . . . What do you need to do to make this work better? Remember anyone can do this . . . this is just a skill . . . like brushing your teeth." This observer also commented: "the teacher used portraits by artists from many different cultures and compared the different moods, textures, atmospheres . . . created in their works and had the students contrast these qualities with their own works." He also noted that the teacher concluded the last class with these words: "You all did extremely well. Remember painting is filled with stress and frustrations, but you can succeed." In addition, he also felt the individual student critiques were valuable and encouraged students to add comments during class critiques, even though he "dominated the discussions and did not pose many questions that might have encouraged further discussion."

Both observers commented on the final exhibition in which work was chosen and hung by the students. Both works in progress and completed pieces were included, as well as excerpts from journals that accompanied the work. One of the observers wrote in her journal about the educational value of the final exhibit and how participating in the painting practicum would affect her future teaching experiences:

> When everything was up in its entirety, I could see what these kids accomplished in a short period of time. I talked to several parents at the exhibit and they seemed proud of their kids and said they learned a lot about art and the processes their children went through to create their "masterpieces." I learned a lot of things that I can take back to my own art classroom; especially, I know I will keep a reflective journal for all my teaching experiences.

Student Assessments

Authentic assessments were conducted to determine student progress and achievement in the painting class through students' sketchbook and journals, photographs and slides of their work in progress and completed portraits, interviews, focus groups, and final institute evaluation forms. In interviews and focus groups, students were unanimous in their approval of the painting class. They said they learned a lot in the class about painting techniques, how to look at art in a "different way," and expressing themselves through paint media. A number of students reported they gained more confidence as they progressed through the class. Group critiques were cited as a means of "learning about our own mistakes and someone else's too." One student said about the painting teacher:

He gives you an idea about what he wants you to do. He makes you go off on your own, too. If he sees you are getting bored he diverts your attention to something else by telling stories. I think he is a really good teacher and a good person, too.

Another student described what she was learning about painting techniques:

> I could never get noses right. I learned how to do that and how to make highlights, the tones, the darks and lights; now I understand how to do it. My style is changing too, and I've learned through examples and class demonstrations.

Still another student expressed his feelings about his frustrations and accomplishments:

> I enjoyed meeting the other students and being with people like myself. The classes were hard and I had to push myself to make my self-portrait look alive and real. I didn't enjoy the work, but I enjoy knowing I will appreciate what happened here in the future.

Student Final Assessments of IUSAI

When students were asked to complete an evaluation form for all programs at the end of the institute, one question they were asked was what they would most likely remember about their experiences at the institute. One fairly typical comment was about grading: "We did not get grades at the institute. I worry about grades all the time. I am not [a bad student] though I have a C average in school subjects. Here at the institute I feel like I am a real person." In respect to understanding values and beliefs about their own and other cultures, one student wrote: "I learned not all the world is as dull as Indiana. There is more out there." Another wrote: "I learned a lot about different people all over the world. I also learned a lot about myself, too." Most students were excited about sessions in which they were looking and talking about art and were able to assess their own art work and that of others. One student wrote: "It's neat to see

Plate 6.4 Students painting "big eyes" in Mark's IU Summer Arts Institute painting class

and understand why other people in other places create art." Another wrote: "My imagination really worked. Nobody ever asked me what I thought about art. I loved it."

Parent Assessments

After the 1988 Summer Arts Institute concluded, parents or guardians of students in the painting class were sent open-ended written evaluations of their children's progress as well as evaluation forms for them to fill out. On forms returned to the institute, parents reported that their children enjoyed the experience, learned about painting techniques and skills, were able to reflect on their experiences, matured socially and emotionally, learned to accept criticism, and appreciated Mark's teaching strategies.

An example of one parent's response to questions on the evaluation form follows:

Question: *What were your child's overall impressions of the painting class? What words were used to describe the class?*

She loved her experience—every aspect. She used words such as "great," "learned so much," "never boring," and "learned so much about myself too."

Question: *What experience was talked about the most? Why was this experience remembered so vividly?*

The painting teacher and the way he constructively criticized and appreciated her work. His respect for the students as young artists was evident when he invited them to his studio for stimulation and to see how he worked.

Question: *What else was remembered about the painting class?*

The teacher's manner—kind, but with specific suggestions for improvement. He started his comments with, "This is good, but it could be better."

Question: *As a parent or guardian, your reactions for future programs are important. On the back of this form, please describe your reactions to the program. What should stay the same? What should be changed?*

My daughter is a farm girl and she enjoyed socializing. . . . There are a lot of kids from different backgrounds and it's a good experience for kids to meet other kids with different life styles. Thank you for letting my daughter attend this summer.

Another parent's response to the last question also involved opportunities her son had to socialize with others with similar interests: "We are very enthusiastic about the program and delighted that our son had an opportunity to participate. It was important for him to be with a large group of kids with similar inclinations. He thoroughly enjoyed the intense instruction and the social setting where he was able to get to know a group of kids and forge friendships in a short period of time." Still another parent commented:

Approaching ordinary items from extraordinary points of view always helps to foster open-minded thinking. Kids really are quite dogmatic in their own groups in an effort to create identity separate from how they view adults. Any process that inspires them to think on their own is a positive one. Introducing students to other cultures and other worlds is terrific.

There were a number of suggestions for improvement from parents. Many of these suggestions were about ways in which the management of the institute as a whole could be improved. There were a few suggestions for improving the painting classes, such as "Featuring an artist or a school, such as Impressionism, and sending a list of resources on these topics to students before they attend the Institute—a few readings could be sent out as well."

Student suggestions for improvement included allowing participants to take more than one painting class during the institute, adding an art careers class or evening sessions on this topic, lengthening the program to 3 weeks to allow for "more in-depth advancement of individual art work. This would also contribute to a more relaxed atmosphere. We could also have a greater number of rest periods or catch-up days for completing art work." A number of these suggestions were discussed with the painting teacher along with his own suggestions for change. Several of these suggestions and critiques from the teacher-observers were incorporated into the painting class that Mark taught at the institute the following summer.

Reflections on the Assessment Process

Most of the goals for the institute, studio classes, and the specific painting class were met as determined by the authentic assessment procedures just described. Students in the painting class did gain new knowledge, skills, and understandings about the visual arts. They also had many opportunities to interact with others with similar interests and abilities. In the painting class, they also became proficient in critiquing their own artwork and that of others, developed vocabulary to discuss works of art, and expanded their abilities to make informed decisions about their own artwork

and that of others. The painting teacher's goals for the students to learn about themselves and their artwork and to experience "what it is like to be an artist" also seem to have been achieved (see Chapter 4 for a description of the painting teacher's strategies).

Authentic assessments reported here were specifically designed for the context in which the institute took place and the variety of students who participated in experiences in the painting class taught by Mark. Authentic assessments, conducted in other settings would employ different tasks and measures to determine whether program goals have been accomplished. Conducting authentic assessments can empower teachers and provide them with effective instructional tools and a new emphasis on teaching relevant problem solving skills.

RECOMMENDATIONS FOR CONDUCTING AUTHENTIC ASSESSMENT

As a result of conducting authentic assessments at Project ARTS, the Indiana University Summer Arts Institute, and a number of other programs for artistically talented students, we would like to make the following recommendations about authentic assessment.

Recommendation 1. Those who employ authentic assessment measures need to adapt their research strategies to meet individual student and community needs. Adoption of authentic assessment as a research tool requires rethinking of relationships between researchers and subjects, data, and the community within which research is conducted. It requires that researchers and subjects become coinvestigators as research instruments are negotiated rather than imposed. In addition, when conducting authentic assessments, both products and processes should be taken into consideration and teachers should collaborate with students to solve difficult technical, expressive, and cognitive problems.

Recommendation 2. In order for authentic assessment goals to be met, we suggest that the following measures be used when conducting authentic assessments

Plate 6.5 A photo-collage by a seventh grader at the IU Summer Arts Institute that represents various factors and circumstances in her life based on the theme My Family and Me

1. Select students for special programs
2. Demonstrate to what extent teachers and students meet their objectives
3. Inform students about what they need to do to improve
4. Provide teachers with information that can help them recognize their successes and make revisions when appropriate
5. Establish a valid assessment system with tasks that are worthwhile, meaningful, and significant
6. Provide a vehicle for translating feedback to parents to help them understand their children's growth
7. Require a final public exhibition where students can demonstrate skills of inquiry and expression and their abilities to respond effectively and imaginatively to a topic.

Recommendation 3. Learning experiences in the visual arts often are difficult to describe with simplistic and predictable outcomes that are not sensitive to students' needs and the processes they experience or the products they create. With the advent of standards in areas of the visual arts and gifted and talented education, it is important that the strengths of authentic assessment—including being integrated, challenging, meaningful, and related to real-life situations, not be compromised. Assessing students authentically can meet requirements of standards at national and state levels and far exceed their minimum requirements.

Recommendation 4. It is important to consider individual student's interests, abilities, cognitive styles, rates of learning, patterns of developed abilities, motivations, work habits, and temperaments, as well as ethnicity, sex, and social class. Authentic assessment measures should be sensitive to pluralistic issues and reinforce achievements of all students, not just those from a particular background or social class. Students' accomplishments should be focused on and celebrated so they are motivated to learn, and teachers will be provided tools that allow them to deliver quality instruction to all students, including those who are artistically talented. In this way, teaching and learning directed toward art talent develop can be nurtured and supported at local, state, and national levels.

Recommendation 5. The emphasis of authentic assessment programs should be to improve teaching and learning at the classroom level. Although authentic assessments make additional demands on teachers, students, and resources, besides requiring extra time to plan and develop materials and arrange meetings between teachers and students, the wealth of information gleaned by engaging in meaningful dialogues that result in better teaching and learning is more than worth the effort.

References

Achter, J. A., Benbow, C., & Lubinski, D. (1997). Rethinking multipotentiality among intellectually gifted: A critical review and recommendatons. *Gifted Child Quarterly, 41*(1), 5–15.

Advanced Placement Program. (1993). Evanston, IL: College Entrance Examination Board.

Anderson, T. (1992). Drawing upon the eye, the brain, and the heart. *Art Education, 45*(5), 45–50.

Anderson, T. (1995). Toward a cross-cultural approach to art criticism. *Studies in Art Education, 36*(4), 198–209.

Andrews, U. (1994). Boxes: Private/Public spaces. In E. Zimmerman (Ed.), *Making a difference: Differentiated curriculum units by teachers in the 1993 Artistically Talented Program* (pp. 3–11). Bloomington: Indiana University, School of Education, and the Indiana Department of Education, Gifted and Talented Program.

Ayer, F. C. (1916). *The psychology of drawing with special reference to laboratory teaching.* Baltimore, MD: Warwick & York.

Banks, J. A. (1993). Approaches to multicultural curriculum reform. In J. A. Banks & C. M. Banks (Eds.), *Multicultural education: Issues and perspectives* (2nd ed., pp. 195–214). Boston: Allyn & Bacon.

Barrett, T. (1990). *Criticizing photographs: An introduction to understanding images.* Mountain View, CA: Mayfield.

Barrett, T. (1995). *Lessons for teaching art criticism.* Bloomington, IN: ERIC/Art.

Becker, H. S. (1964). Introduction. In H. S. Becker (Ed.), *The other side: Perspectives on deviance* (pp. 1–5). New York: Free Press.

Belenky, M. F., Clinchy, B. M., Goldberger, N. R., & Tarule, J. M. (1986). *Women's ways of knowing: The development of self, voice, and mind.* New York: Basic Books.

Blandy, D., & Hoffman, E. (1993). Toward an art education of place. *Studies in Art Education, 35*(1), 22–33.

Bloom, B. S. (1985). *Developing talent in young people.* New York: Ballantine.

Borland, J. H. (1986). IQ tests: Throwing out the bath water, saving the baby. *Roeper Review, 8*(2) 163–167.

Brittain, W. L. (1961). Creative art. In L. A. Fliegler (Ed.), *Curriculum planning for the gifted* (pp. 201–221). Englewood Cliffs, NJ: Prentice-Hall.

Broudy, H. S. (1972). *Enlightened cherishing.* Urbana: University of Illinois Press.

Broudy, H. S. (1987). *The role of imagery in learning.* Los Angeles: Getty Center for Education in the Arts.

Buescher, T. M. (1985). Seeking the roots of talent: An interview with Howard Gardner. *Journal of Education of the Gifted, 8*(3), 179–187.

Buros, O. (Ed.). (1972). *The seventh mental measurements yearbook.* Highland Park, NJ: Gryphon Press.

Burton, J., Horowitz, R., & Ables, H. (2000). Learning in and though the arts: The question of transfer. *Studies in Art Education, 41*(3), 228–257.

Chapman, L. H. (1978). *Approaches to art in education.* New York: Harcourt, Brace, Jovanovich.

Chetelat, F. J. (1982). *A preliminary investigation into the life situations and environments which nurture the artistically gifted and talented child.* Unpublished doctoral dissertation, Pennsylvania State University, College Park.

Clark, B. (1979). *Growing up gifted: Developing potential of children at home and at school.* Columbus, OH: Merrill.

Clark, G. (1984). Establishing reliability of a newly designed visual concept generalization test in the visual arts. *Visual Arts Research, 10*(2), 73–78.

Clark, G. (1987). Early inquiry, research, and testing of children's art abilities. In G. Clark, E. Zimmerman, & M. Zurmuehlen, (Eds.), *Understanding art testing* (pp. 1–18). Reston, VA: National Art Education Association.

Clark, G. (1989). Screening and identifying students talented in the visual arts: Clark's Drawing Abilities Test. *Gifted Child Quarterly, 33*(3), 98–105.

Clark, G. (1992). Child art, art teachers and gifts: Implications of the concept of artistic giftedness. *Images, 3*(3), 2.

Clark, G. (1993). Judging children's drawings as measures of art abilities. *Studies in Art Education, 34*(2), 72–81.

Clark, G. (1997). Identification. In G. Clark, & E. Zimmerman, *Project ARTS: Programs for ethnically diverse, economically disadvantaged, high ability, visual arts students in rural communities* (pp. 17–87). Washington, DC: U.S. Department of Education. (ERIC Document Reproduction Service No. ED 419 762 and ED 419 765)

Clark, G., Day, M., & Greer, W. D. (1987). Discipline-based art education: Becoming students of art. *Journal of Aesthetic Education, 24*(2), 129–193. (Republished in *Discipline-based art education: Origins, meaning, and development,* pp. 129–193, by R. A. Smith, Ed., 1989, Urbana: University of Illinois Press)

Clark, G., & Wilson, T. (1991). Screening and identifying gifted/talented students in the visual arts with Clark's Drawing Abilities Test. *Roeper Review, 13*(2), 92–97.

Clark, G., & Zimmerman, E. (1978a). *Art/design: Communicating visually.* Blauvelt, NY: Art Education.

Clark, G., & Zimmerman, E. (1978b). A walk in the right direction: A model for visual arts education. *Studies in Art Education, 19*(2), 34–49.

Clark, G., & Zimmerman, E. (1981). Toward a discipline of art education. *Phi Delta Kappan, 63*(1), 53–55.

Clark, G., & Zimmerman, E. (1983). Toward establishing first class, unimpeachable art curricula prior to implementation. *Studies in Art Education, 24*(2), 77–85.

Clark, G., & Zimmerman (1984). *Educating artistically talented students.* Syracuse, NY: Syracuse University press.

Clark, G., & Zimmerman, E. (1986). A framework for educating artistically talented students based on Feldman's and Clark and Zimmerman's models. *Studies in Art Education, 27*(3), 115–122.

Clark, G., & Zimmerman, E. (1987). *Resources for educating artistically talented students.* Syracuse, NY: Syracuse University Press.

Clark, G., & Zimmerman, E. (1988a). Professional roles and activities as models for art education. In S. M. Dobbs (Ed.), *Research readings in discipline-based art education: A journey beyond creating* (pp. 78–97). Reston, VA: National Art Education Association.

Clark, G., & Zimmerman, E. (1988b). Views of self, family background, and school: Interviews with artistically talented students. *Gifted Child Quarterly, 32*(4), 340–346.

Clark, G., & Zimmerman, E. (1992). *Issues and practices related to identification of gifted and talented students in the visual arts* (Javits Act Program Grant No. R206R0001) Storrs, CT: National Research Center on the Gifted and Talented.

Clark, G., & Zimmerman, E. (1994). *Programming opportunities for students talented in the visual arts* (Javits Act Program Grant No. R206R0001) Storrs, CT: National Research Center on the Gifted and Talented.

Clark, G., & Zimmerman, E. (1997). *Project ARTS: Programs for ethnically diverse, economically disadvantaged, high ability, visual arts students in rural communities* (Javits Act Program, Grant No. R206A30220). Washington, DC: U. S. Department of Education. (ERIC Document Reproduction Service No. ED 419 762 and No. ED 419 765)

Clark, G., & Zimmerman, E. (1998). Nurturing the arts in programs for gifted and talented students. *Phi Delta Kappan, 79*(10), 747–756.

Clark, G., & Zimmerman, E. (2000). Greater understanding of the local community: A community-based art education program for rural schools. *Art Education, 53*(2), 33–39.

Clark, G., & Zimmerman, E. (2001a). Art talent development, creativity, and enrichment programs for artistically talented students in grades K–8. In M. D. Lynch & C. R. Harris (Eds.), *Fostering creativity in children, K–8: Theory and practice* (pp. 211–226). Boston: Allyn & Bacon.

Clark, G., & Zimmerman, E. (2001b). Identifying artistically talented students in four rural communities in the United States. *Gifted Child Quarterly, 45*(2), 104–114.

Clark, G., & Zimmerman, E. (2003, April), *A pilot project for developing visual art talent in Hong Kong.* Paper presented at the convention of the National Art Education Association, Minneapolis, MN.

Cole, C. (1993). More than meets the eye: Architectural preservation awareness. In G. Clark & E. Zimmerman (Eds.), *Making a difference: Differentiated curriculum units by teachers in the 1993 Artistically Talented Program* (pp. 68–80). Bloomington: Indiana University, School of Education, and the Indiana Department of Education, Gifted and Talented Program.

Committee of Ten. (1893). In *Report of the Committee of Education for the year 1892–93* (Vol. 2). Washington, DC: U.S. Government Printing Office.

Cooke, E. (1985). On art teaching and child nature. *Journal of Education, 8*(198), 12–15.

Csikszentmihalyi, M. (1990). *Flow: The psychology of optimal experence.* New York: Harper.

Csikszentmihalyi, M. (1996). *Creativity: Flow and the psychology of discovery and invention.* New York: HarperCollins.

Darling-Hammond, L. D. (1993). Re-framing the school reform agenda: Developing capacity for school transformation. *Phi Delta Kappan, 74*(10), 753–761.

Davis, J. (1997a). Does the "U" in the U-curve also stand for universal? Reflections on provisional doubts. *Studies in Art Education, 38*(3), 179–185.

Davis, J. (1997b). Drawing's demise: U-Shaped development in graphic symbolization. *Studies in Art Education, 38*(3), 132–157.

DiLeo, J. H. (1977). *Child development: Analysis and synthesis.* New York: Brunner/Mazel.

Efland, A. (Ed.). (1970). *Guidelines for planning art instruction in the elementary schools of Ohio.* Columbus: Ohio Department of Education.

Efland, A., Freedman, K., & Stuhr, P. (1996). *Postmodern art education: An approach to curriculum.* Reston, VA: National Art Education Association.

Eisner, E. W. (1972). *Educating artistic vision.* New York: Macmillan.

Eisner, E. W. (1994). *Cognition and curriculum reconsidered.* New York: Teachers College Press.

Evans, K. M., & King, J. A. (1994). Outcome-based gifted education: Can we assume contined support? *Roeper Review, 16*(4), 260–264.

Feldhusen, J. F. (1992). *Talent and identification and development in education (TIDE).* Sarasota, FL: Center for Creative Learning.

Feldhusen, J. F. (1994). A case for developing America's talent: How we went wrong and where we go now. *Roeper Review, 16*(4), 231–322.

Feldhusen, J. F. (1995). Talent development as the alternative in high school programs. *Understanding Our Gifted, 7*(4), 1, 11–14.

Feldhusen, J. F., Asher, J. W., & Hoover, S. M. (1984). Problems in the identification of giftedness, talent, or ability. *Gifted Child Quarterly, 28*(4), 149–151.

Feldhusen, J. F., & Hoover, S. M. (1986). A conception of giftedness: Intelligence, self-concept, and motivation. *Roeper Review, 8*(3), 140–143.

Feldman, D. H. (1979). The mysterious case of extreme giftedness. In A. H. Passow (Ed.), *The gifted and the talented: Their education and development* (pp. 335–351). Chicago: University of Chicago Press.

Feldman, D. H. (1980). *Beyond universals in cognitive development.* Norwood, NJ: Ablex.

Feldman, D. H. (1982). *Developmental approaches to giftedness and creativity.* San Francisco: Jossey-Bass.

Feldman, D. H. (1983). Developmental psychology and art education. *Art Education, 36*(2), 19–21.

Feldman, D. H. (1985). The concept of non-universal developmental domains: Implications for artistic development. *Visual Arts Research, 11*(1), 82–89.

Feldman, D. H. (1999). The development of creativity. In R. J. Sternberg (Ed.), *Handbook of creativity* (pp. 169–186). Cambridge, UK: Cambridge University Press.

Feldman, D. H., & Goldsmith, L. (1986a). *Nature's gambit: Child prodigies and the development of human potential.* New York: Basic Books.

Feldman, D. H., & Goldsmith, L. (1986b). Transgenerational influences on the development of early prodigious behavior: A case study approach. In W. Fowler (Ed.), *Early experience and the development of competencies* (pp. 83–97). San Francisco: Jossey-Bass.

Feldman, E. B. (1973). The teacher as model critic. *Journal of Aesthetic Education, 7*(1), 50–57.

Feldman, E. B. (1981). *Varieties of visual experience.* Englewood Cliffs, NJ: Abrams.

Fine, M. J. (1970). Facilitating parent-child relationships for creativity. *Gifted Child Quarterly, 21*(4), 487–500.

Ford, B. (1978). Student atttudes toward special programming and identification. *Gifted Child Quarterly, 22*(4), 402–491.

Fritz, H. E. (1930). A search for the conservation of the gifted. *Bulletin of High Points, 12*(8), 19–25.

Gallagher, J. J. (1985). *Teaching the gifted child* (3rd ed.). Boston: Allyn & Bacon.

Gallagher, J. J. (1993). Comments on McDaniel's education of the gifted and the excellence-equity debate. In C. J. Maker (Ed.), *Critical issues in gifted education: Vol. 3. Programs for the gifted in regular classrooms* (pp. 19–21). Austin, TX: Pro-Ed.

Gallagher, J. J., & Gallagher, S. A. (1994). *Teaching the gifted child* (4th ed.). Needham, MA: Allyn & Bacon.

Gardner, H. (1980). *Artful scribbles: The significance of children's drawings.* New York: Basic Books.

Gardner, H. (1983). *Frames of mind: The theory of multiple intelligences.* New York: Basic Books.

Gardner, H. (1989). Toward more effective arts education. In H. Gardner & D. Perkins (Eds.), *Art, mind, and education* (pp. 157–167). Urbana: University of Illinois Press.

Gardner, H. (1996). The creator's patterns. In M. A. Boden (Ed.), *Dimensions of creativity* (pp. 143–158). Cambridge, MA: MIT Press.

Gardner, H., & Winner, E. (1982). First intimations of artistry. In S. Strauss (Ed.), *U-shaped development* (pp. 147–168). New York: Academic Press.

Gardner, J. W. (1961). *Excellence: Can we be excellent and equal too?* New York: Harper Colophon Books.

Getzels, J. W., & Csikszentmihalyi, M. (1976). *The creative vision: A longitudinal study of problem finding in art.* New York: John Wiley & Sons.

The gifted and talented children's act, Pub. L. No. 95-561, §902 (1978).

Gilligan, C. (1982). *In a different voice: Psychological theory and women's development.* Cambridge, MA: Harvard University Press.

Gitomer, D., Grosh, S., & Price, K. (1992). Portfolio culture in arts education. *Art Education, 45*(1), 7–15.

Goldsmith, L. T. (1992). Wang Yani: Stylistic development of a Chinese painting prodigy. *Creativity Research Journal, 5*(3), 281–293.

Golomb, C. (1992a). *The child's creation of a pictorial world.* Berkeley: University of California Press.

Golomb, C. (1992b). Eitan: The early development of a gifted child artist. *Creativity Research Journal, 5*(3), 265–27 framework.

Golomb, C. (1995). Eitan: The artistic development of a child prodigy. In C. Golomb (Ed.), *The development of artistically gifted children: Selected case studies* (pp. 171–196). Hillside, NJ: Lawrence Erlbaum.

Graves, M. (1978). *Graves Design Judgment Test.* New York: Psychological Corporation.

Gross, M. U. M., MacLeod, B., Drummond, D., & Merrick, C. (2001). *Gifted students in primary schools: Differentiating the curriculum.* University of New South Wales. Sydney: GERRIC.

Gross, M. U. M., Sleap, B., & Pretorius, M. (1999). *Gifted students in secondary schools: Differentiating the curriculum.* University of New South Wales, Sydney: GERRIC.

Grube, L. (1993). Social problems and art: How artists can use their talents to help their community. In G. Clark & E. Zimmerman (Eds.), *A community of teachers: Art curriculum units by teachers in the 1992 Artistically Talented Program* (pp. 1–7). Bloomington: Indiana University, School of Education, and the Indiana Department of Education, Gifted and Talented Program.

Guskin, S. (1978). Theoretical and empirical strategies for the study of the labeling of mentally retarded persons. In N. R. Ellis (Ed.), *International Review of Research in Mental Retardation* (pp. 34–47). New York: Academic Press.

Guskin, S., Zimmerman, E., Okola, C., & Peng, J. (1986). Being labeled gifted or talented: Meanings and effects perceived by students in special programs. *Gifted Child Quarterly, 30*(2), 61–65.

Hamblen, K. (1984). An art criticism questioning strategy within the framework of Bloom's taxonomy. *Studies in Art Education, 26*(1), 41–50.

Harris, D. B. (1963). *Children's drawings as measures of intellectual maturity: A revision and extension of Goodenough's Draw-A-Man Test.* New York: Harcourt, Brace & World.

Hausman, J. (1994). Standards and assessment: New initiative and continuing dilemmas. *Art Education, 47*(2), 9–13.

Herman, J. L., Aschbacher, P. K., & Winters, L. (1992). *A practical guide to alternative assessment.* Alexandria, VA: Association for Supervision and Curriculum Development.

Hildreth, G. H. (1941). *The child mind in evolution: A study of developmental sequences in drawing.* New York: Kings Crown.

Horn, C. C. (1953). *Horn Art Aptitude Inventory.* Chicago: Stoelting.

Hunsaker, S. L., & Callahan, C. (1995). Creativity and giftedness: Instrument uses and abuses. *Gifted Child Quarterly, 39*(2), 110–114.

Hurwitz, A. (1983). *The gifted and talented in art: A guide to program planning.* Worcester, MA: Davis.

Hurwitz, A., & Day, M. (2001). *Children and their art: Methods for the elementary school* (7th ed.). San Diego, CA: Harcourt College Publishers.

Jellen, H. G., & Verduin, J. R. (1986). *Handbook for differential education of the gifted: A taxonomy of 32 key concepts.* Carbondale: Southern Illinois University Press.

Johnson, N. (1985). Teaching and learning in art: The acquisition of art knowledge in an eighth-grade class. Arts and Learning SIG: *Proceedings of the American Educational Research Association, 3,* 14–32.

Johnson, R. (1993). How mpressionism reflected social impacts of the 1980s. In G. Clark & E. Zimmerman (Eds.), *A Community of teachers: Art curriculum units by teachers in the 1992 Artistically Talented Program* (pp. 8–20). Bloomington: Indiana University, School of Education, and the Indiana Department of Education, Gifted and Talented Program.

Kaufman, A. S., & Harrison, P. L. (1986). Intelligence tests and gifted assessment: What are the positives? *Roeper Review, 8*(3), 154–159.

Kerr, B. A. (1987). *Smart girls, gifted women.* Columbus, OH: Ohio Psychology Publishing.

Kerschensteiner, I. G. (1905). *Die entwickelung der zeichnerischen begabung* [The development of drawing ability]. Munich: Gerber.

Khatena, J. (1982). *Educational psychology of the gifted.* New York: Wiley & Sons.

Khatena, J. (1989). Intelligence and creativity to multi-talent. *Journal of Creative Behavior, 23*(2), 93–97.

Khatena, J. (1992). *Gifted: Challenge and response for educators.* Itasca, IL: Peacock.

Kindler, A. (2000). From the U-Curve to dragons: Culture and understandings of artistic development. *Visual Arts Research, 26*(2), 15–28.

Kindler, A., & Darras, B. (1998). Culture and development of pictorial repertoires. *Studies in Art Education, 39*(2), 47–67.

Kindler, A., Pariser, D., van den Berg, A., & Lui, W. (2001). Visions of Eden: The differential effect of skill on adult's judgments of children's drawings: Two cross-cultural studies. *Canadian Review of Art Education, 28*(2), 35–63.

Kleinsasser, A. M. (1986). Equity in education for gifted rural girls. *Rural Special Education Quarterly, 8*(4), 27–30.

Kruse, S. (1991). Multi-cultural enrichment for fourth grade students. In G. Clark, & E. Zimmerman (Eds.), *Programs for artistically talented students* (pp. 58–61). Bloomington: Indiana University, School of Education, and the Indiana Department of Education, Gifted and Talented Program.

Kulik, J. A. (1992). *An analysis of the research on ability grouping: Historical and contemporary perspectives.* Storrs, CT: National Research Center on the Gifted and Talented.

Kulik, J. A., & Kulik, C. L. (1992). Meta-analytic findings on grouping programs. *Gifted Child Quarterly, 36*(2), 73–77.

Landrum, M. S., Callahan, C. M., Shaklee, B. D. (2001). *Aiming for excellence: Gifted program standards.* Waco, TX: Prufrock Press.

Lark-Horovitz, B., Lewis, H. P., & Luca, M. (1967). *Understanding children's art for better teaching.* Columbus, OH: Charles E. Merrill.

Lark-Horovitz, B., & Norton, J. A. (1960). Children's art abilities: The interrelations and factorial structure of ten characteristics. *Child Development, 31*(1), 453–462.

Lewis, M. G. (1993). *Without a word: Teaching beyond women's silence.* New York: Routledge.

Loeb, R. C., & Jay, G. (1987). Self-concept in gifted children: Differential impact in boys and girls. *Gifted Child Quarterly, 31*(1), 9–14.

Lowenfeld, V. (1954). *Your child and his art: A guide for parents.* New York: Macmillan.

Lubart, T. L. (1999). Creativity across cultures. In R. Sternberg (Ed.), *Handbook of creativity* (pp. 339–350). Cambridge, UK: Cambridge University Press.

Luca, M., & Allen, B. (1974). *Teaching gifted children art in grades one through three.* Sacramento: California Department of Education.

Lutz, F., & Lutz, S. B. (1980). Gifted pupils in the elementary school setting: An ethnographic study. Paper presented at the annual meeting of the American Educational Research Association, Boston.

Maeroff, G. I. (1988). A blueprint for empowering teachers. *Phi Delta Kappan, 69*(7), 473–477.

Maker, C. J. (1982). *Curriculum development for the gifted.* Austin, TX: Pro-Ed.

Manuel, H. T. (1919). Talent in drawing: An experimental study of the use of tests to discover special ability. *School and Home Education Monograph No. 3.* Bloomington, IL: Public School Publishing.

Marché, T. (1997). Community-based art education: Curriculum development. In G. Clark & E. Zimmerman, *Project ARTS: Programs for ethnically diverse, eco-*nomically disadvantaged, high ability, visual arts students in rural communities* (pp. 88–111). Washington, DC: U.S. Department of Education. (ERIC Document Reproduction Service No. ED 419 762 and ED 419 765)

Marché, T., & Zimmerman, E. (2000). Assessment methods for students from diverse populations. In S. D. LaPierre, M. Stokrocki, & E. Zimmerman (Eds.), *Research methods and methodologies for multicultural and cross-cultural research in art education* (pp. 31–36). Tempe, AZ: Arizona Arts Education Research Institute.

Marland, S. P. (1972). *Education of the gifted and talented, Vol. 1: Report to the Congress of the United States by the U.S. Commissioner of Education.* Washington, DC: U.S. Government Printing Office.

Meier, N.C. (Ed.). (1939). Studies in the psychology of art Vol. III. *Psychological Monographs, 51* (1). Iowa City, IA: University of Iowa Press.

Meier, N. C. (1942). *Art in human affairs: An introduction to the psychology of art.* New York: McGraw-Hill.

Milbrath, C. (1995). Germinal motifs in the work of a gifted child artist. In C. Golomb (Ed.), *The development of artistically gifted children: Selected case studies* (pp. 101–134). Hillside, NJ: Lawrence Erlbaum.

Milbrath, C. (1998). *Patterns of artistic development: Comparative studies of talent.* Cambridge, UK: Cambridge University Press.

Mittler, G. A. (1980). Learning to look/looking to learn: A proposed approach to art appreciation at the secondary school level. *Art Education, 33*(3), 17–21.

Mittler, G. A. (1985). *Art in focus.* Mission Hills, CA: Glencoe.

Mostyn, B. (1985). The content analysis of qualitative research data: A dynamic approach. In M. Brenner, J. Brown, & D. Canter (Eds.), *The research interview: Uses and approaches* (pp. 115–145). London: Academic Press.

Mullins, F. (1993). Considerations of the geometric proportions and terrestrial observations of the Serpent Mound as a model cosmology. In G. Clark & E. Zimmerman (Eds.), *Making a difference: Differentiated curriculum units by teachers in the 1993 Artistically Talented Program* (pp. 78–88). Bloomington: Indiana University, School of Education, and the Indiana Department of Education, Gifted and Talented Program.

Mumford, M. D., Connely, M. S., Baughman, W. A., & Marks, M. A. (1994). Creativity and problem solving: Cognition, adaptability, and wisdom. *Roeper Review, 16*(4), 241–246.

Nachitgal, P. N. (1992). Rural schools: Obsolete . . . or barbingers of the future? *Educational Horizons, 70,* 66–70.

National Assessment of Educational Progress. (1977). *Design and drawing skills* (Art report No. D6-A-01). Washington, DC: U.S. Government Printing Office.

National Assessment of Educational Progress. (1981). *Art and young Americans* (Art report No. 10-A-01). Denver, CO: Education Commission of the States.

National Center for Education Statistics. (1998). *The NAEP 1997 art report card: Eighth-grade findings from the National Assessment of Educational Progress* (NCES No. 1999-486). Washington, DC: U.S. Department of Education.

Nelson, K. C., & Janzen, P. (1990). Diane: Dilemma of the artistically talented in rural America. *Gifted Child Today*, *13*(1), 12–15.

Pandiscio, R. (1999, October). Thirty to watch. *Interview*, pp. 150–154.

Pariser, D. (1991). Normal and unusual aspects of juvenile artistic development in Klee, Lautrec and Picasso: A review of findings and direction for future research. *Creativity Research Journal*, *4*(1), 51–67.

Pariser, D. (1995). Lautrec: Gifted child-artist and artistic monument: Connections between juvenile and mature work. In C. Golomb (Ed.), *The development of gifted child artists: Selected case studies* (pp. 31–71). Hillsdale, NJ: Lawrence Erlbaum.

Pariser, D. (1997). Conceptions of children's artistic giftedness from modern and postmodern perspectives. *Journal of Aesthetic Education*, *31*(4), 35–47.

Pariser, D., & van den Berg, A. (1997a). Beholder beware: A reply to Jessica Davis. *Studies in Art Education*, *38*(3), 186–192.

Pariser, D., & van den Berg, A. (1997b). The mind of the beholder: Some provisional doubts about the U-curved aesthetic development thesis. *Studies in Art Education*, *38*(3), 158–178.

Peat, F. D. (2000). *The black winged night: Creativity in nature and mind*. Cambridge, MA: Perseus.

Potok, C. (1972). *My name is Asher Lev*. Greenwich, CT: Fawcett.

Reis, S. M. (1987). We can't change what we don't recognize: Understanding the special needs of gifted females. *Gifted Child Quarterly*, *31*(2), 83–89.

Reis, S. M. (1991). The need for clarification in research designed to examine gender differences in achievement and accomplishment. *Roeper Review*, *13*(4), 193–202.

Renzulli, J. S. (1977). *The enrichment triad model: A guide for developing defensible programs for the gifted and talented*. Mansfield Center, CT: Creative Learning.

Renzulli, J. S. (1982). The enrichment triad. In C. J. Maker (Ed.), *Teaching models in education of the gifted* (pp. 207–236). Austin, TX: Pro-Ed.

Renzulli, J. S., & Reis, S. M. (1994). Research related to the school-wide enrichment triad model. *Gifted Child Quarterly*, *38*(1), 7–20.

Renzulli, J. S., Reis, S. M., & Smith, L. H. (1981). *The revolving door identification model (RDIM)*. Mansfield Center, CT: Creative Learning.

Ricci, C. (1887). *L'Arte dei bambini* [The art of the child]. Bologna, Italy: N. Zanchelli.

Richert, E. S. (1987). Rampant problems and promising practices on the identification of disadvantaged gifted students. *Gifted Child Quarterly*, *31*(4), 149–154.

Robinson, A. (1991). *Cooperative learning and the academically talented student*. Storrs, CT: National Research Center on the Gifted and Talented.

Robinson, H., Roedell, W. C., & Jackson, N. E. (1979). Early identification and intervention. In H. Passow (Ed.), *The gifted and the talented: Their education and development* (pp. 138–154). Chicago, IL: University of Chicago Press.

Rogers, K. B. (1991). *The relationship of grouping practices to the education of the gifted and talented learner*. Storrs, CT: National Research Center on the Gifted and Talented.

Runco, M. (1993). *Creativity as an educational objective for disadvantaged students*. Storrs, CT: National Center on the Gifted and Talented.

Runco, M., & Nemiro, J. (1993). Problem finding and problem solving. *Roeper Review*, *16*(4), 235–241.

Sabol, F. R. (1994). *A critical examination of visual arts achievement tests from state departments of education in the United States*. Unpublished doctoral dissertation, Indiana University, Bloomington.

Sandberg, S. (2003, November). *Issues surrounding Thomas Hart Benton's Indiana murals*. Paper presented at the convention of the National Association of Gifted Children, Indianapolis, IN.

Sandborn, M. P. (1979). Counseling and guidance needs of the gifted and talented. In A. H. Passow (Ed.), *The gifted and talented: Their education and development* (pp. 396–401). NSSE Yearbook, Part 1. Chicago: University of Chicago Press.

Schavelson, R., Baxter, G., & Pine, J. (1992). Performance assessment: Political rhetoric and measurement reality. *Educational Researcher*, *21*(4), 22–27.

Schubert, D. S. P. (1973). Intelligence as necessary but not sufficient for creativity. *Journal of Genetic Psychology*, *122*, 45–47.

Shore, B. (1987). *Recommended practices in the education and upbringing: A progress report on an assessment of the knowledge base*. Indianapolis: Indiana Department of Education.

Silver, R. (1983). *Silver Drawing Test of cognitive and creative skills*. Seattle, WA: Special Child Publications.

Silverman, L. K. (1986). What happens to the gifted girl? In C. J. Maker (Ed.), *Critical issues in gifted education: Vol. 1. Defensible programs for the gifted* (pp. 43–89). Austin, TX: Pro-Ed.

Slavin, R. E. (1980). Cooperative learning. *Review of Educational Research, 50*, 315–342.

Slavin, R. E. (1990). Ability grouping, cooperative learning, and the gifted. *Journal of Education of the Gifted, 14*(1), 3–8.

Sleeter, C. E., & Grant, C. A. (1987). An analysis of multicultural education in the United States. *Harvard Educational Review, 57*(4), 421–444.

Sloan, K. D., & Sosniak, L. A. (1985). The development of accomplished sculptors. In B. Bloom (Ed.), *Developing talent in young people* (pp. 90–138). New York: Ballantine.

Smith, N. (1998). *Observation drawing with children. A framework for teaching*. New York: Teacher's College Press.

Smith, P. L., & Traver, R. (1983). Classical living and classical learning: The search for equity and excellence. In M. C. Smith, *Proceedings of the Annual Conference of the Midwest Philosophy of Education Society* (pp. 79–92). Chicago: Midwest Philosophy of Education Society.

Stalker, M. Z. (1981). Identification of the gifted in art. *Studies in Art Education, 22*(2), 49–56.

Stanley, J. C. (1977). Rationale of the study of mathematically precocious youth (SYMPY) during the first five years of promoting educational acceleration. In J. C. Stanley, W. C. George, & C. H. Solano (Eds.), *The gifted and creative: A fifty-year perspective* (pp. 75–112). Baltimore, MD: Johns Hopkins University Press.

Starko, A. J. (2001). *Creativity in the classroom: Schools of curious delight* (2nd ed.). Mahwah, NJ: Lawrence Erlbaum.

Sternberg, R. J. (1985). *Beyond IQ: A triarchic theory of human intelligence*. New York: Cambridge University Press.

Sternberg, R. J. (1986). Identifying the gifted through IQ: Why a little bit of knowledge is a dangerous thing. *Roeper Review, 8*(3), 143–150.

Sternberg, R. J. (Ed.). (1999). *Handbook of creativity*. Cambridge, UK: Cambridge University Press.

Sternberg, R. J. (2001). What is the common thread of creativity? *American Psychologist, 56*(4), 360–362.

Sternberg, R. J., & Lubart, T. I. (1999). Concept of creativity: Prospects and paradigms. In R. J. Sternberg (Ed.). *Handbook of creativity* (pp. 3–15). Cambridge, UK: Cambridge University Press.

Sternberg, R. J., & Williams, W. M. (1996). *How to develop student creativity*. Alexandria, VA: Association for Supervision and Curriculum Development.

Stevens, M. (1992). School reform and restructuring: Relationship to gifted educaiton. In Ohio Department of Education, *Challenges in gifted education: Developing potential and investing knowledge for the 21st century* (pp. 49–55). Columbus: Ohio Department of Education.

Stokrocki, M. (1986). A portrait of an effective elementary art teacher. *Studies in Art Education, 27*(2), 82–93.

Stokrocki, M. (1990). A portrait of a black art teacher of preadolescents in the inner city. In B. Young (Ed.), *Art, culture, and ethnicity* (pp. 201–218). Reston, VA: National Art Education Association.

Stokrocki, M. (1995). Understanding young children's ways of interpreting their experiences through participant observation. In C. M. Thompson (Ed.), *The visual arts and early childhood learning* (pp. 67–72). Reston, VA: National Art Education Association.

Sullivan, G. (1993). Art-based art education: Learning that is meaningful, authentic, critical and pluralist. *Studies in Art Education, 35*(1), 5–21.

Taylor, R. (1986). *Educating for art*. London: Longman.

Terman, L., & Oden, M. (1947). Genetic studies of genius. Vol. 4. *The gifted child grows up: Twenty-five year's follow-up of a superior group*. Stanford, CA: Stanford University Press.

Thorndike, E. L. (1916). Tests of esthetic appreciation. *Journal of Educational Psychology, 7*(10), 509–517.

Thurber, F., & Zimmerman, E. (1997). Voice to voice: Developing in-service teachers' personal, collaborative, and public voices. *Educational Horizons, 75*(4), 20–26.

Tiebout, C., & Meier, N. C. (1936). Artistic ability and general intelligence. *Psychological Monographs, 48*(213), 95–125.

Tomlinson, C. A. (1995). *How to differentiate instruction in mixed-ability classrooms*. Alexandria, VA: Association for Supervision and Curriculum Development.

Tomlinson, C. A., Kaplan, S. N., Renzulli, J. S., Purcell, J., Leppin, J., & Burns, D. (2002). *The parallel curriculum: A design to develop high potential and challenge high ability learners*. Thousand Oaks, CA: Corwin Press.

Torrance, E. P. (1963). *Education and the creative potential*. Minneapolis: University of Minnesota Press.

Torrance, E. P. (1972). Career patterns and peak creative achievements of creative high school students twelve years later. *Gifted Child Quarterly, 26*(2), 75–88.

Treffinger, D. J., & Renzulli, J. (1986). Giftedness as potential for creative productivity: Transcending IQ issues. *Roeper Review, 8*(3), 150–163.

Treffinger, D. J., Sortore, M. R., & Cross, J. A. (1993). Programs and strategies for nurturing creativity. In K. A. Heller, F. J. Monk, & A. H. Passow (Eds.), *International handbook of research and development of giftedness and talent* (pp. 555–567). New York: Pergamon.

Tuttle, F., & Becker, L. (1980). *Characteristics and identification of gifted and talented students.* Washington, DC: National Education Association.

VanTassel-Baska, J. (1986). Acceleration. In C. J. Maker (Ed.), *Critical issues in gifted education: Vol. 1. Defensible programs for the gifted* (pp. 179–196). Rockville, MD: Aspen.

VanTassel-Baska, J. (1987). The ineffectiveness of the pull-out program model in gifted education: A minority perspective. *Journal of Education of the Gifted, 10*(4), 255–264.

VanTassel-Baska, J. (1992). Educational decision making on acceleration and grouping. *Gifted Child Quarterly, 36*(2), 68–72.

VanTassel-Baska, J. (1998). *Excellence in educating gifted and talented learners* (3rd ed.). Denver, CO: Love Publishing.

Vernon, P. E., Adamson, G., & Vernon, D (1977). *The psychology and education of gifted children.* Boulder, CO: Viewpoint.

Viola, W. (1942). *Child art* (2nd ed.). London: University of London Press.

Walters, J., & Gardner, H. (1984, March). *The crystallizing experience: Discovering an intellectual gift.* Technical paper, supported by grants from the Social Science Research Council and the Bernard van Leer Foundation of The Hague. (ERIC Document Reproduction Service No. ED 254 544)

Weiner, J. L. (1968). Attitudes of psychologists and psychometrists toward gifted children and programs for the gifted. *Exceptional Children, 34*(5), 364.

Weiner, J. L., & O'Shea, H. E. (1963). Attitudes of university faculty, administrators, teachers, supervisors, and university students toward the gifted. *Exceptional Children, 30*(4), 163.

Weitz, M. (1961, March 24). *The nature of art.* Address given at the conference of the National Committee on Art Education, Columbus, Ohio.

Wenner, G. C. (1985). Discovery and recognition of the artistically talented. *Journal for the Education of the Gifted, 8*(3), 221–238.

Whipple, G. M. (1919). *Classes for gifted children.* Bloomington, IL: Public School Publishing.

Willats, J. (1997). *Art and representation. New principles in the analysis of pictures.* Princeton, NJ: Princeton University Press.

Wilson, B., Hurwitz, A., & Wilson, M. (1987). *Teaching drawing from art.* Worcester, MA: Davis.

Wilson, B., & Wilson, M. (1976). Visual narrative and the artistically gifted. *Gifted Child Quarterly, 20*(4), 423–447.

Wilson, B., & Wilson, M. (1980). Beyond marvelous: Conventions and inventions in John Scott's Gemini. *School Arts, 80*(2), 19–26.

Wilson, T., & Clark, G. (2000). Looking and talking about art: Strategies of an experienced art teacher. *Visual Arts Research, 52*(2), 33–39.

Winner, E. (1996). *Gifted children: Myths and realities.* New York: Basic Books.

Winner, E., & Martino, G. (1993). Giftedness in the visual arts and music. In K. A. Keller, F. J. Monk, & A. H. Passow (Eds.), *International handbook of research and development of giftedness and talent* (pp. 253–281). New York: Pergamon.

Winter, G. W. (1987). *Identifying children in grades 1–3 who are gifted and talented in the visual and performing arts using performance rated criteria.* A report presented in partial fulfillment of requirements for the Doctor of Education degree, Nova University, Fort Lauderdale, FL.

Witzling, M. R. (1994). *Voicing today's visions: Writings by contemporary women artists.* New York: Universe.

Wolf, D. P., & Perry, M. (1988). From endpoints to repertoires: New conclusions about drawing development. In H. Gardener, & D. Perkins (Eds.), *Art, mind, and education* (pp. 17–34). Urbana: University of Illinois Press.

Worthen, B. R., & Spandel, V. (1991). Putting the standardized test debate in perspective. *Educational Leadership, 48*(5), 65–69.

Zaffrann, R. T. (1978). Gifted and talented students: Implications for school counselors. *Roeper Review, 1*(2), 9–13.

Ziegfeld, E. (1961). *Art for the academically talented student.* Washington, DC: National Art Education Association.

Zimmerman, E. (1991). Rembrandt to Rembrandt: A case study of a memorable painting teacher of artistically talented 13- to 16-year-old students. *Roeper Review, 13*(2), 174–185.

Zimmerman, E. (1992a). Assessing students' progress and achievements in art. *Art Education, 45*(6), 34–38.

Zimmerman, E. (1992b). A comparative study of two painting teachers of talented adolescents. *Studies in Art Education, 33*(2), 174–185.

Zimmerman, E. (1992c). Factors influencing the graphic development of a talented young artist. *Creativity Research Journal, 5*(3), 295–311.

Zimmerman, E. (1992d). How should students' progress and achievements be assessed? A case for assessment that is responsive to diverse students' needs. *Visual Arts Research, 20*(1), 29–35.

Zimmerman, E. (1994–1995). Factors influencing the art education of artistically talented girls. *Journal of Secondary Gifted Education, 6*(2), 103–112.

Zimmerman, E. (1995). It was an incredible experience: The impact of educational opportunities on a talented student's art development. In C. Golomb (Ed.), *The development of artistically gifted children: Selected case studies* (pp. 135–170). Hillside, NJ: Lawrence Erlbaum.

Zimmerman, E. (1997a). Assessment. In Clark, G., & Zimmerman, E. (1997a). *Project ARTS: Programs for ethnically diverse, economically disadvantaged, high ability, visual arts students in rural communities* (pp. 163–184). Washington, DC: U. S. Department of Education. (ERIC Document Reproduction Service No. ED 419 762 and ED 419 765)

Zimmerman, E. (1997b). Authentic assessment in art education. In S. La Pierre & E. Zimmerman (Eds.), *Research methods in art education* (pp. 149–169). Reston, VA: National Art Education Association.

Zimmerman, E. (1997c). Authentic assessment of a painting class: Sitting down and talking with students. In G. D. Phye (Ed.), *Handbook of classroom assessment: Learning, achievement, and adjustment* (pp. 448–458). New York: Academic Press.

Zimmerman, E. (1997d). Building leadership roles for teachers in art education. *Journal of Art and Design Education, 6*(3), 281–284.

Zimmerman, E. (1997e). Excellence and equity issues in art education: Can we be excellent and equal too? *Arts Education Policy Review, 98*(4), 281–284.

Zimmerman, E. (1997f). I don't want to sit in the corner cutting out valentines: Leadership roles for teachers of talented art students. *Gifted Child Quarterly, 41*(1), 37–41.

Zimmerman, E. (1999). A cautionary tale for those involved in large-scale arts assessments. *Art Education, 5*(5), 44–50.

Index

About the Authors

Gilbert Clark and **Enid Zimmerman** are a husband/wife team who have been writing about art talent development and educating artistically talented students for over two and a half decades. They have authored many articles, book chapters, books, and monographs on this topic including: *Educating Artistically Talented Students, Resources for Educating Artistically Talented Students, Understanding Art Testing, Issues and Practices Related to Identification of Gifted and Talented Students in the Visual Arts*, and *Programming Opportunities for Students Talented in the Visual Arts*. They also authored a middle school textbook, *Art/Design: Communicating Visually*.

They received the National Association for Gifted Children's Paper of the Year award and a Jacob Javits Gifted and Talented Children's grant. Both served as World Councilors for the International Society for Education Through Art (INSEA), edited *INSEA News*, and have been invited speakers or workshop presenters in over 20 countries. They received a number of national and international awards from the National Art Education Association (NAEA) and INSEA and are NAEA Distinguished Fellows.

Gilbert Clark, a professor emeritus at Indiana University, also investigates art curricula, child art development, art test development, and assessment of art learning. He helped develop several major curriculum projects, including discipline based art education sponsored by the Getty Foundation.

Enid Zimmerman, professor and coordinator of Art Education and Gifted and Talented Education programs at Indiana University, researches issues related to woman art educators, educational leadership, and art teaching and art teacher education. She has co-authored several books on these topics, including *Woman Art Educators, I-V* and *Research Methods and Methodologies for Art Education*. She was named the NAEA Art Educator of the Year and has served as chairperson of the NAEA Commission on Research. Zimmerman recently edited the Teacher and Teacher Education section for the *Handbook on Research and Policy in Art Education* and co-authored a chapter in this handbook, Art Learning of Gifted and Talented Students.